Advance Praise for *Squandering A*

"Susan Ochshorn has written an ambitious book, unlike any other in early childhood policy. With a broad canvas, a strong moral compass, and pragmatism, she connects the dots between the diverse influences on the lives of children, her passion for their well-being shining through. It's a must-read for all who care about kids."

—Nancy Carlsson Paige, founder, Defending the Early Years, author, *Taking Back Childhood*

"In this eye-opening book, Susan Ochshorn reveals the enormous gap between the policies we need to support our youngest children and the aggressive neglect so many currently experience. An urgent call to action that could change the course of the nation's future."

—Linda Darling-Hammond, Stanford University, author, *The Flat World and Education*

"Susan Ochshorn has created a kaleidoscope of stories and statistics to illustrate the profound injustices we are visiting on our children and the corresponding injuries we are inflicting on ourselves. We can only hope that *Squandering America's Future* will help to turn the tide."

—Anne-Marie Slaughter, president and CEO, New America

"I was riveted by *Squandering America's Future*. Susan Ochshorn offers a sweeping, and hopeful, vision of human capital creation, one that respects children and values the work of those who nurture their formidable capabilities. Indispensable for policymakers, educators, and all who care about our future."

—Riane Eisler, author of *The Chalice and the Blade* and *The Real Wealth of Nations*

"This remarkable book manages to pinpoint the critical issues in the care and education of young children with up-to-date research, and all of this in a pleasurable and lively style. This needs to be read widely, and right away."

—Deborah Meier, New York University, author, *The Power of Their Ideas*

"Thank you for being the voice of the voiceless and for continuing to fight for many of us who choose to do quality work with children and families but who are too tired to speak out."

—Bonnie Mallonga, COO, 1199SEIU Future of America Learning Center

"Beyond the talking/selling points of investing in early childhood education, Ochshorn's Squandering America's Future strives to ask critical questions about our current world while marveling at the potential of all children."

—Jose Vilson, math educator and author, This is Not A Test

"Susan Ochshorn paints a picture of children and families in America exposed to risks and circumstances that threaten their lives, happiness, and future. Fortunately, she doesn't leave us in despair but shows us how a few dedicated people, schools, agencies, and institutions have made a difference in children's lives—a difference that is enhancing early development in this generation and those to come."

—Samuel J. Meisels, founding executive director,
Buffett Early Childhood Institute, University of Nebraska

"In *Squandering America's Future*, Susan Ochshorn introduces her readers to a vast community of innovative and indefatigable individuals, all converging around an urgent cry for more effective and more egalitarian investments in our young children. This unconventional book is sharp eyed, warm, and lively— a delightful read on a dead-serious topic."

—Janet Gornick, director, Luxembourg Income Study Center, CUNY,
coauthor, *Families That Work*

"Susan Ochshorn's book is a must-read, skillfully weaving science, theory, and passion. Her voice—on the dynamic and ecological nature of development— comes through loud and clear, setting the direction for policy and practice."

—Elizabeth Isakson, codirector, Docs for Tots

Squandering America's Future

Why ECE Policy Matters for Equality, Our Economy, and Our Children

Susan Ochshorn

Foreword by David L. Kirp

TEACHERS COLLEGE PRESS

TEACHERS COLLEGE | COLUMBIA UNIVERSITY

NEW YORK AND LONDON

Published by Teachers College Press, 1234 Amsterdam Avenue, New York, NY 10027

Library of Congress Cataloging-in-Publication Data

Ochshorn, Susan.
  Squandering America's future : why ECE policy matters for equality, our economy, and our children / Susan Ochshorn ; foreword by David L. Kirp.
    pages cm
  Includes bibliographical references and index.
  ISBN 978-0-8077-5670-6 (pbk. : alk. paper)—
  ISBN 978-0-8077-7388-8 (ebook)
    1. Child care services—Government policy—United States. 2. Children—Services for—Government policy—United States. 3. Early childhood education—Government policy—United States. 4. Early childhood education—Social aspects—United States. I. Title.
  HQ778.63.O24 2015
  362.71'20973—dc23   2015005713

ISBN 978-0-8077-5670-6 (paper)
ISBN 978-0-8077-7388-8 (ebook)

Printed on acid-free paper
Manufactured in the United States of America

22 21 20 19 18 17 16 15   8 7 6 5 4 3 2 1

For the nation's real wealth producers and all our children

Contents

Foreword

The Public Equivalent of Love

Just as we know, on the basis of irrefutable research, that human activity affects climate change and smoking causes cancer, we know that children's earliest years shape the arc of their lives.

Multiple strands of research buttress this assertion. Neuroscientists have mapped the astonishing changes occurring in the brain during the first years of a child's life. Geneticists have debunked the argument that an individual's genetic endowment is decisive—the correct formulation isn't nurture *versus* nature but nurture *through* nature. Long-term studies of iconic programs like Perry Preschool and Abecedarian have shown the lifelong impact of early experiences on education, income, and incarceration. Contemporary studies of large-scale programs, such as the Tulsa and Boston pre-K programs and the statewide preschool initiative in New Jersey, confirm the substantial positive impact of a good early education. "Skills beget skills," asserts University of Chicago Nobel Prize winner James Heckman, one of many economists who have calculated the return on investment in high-quality preschool. Their conclusions would make Warren Buffett envious. (In fact, when Buffett asked his daughter, Susan Buffett, to identify a social investment as solid as the companies he bankrolled, she decided to focus on early education.)

Sixty years ago, the Supreme Court unanimously declared, in *Brown v. Board of Education*, that "it is doubtful that any child may reasonably be expected to succeed in life if he is denied the opportunity of an education. Such an opportunity, where the state has undertaken to provide it, is a right which must be made available to all on equal terms." We know now that the same holds true for early education, which merits being treated as the civil rights issue of our time.

None of this counts as news. In recent years, scores of books, as well as countless articles, blogs, tweets, and TV and radio programs have extolled the virtues of early education. The public has gotten the message—polls show that an overwhelming majority supports expanding early education and support cuts across ideological and party lines, a rarity in today's fractured political climate.

Sadly, this popular backing hasn't translated into wise policy. Early education remains a patchwork quilt. Just 28 percent of four-year-olds—a far lower figure than in any other postindustrial nation—attended a state-funded preschool program during the 2012–2013 school year, according to the National Institute of Early Education Research (NIEER). And many of these preschoolers received a bare-bones education. Per-child expenditures averaged $4,000—less than half of what states spend on K–12. High-quality pre-K means a full-day program, with well-trained teachers, small classes, a well-equipped classroom and an evidence-based curriculum, and $4,000 isn't nearly enough to pay for that kind of opportunity. As Steven Barnett, the director of NIEER, says, "preschool without quality is just high-class day care."

The topic at hand is no less than our future. For the sake of these children—in the interest of the rest of us as well—it's essential to close this gap between what young children need and what they receive. Potentially, *Squandering America's Future* will help to bring about this transformation.

As psychologists have learned, we form our opinions mainly on the basis of stories and rely on quantitative evidence to buttress those opinions. Susan Ochshorn, a veteran journalist, has scoured the early education field. She has done a remarkable job of weaving together narratives and analysis, stories and statistics. The profiles of changemakers that dot the book are inspiring to any reader and offer a road map for those who want to make things happen.

Squandering America's Future takes a clear-eyed view of the present situation. It shows how hard it will be to give young children the caliber of education and care that they need to flourish—how hard it is to make "high-quality" preschool more than a slogan. What's more, as Ochshorn contends, the "child problem" is also a poverty problem. Nearly a quarter of young children under the age of six live in poverty and too often they live in what Jack Shonkoff, director of the Harvard Center on the Developing Child, describes as a toxic environment. Although parents want to do the right thing, poor families often lack the resources to give their children what they need to realize their fullest potential. By the time they turn four, these children have heard 30 million fewer words than the offspring of professionals. They start kindergarten a full year behind their middle-class peers, and must play catch-up from the outset. What's more, early education is necessary but not sufficient. We need to make wise investments, not only from birth to age five but from cradle to college.

Obviously, all of this costs money. For now, neither Washington nor the states will pick up the tab, but long-term prospects may be brighter. Sixty years ago, the federal government spent less on seniors than on any other age group. How things have changed—today, for every dollar Washington spends on a child it spends six dollars on a senior. This turnabout didn't just happen. The AARP, nearly 40 million members strong, won the day by exerting tremendous pressure on politicians. If America's 75 million children are to prosper, they must be represented by the kids' version of the AARP, a "children's crusade" organization with comparable clout.

The measure of what's wanted is the policy version of the Golden Rule: *Every child deserves what you want for a child you love.* Combining compelling narratives and convincing argument, *Squandering America's Future* shows what is required to turn this aspiration into a reality. It should be read by anyone committed to children's lives and America's future.

David L. Kirp is a professor at the Goldman School of Public Policy, University of California at Berkeley. His recent books include *Improbable Scholars: The Rebirth of a Great American School District and a Strategy for America's Schools* and *Kids First: Five Big Ideas for Transforming Children's Lives and America's Future.*

Acknowledgments

They say that it takes a village to raise a child. The same could be said of a book. The process of writing, like parenting, is marked by isolation, self-doubt, and those moments of pure joy when you get it just right. But as I worked on this project, I had the support of more people than I could ever have hoped for.

This baby gestated for five years, conceived in my growing despair over the state of America's children and those who nurture their development. In midcareer, I had switched gears, moving from magazine journalism to policy analysis and advocacy. In this new field, focused on early childhood, I found my people. They shared my deep concern for the well-being of our nation's most precious resource and the stewards of their future, and they were working overtime to change the calculus.

To ensure a solid foundation, I conducted interviews with more than 50 thought leaders in early development and education. A number of them I met in person, on site visits across the country. I am especially indebted to Terrie Rose, Talina Jones, Jessica Sager, Ericka Guynes, Gerrit Westervelt, and Kristin Eno, the subjects of the book's "Changemaker" profiles. They are ingenious gymnasts—keeping their balance, with a deep sense of equity and social justice, on the three-legged, wobbly stool of research, practice, and policy.

I am also grateful for the hospitality and thinking of Rahil Briggs; Deb Lund; Takiema Bunche Smith; Marjorie Brickley, Alanna Navitski, Cristina Mendonca, and her conference group peers; Julie Zuckerman, Tatiana Rosa, Thomas Vorsteg, and Sally Cleaver; Anne Smith, Alexandra Papadopoulos, and their kindergarten and first- and second-grade colleagues; and Geralyn McLaughlin. They welcomed me into their places of work, where they nurture babies, toddlers, preschoolers, kindergartners, and children at the borders of early childhood, and collaborate with parents, teachers, social workers, psychologists, speech therapists, pediatricians, early intervention specialists, and the others of this sprawling village. To protect their privacy, the names and identifying details of the children were changed in all the settings depicted in the book. I also extend thanks to Swati Adarkar, Andreina Velasco, Nina Auerbach, and

Betty Hyde, who have held up the western flank of the American children's crusade with tremendous energy and dedication.

Others talked to me about the big issues and challenges of making change in a telephonic policy salon—or face to face over coffee, tea, and oatmeal. Some of their voices punctuate the book's narrative; others remain unheard but are no less important. I am grateful for the experience and wisdom of this brain trust: Portia Kennel, Kenneth Braswell, Cherie Craft, Brooke Richie-Babbage, Cynthia Lamy, Elizabeth Isakson, Dina Lieser, Margaret Sampson, Lauren Hipp, Linda Espinosa, Hirokazu Yoshikawa, Rebeca Itzkowich, M. Starita Boyce Ansari, Renee Smith-Maddox, Beverly Falk, Marcy Whitebook, Valora Washington, Sherry Cleary, Teri Talan, Jill Bella, Pamela Winton, Janna Wagner, Sheri Marlin, Tracy Benson, Peter Mangione, Samuel Meisels, Deborah Leong, Robert Pianta, Steven Barnett, Kathy Hirsh-Pasek, Roberta Michnick Golinkoff, Nicholas Clement, Jason Sachs, Laura Morana, Steven Antonelli, Jacqueline Jones, Beverly Falk, Sharon Lynn Kagan, Kris Perry, Kristie Kauerz, Kathryn Tout, Geoffrey Nagle, Elizabeth Groginsky, Elliot Regenstein, Lisa Stanley, Naomi Eisenstadt, Marsha Basloe, Stephanie Fanjul, Charles Bruner, Kate Sachnoff, Harriet Dichter, and Ruby Takanishi.

For leading this reluctant immigrant into the "digital Wild West," I am grateful for the guidance of Chip Donohue, Lisa Guernsey, Cari Frisch, Michael Rich, Bonnie Blogojevic, Roberta Schomburg, Michael Levine, and Erin Klein, as well as Aubrey Rubin and Angel Nasseh, who awakened me to the promise of technology for children with special needs.

I am lucky to have had a number of skilled midwives in birthing this book. Marie Ellen Larcada, my editor at Teachers College Press, was the consummate cheerleader. She endured my writer's moodiness and was a model of patience. Sarah Biondello gracefully stepped in, taking my separation anxiety in stride, when Marie Ellen left the Press for her next act. Sarah ensured a smooth transition for the book as we entered the final stages, along with Brian Ellerbeck, Karl Nyberg, John Bylander, Emily Renwick, and Nancy Power— all under the direction of Carole Saltz. Paula Jorde Bloom was an early supporter of the book, assuring me that it would have a future. And David Kirp supplied a foreword with a title that nearly brought me to tears.

I am also grateful for the able assistance of Phoebe Jiang, who brought efficiency, "smarts," and spirit to the process of fact-checking, research, and manuscript preparation. In the end, I take responsibility for any misstatements of fact, omissions, or other errors.

Didi Goldenhar, my dear friend and colleague, pushed me into the blogosphere, where I created *ECE Policy Matters*. Her acute intelligence and expertise on leadership and social impact greatly informed this book's chapter on professional identity. Didi also introduced me to Katie Orenstein, CEO of the Op-Ed Project, who inspired the construction of my virtual soapbox at the *Huffington Post*. Katie's mission to diversify the voices we hear in the world is a model for marginalized early childhood educators, long silenced in the national conversation. Bridget Marmion and her team at Your Expert Nation, including the irrepressible Tammy Richards, have urged me to keep sounding the alarm. Their energy and faith in me and in the book have been a source of great comfort and inspiration.

Naomi Karp is one of the "grandmothers" of this book. She came upon my first policy report, *Partnering for Success*, when she was at the U.S. Department of Education, and championed it like no other. Naomi is an exotic species, a progressive in her home state of Arizona, where she has spearheaded a professional-development initiative that keeps the whole child at its center. I am grateful to have had such a stalwart mentor. In that same category, I also thank Virginia Casper, an open-minded, innovative partner in my midcareer change who worked with me to fashion a hybrid early childhood–public policy master's degree program.

To write a book, you need a quiet, peaceful place. I had the good fortune to spend several weeks at Mesa Refuge, an idyllic sanctuary at Point Reyes Station in northern California, and at Blue Mountain Center in the glorious Adirondacks of New York. I extend thanks for the hospitality and support of Peter Barnes, Harriet Barlow, and Ben Strader, and to my fellow residents, who spurred me on in the early stages of writing.

None of the above, of course, would have been possible without my family. Ours is one of those unwieldy, reconfigured ones. First, there were the original nurturers, Joan and Elliot, who provided the soil and sunlight for me and David, my brother. He and my sister-in-law, Allison, have been steadfast in their support, through thick and thin. My own children, Sam and Eliza, fill my heart with swing—as my protohipster, bebop-loving father once said. Watching them grow, thrive, and launch has been the supreme pleasure of my life. In reconnecting with my first grown-up love, I also got to play a bit part in this process with his children, Amanda and Liam, who have added more fun to the mix.

During the seasons of writing this book, our young men started families with their partners, Camille and Valerie, and a new generation emerged. First came Fox, Sam's son (the new light of my life), and then Madeline, Liam's spunky daughter. As this book goes into production, another baby is about to pop. My husband, Marc, is my partner in this adventure. We never stop marveling at the serendipity of our path. As the family chef, he feeds me delicious meals, in bursts of growing creativity. But his sustenance goes so much deeper—a gift of fate and his deeply generous spirit.

Prologue

The arc of the moral universe is long, but it bends towards justice.

—Martin Luther King Jr.

The failure of most current economic systems to give real value to caring and caregiving, whether in families or in the larger society, continues to lie behind massive economic inequities and dysfunctions.

—Riane Eisler

One December in the early 21st century, the United States lost its position as the largest economy in the world. Our Gross Domestic Product of $17.4 trillion was just not good enough. "It doesn't matter a darn," proclaimed *Forbes*, "the Capitalist Tool," ever optimistic about America's potential. Within a matter of days, China had missed its annual-growth target, hitting a 24-year low. That's the way the cookie crumbles on the global economic scene.

But we have a big problem here in the land of plenty. America is squandering its human capital, the real wealth of our nation. Our policies give short shrift to children, our budding innovators. They also leave families and educators, venture capitalists for these future wealth producers, in the lurch. The list of our sins is long—and dispiriting. Childrearing has now achieved the status of luxury item. Education is seen as expenditure, not investment. We tolerate child-poverty rates that put us to shame on the world's social justice index. The hard, essential work of caregiving and nurturing appear nowhere on the ledger sheets for our GDP.

Fortunately, changemakers across America are following the arc of the moral universe, bending it with solutions. A new economic paradigm is emerging. It measures a different kind of capital—social wealth—including human capability and the cost of its nurturance. Social entrepreneurs, among them parents and teachers of young children, are raising their voices, sounding the alarm in a nation that purports to leave no child behind but that has failed miserably in that noble and necessary endeavor.

POLICY TALES

I'm a writer by training, and I like telling stories. While this book was gestating, I discovered Timothy Wilson, a psychology professor at the University of Virginia, who does double duty at the Frank Batten School of Leadership and Public Policy. The author of *Redirect*, a book about how we change our minds and behavior, Wilson once told a *New York Times* interviewer that "stories are more powerful than data, because they allow individuals to identify emotionally with ideas and people they might otherwise see as 'outsiders.'" His observation seems to fly in the face of the conventional wisdom about policymakers. They want "the facts, ma'am," don't they? And they're happy to drown in an ocean of big data.

I thought Wilson was on to something. I was reminded of a visit to Capitol Hill one snowy February, when I met with a young aide to New York senator Charles Schumer. Here I was, armed with a wonkish briefing on QUALITYstarsNY, the latest initiative to assess, improve, and communicate to parents the quality of early childhood programs. But guess who stole the show: one of my team partners, the director of a child care center in the western reaches of the state. She told the story of children in her program, painting a vivid picture of their hunger in the face of cuts to the Women, Infant, and Children Special Supplemental Nutrition Program. They were missing their snacks, she said. These federal grants to states sustain low-income families with food, health care referrals, and nutrition during pregnancy, postpartum, and the years before children enter kindergarten. And they're perennials on the chopping block.

All short stories are defined by a series of elements: characters, setting, plot, point of view, and theme. Conflict is also an essential ingredient. This book's bold-faced protagonists are parents, teachers, and all their partners in the creation of human capital—eternally under siege. Theorists and researchers, the keepers of early childhood's robust evidence base, also play a role. So do policymakers, toggling back and forth among the groups, their eyes on the bottom line. Politicians struggle to keep their heads above water, dependent on ever-growing quantities of money to ensure their future.

All of these people figure in the arduous process of translating research into practice and policy. Sometimes it works, but too often we're caught between the words and the lines, looking for a real solution that meets the need. Finally, we have the children, whose voices have been silenced. They depend on us. We're supposed to be the adults. But we're constantly letting them down.

The setting for this collection of stories is the national conversation, filled with commentary from all of the above and defined by lots of that requisite conflict. I also throw in some scenes from the early childhood universe across the country, taking you to Oregon, Washington, Minnesota, Massachusetts, and my home city and state of New York. In towns and neighborhoods, people are making change, in spite of the odds. You'll see profiles of them and their work in each of the chapters. New voices are emerging in our state capitals; in Washington, DC; and in the nation's kindergarten classrooms, where the defenders of children are growing stronger. I'm cheering them on—with every fiber of my being.

Most of them are women, whom Horace Mann, the first secretary of education in Massachusetts, thought were endowed with heavenly virtue. That may be so, but virtue rarely prevails. Those who nurture the wealth of our nation have long been clustered in the "pink ghetto," a bastion of the disenfranchised. The old guard—many of them, male—persists, stuck on antiquated ideas about intervention in the earliest years, waving the flag of family values, rugged individualism, and self-sufficiency. That's what I say in polite company. Among friends, family, and colleagues who know my bent, I've been known to refer to them as Neanderthals. Or dinosaurs—soon, I hope, to be extinct.

Historically, policymaking has been an incremental process. It still is. But increasingly, how the message gets out is critical for rising above the daily assault of information. The medium is the message, said Marshall McLuhan, whom some have called a prophet of the digital age. The stewards of human capital must be consummate "spinmeisters." The drone of the conversation is relentless; the competition, fierce. The process has become faster and more dynamic—people with opinions of all stripes hawking positions on Twitter, Google+, TED talks, and a dizzying array of emerging platforms. The same applies to making social change, a slog fueled by inexhaustible energy and moral outrage at the abysmal status quo.

Today, these arenas demand more complex skills and knowledge. The good news is that the latest research on children and incursions against their healthy development has infiltrated the mainstream. Public opinion is coming around. Men are also staking their claim, declaring time and engagement with children and family a top priority. Notions of community, interdependence, and the role of government are all up in the air, with historically marginalized groups emboldened. In a nation where the poverty rate for children under age six hovers at 25 percent, and the best interests of the child are perpetually at risk, this sea change could not be more welcome.

Above all, the producers of the nation's real wealth need to claim their seat at the table—to "lean in," as Sheryl Sandberg urged America's women. A billionaire who crashed through the glass ceiling, she couldn't be more removed from the low-wage mothers juggling offspring and jobs, not to mention early childhood teachers. But the spirit is right, and the alternative is not acceptable. Otherwise, those who know little about children, and are woefully inadequate to the task, end up making big decisions with dangerous repercussions.

URIE BRONFENBRENNER AND HIS RUSSIAN DOLLS

Urie Bronfenbrenner, born in Moscow in 1917 amid revolutionary turmoil, is one of my heroes. After emigrating to the United States as a six-year-old, he went on to a distinguished career as a child psychologist. He makes a cameo appearance in a number of the chapters, his influence casting a long shadow. Cornell University, where Bronfenbrenner taught for more than half a century, has named a center for translational research in his honor. Here, his legacy lives on.

Bronfenbrenner well understood the need for interdependence. But he wasn't interested in the individual psyches of little ones—although he got right to the heart of the matter in his belief that all children, first and foremost, need someone who is crazy about them. He envisioned a human ecosystem, which he likened to a set of nested structures, one inside the next like a set of Russian dolls, with children in the innermost sanctum.

Children, Bronfenbrenner proposed, don't develop in isolation. Nor do their parents. They blossom in relation to the institutions and values in which they're embedded: home, school, community, workplace, and the larger society. His elegant bioecological theory undergirds America's barebones social policy, including Community Schools, Promise Neighborhoods, and Head Start, the nation's early childhood program for low-income children, which he helped to design. It's also the foundation for the work of the book's changemakers and systems architects, all of whom look at the child in context.

This wise scientist saw children whole, not as a collection of spare parts. Their intellectual, emotional, and social selves could not be separated. He understood that what happened out there—in the larger Russian dolls—had everything to do with a healthy developmental trajectory. He also knew that how parents fared at home, and in their relationships across society, had a profound impact on their youngsters' chances of making it in the world. We ignore his wisdom at our peril. We continue to leave the shepherds of children's early development and education high and dry, starving the human ecosystem.

MY OWN NARRATIVE

This story begins, as all do, with an infant's primal wail. The leap to parenthood is unfathomable, a journey from one planet to another, if not across galaxies. When my son was born—in the year *A Nation at Risk* was released—my perspective shifted 180 degrees. Suddenly his needs trumped everything on my to-do list. Concern for his well-being reordered my priorities like nothing before had managed to do, the life that I had known upended.

No sooner had I emerged from my postlabor fever than I jumped into this terra incognita. Just as Sam completed his 13th week on the earth, I returned to my magazine editor's job from a maternity leave cobbled together with temporary disability insurance and my own sweat equity. I was the beneficiary of the largesse of an enlightened corporation—although I did have to place a frantic phone call to the CEO just before I resumed work. He had been thinking of kicking me out of my office, barrel cactus and all.

The transition was tough. Each day, I left my newborn at home in the loving care of his child care provider. But I was miserable. And those breastfeeding sessions with a handheld pump astride a toilet in the company restroom didn't help. Working nine to five, often later, in midtown Manhattan, I rushed home each night on the subway to take back what I felt had been stolen. Most of all, I craved time. I wanted to be there, first, with my curious, babbling, and fascinating infant and then with my toddler, whose world was opening up, his words rushing like a stream, new discoveries coming every minute.

I felt so deprived that I quit to freelance when Sam was 19 months old, hoping to find that elusive work-family balance. Soon after, his father and I enrolled him at Purple Circle Day Care Center, becoming part of the village it takes to raise a child. Who were these amazing people, our new lifeline in this daunting task of rearing the next generation? I was awed by what they knew and their dedication—for which they received little respect and recognition, some of them paid on par with embalmers and parking attendants.

The epic challenges of parenthood had sent me back to the rich, progressive soil of my childhood, tilled by my own mother and father. Something was beginning to stir in me—and it wasn't another baby. My own two offspring were thriving. But I knew they were lucky. They'd been born to upward mobility—now off-limits to millions of children in a country with deep income inequality. I was lucky too. I struggled in the aftermath of a difficult divorce from their father, my dreams for further education saved by the loving support of my next of kin.

Still, I've never forgotten those days when my checking account showed a negative balance. How terrified I was to be on the brink—where so many single mothers today find themselves. Of course I had a safety net, an anomaly in modern America. Soon, I looked up and out, setting my sights beyond our own reconfigured nuclear family to other people's children in a nation that seemed to have left them behind.

A SNEAK PREVIEW OF THE BOOK

In the chapters that follow, the themes emerge, the plot thickens, and the conflicts intensify. Here, you'll find my adventures in the confounding world of public policy, where early childhood has unwittingly ascended to the top of the agenda. Some are fighting this development tooth and nail. They're defenders of the sacred realm of the family, proponents of lean, mean government. But I have to keep on reminding myself that they're also interlocutors in our national conversation, a mainstay of our vibrant, messy democracy. My private, less generous fantasies about their fate remain hidden—most of the time.

This is where the author's "point of view" comes in. Someone has to be the grown-up around here. These naysayers just don't have their priorities straight. They're clinging to antiquated ideas about gender roles. Worst of all, their proposed methods of nurturing the young are mad—and destructive. Many would say (and I do) that they verge on child abuse. See that five-year-old boy over there filling in the bubbles of a test? Or the six-year-old who—heaven forbid—is not yet reading fluently? He feels like a failure before he's even hit first grade. And what about play, the primary engine of human development? It's vanishing—along with recess and those smooth, solid blocks of all shapes and sizes in the corner.

In the opening chapter, I take a look at the period from conception to age three, when babies' hundred billion neurons are in play. Today, we know more than ever about our origins and the earliest years. Researchers are pushing boundaries, exploring the physical, cognitive, social-emotional, and moral lives of little humans. Yet we're stunting them from the get-go. Toxic stress and violence are proliferating along with the growing number of homeless and hungry children. The nation's food banks can barely keep up with demand, using something called "hungry calculus" to determine the level of incidence.

Nor can we get over our bad habit of demonizing the poor. They're still on the margins, most of them women. Never mind that we condemn their children to the bottom rungs of the ladder, to a cycle of intergenerational dysfunction. We think nothing of spending billions on fleets of fighter jets, while we hack away at the children's tiny share of the budget pie with impunity. And then we blame the parents, sticking them with the bill for child care, which costs more than tuition for college in some states.

The United States pales by comparison with Europe—especially Scandinavia, which offers all kinds of goodies to new parents. For starters, there's the well-stocked Finnish baby box, with onesies and pads for mother's leaky milk ducts. In America, a threadbare quilt of cash assistance and modest tax credits is the extent of our natal offering—unless you count the free tee-shirts given to babies just lucky enough to be born near a big football school looking for future fans. And then, how about those generous paid-leave policies in civilized social democracies? Millennials are dying of envy, living in a nation cited by Human Rights Watch for failing its families.

Equity is a leitmotif across the book's stories. In Chapter 2, I'll uncover the connections between poverty and academic outcomes, zeroing in on deep inequality in the United States, what Linda Darling-Hammond, one of our foremost equity analysts—not *that* kind—called the Achilles' heel of American education. Persistent achievement gaps have driven education reform since the National Assessment of Educational Progress issued its first report card in 1969. We know that less segregated communities with lower levels of income inequality, better schools, greater social capital, and more stable families are fertile ground for dream weaving.

But our children's sleep is troubled. The same holds true for their parents, who live in a time when the pursuit of life, liberty, and happiness butts up against a gap in income on par with that of El Salvador. Our child poverty levels—soaring beyond the 50-percent mark in Louisiana after Hurricane Katrina—place us in an ignominious position in rankings across the globe. The progressive mayor of New York City, where social critic Jonathan Kozol documented savage inequalities in the South Bronx decades ago, has taken a stab at changing the odds, making universal prekindergarten the foundation of a crusade to fight inequality.

The bandwidth of social change is broader than ever. Still, activism has a different cast these days, energized but also trivialized by social media, where advocates promote causes in tweets of 140 characters. The universe of need is expanding exponentially, families morphing into different forms, colors, and identities. The majority of babies born in the United States are now ethnic and racial minorities. By 2018, the majority of the U.S. workforce will be people of color, and by midcentury—if not sooner—no single racial group will dominate the population. I'll explore the confluence of these societal trends and how innovative people are coping, offering solutions to the urgent challenges at hand.

As debates about teacher effectiveness have reached a crescendo, America's early childhood practitioners are adrift, navigating uncharted seas. In Chapter 3, I tell the story of their journey, starting with Catherine Beecher, the 19th-century normal school pioneer, who saw home and school, the feminine realms, as inextricably linked. Women's rights activist Susan B. Anthony also weighs in. A teacher at Canajoharie Academy in Palatine Bridge, New York, she wrote a letter to her mother, giving vent to her frustration about a salary raise denied.

We then fast-forward two and a half centuries to the Worthy Wage campaign led by second-wave feminist Marcy Whitebook. Dan Rather covered one of the movement's days of protest on the CBS Evening News. "Why did the child care worker cross the road?" he asked, riffing on the well-worn riddle. "To get to her second job." At last count, the median hourly wage of teachers working within child care had inched up to a paltry $10.60. Millennial "child care workers"—exiled to the Siberia of a personal service category in the Bureau of Labor Statistics—earn less than animal trainers and barely a hair above preparers of fast food.

As important as they are, wages are only part of the story. Teacher preparation is in major flux. The professional identity of early childhood educators is still unformed. The rest of society sees them as babysitters—a perception that's hard to shake. Besides, the work they do has no value in the marketplace, where our eyes are on Wall Street and the Gross Domestic Product. Economist Nancy Folbre has bluntly warned us of the consequences for our future. A society that puts such a premium on individual success to the exclusion of nurturing the next generation is doomed.

America is a can-do nation. We pride ourselves on our creativity, innovation, and entrepreneurial moxie. Yet, we hold out ideas, often radically different, about what it takes to produce that potent mix. In Chapter 4, I'll explore the promise and pitfalls of the union between early childhood and the K–12 system. I'll take a look at the yin and the yang of education reform in this rambunctious blended family—a process that education historians David Tyack and Larry Cuban likened to "tinkering toward utopia."

The United States has always believed deeply in education as a way of perfecting the future and improving the young—a silver bullet for the ravages of poverty. We also see it as the tried-and-true route to preeminence on the world stage. To that end, America's leading the way among advanced economies, applying the dubious process of disruptive innovation, a popular business strategy, to human development, learning, and teaching. Nothing is off-limits in our pursuit of cognitive complexity. That includes the subconscious. A patent-pending product called Sleep'n Sync promises a multifaceted brain lift for children after they've drifted off to dreamland.

As a symptom of our very own obsessive-compulsive disorder, we're measuring children's progress every step of the way. Are they prepared for school? Can they count up to 20? Are they reading *The Sorcerer's Stone?* Watch out for those third-grade benchmarks. We keep pushing them along—ignoring the pesky emotions that get in the way of regulation and executive function. Lately, the guardians of childhood have declared they've had enough. They're putting their feet down, opting out of the growing number of standardized tests that are casting a blight on the "gardens of delight" envisioned by Johann Comenius, a 17th-century Moravian bishop disturbed by the violence of the Thirty Years' War.

Designing a system to ensure children get what they need is not for the faint of heart. In Chapter 5, I've taken a page from John F. Kennedy's classic, *Profiles in Courage*, highlighting the architects on this master project. Before you build, you need a blueprint to determine the extent of the work. Early childhood has had to start from the ground up—a process requiring great leaps of imagination, faith, and lots of pluck. System building isn't sexy. Just think about the terms of art: infrastructure, linkages, coordination, alignment. And the process couldn't be more fraught. It's not easy wrestling with the field's big issues—equity, sustainability, and accountability—day to day over time.

Then there's the long and winding road to quality, another of our national obsessions. We haven't yet produced a universally accepted definition—this, in spite of all we know about children and the conditions that support their development and academic skill formation. Some of today's senior architects identify with Sisyphus, pushing his heavy boulder up the mountain. A newer, more energetic crop, weaned on unprecedented support for their work at the highest levels of policymaking, is more sanguine; they see a glass half full.

Wherever they sit, the architects navigate a polarized and dysfunctional political system. Internecine squabbling is rife. The budget pie is miniscule, and priorities constantly shift. Most politicians couldn't care less about the long-term outcomes. How anyone moves the needle is a wonder. Still, they believe—as all converts do—that early childhood is the most powerful leverage point for changing the trajectory of children. All are alchemists, their own early experiences transmuted into the drive for reform.

The book's final chapter started out as an elegiac meditation on the impact of technology on young children in their most tender years. But I ended up embracing this brave, new world—with reservations. How could I scorn iChat, which helps children without speech communicate? Electronic media use in the United States is exploding, our preschoolers and babies swiping their sweet, little fingers across a plethora of magnetizing screens. I chronicle the movement from analog to digital—a transformation, some say, on par with the huge leaps from oral to written language and onward to the printing press. What would life be without the World Wide Web, which was born in the same year as my daughter? Victoria Rideout has been reporting from the front, at Common Sense Media, suffering from battle fatigue.

For parents, technology is just one more thing on a long list of things that they need to perfectly navigate. Researchers in child development, working on academia's pokey timeline, can barely keep up with their questions. Is that video frying or firing the synapses of my child's brain? Will the green room in *Goodnight Moon* lose its magic on an electronic reader? Can little Olivia master, much less understand, fractions via a math app online? The answers emerge slowly, but they're inadequate to the task of assuaging parents' anxieties.

In the classrooms of the nation's early educators, this profound paradigm shift is well under way, shaking the foundations of the field. Whatever happened to Jean Piaget and Lev Vygotsky? Those legendary theorists believed that young children learn best through their senses, exploring their world with adults and their peers. Technology's virtual toys seem a poor substitute for the real thing. A new breed of professional-development specialist is bringing them along—including Erin Klein, a "Tweet loving, technology integrating mom of two with a passion for classroom design." A pioneer into the digital Wild West, she's leading the way.

This contentious, uniquely American conversation continues, the protagonists changing with the seasons. But children's needs remain fixed. And we must do a better job of meeting them. The future of our civilization is at risk.

CHAPTER 1

In the Beginning

Here in the land of self-sufficiency and family values . . . anything that smacks of social welfare statehood is a tough sell. Never mind that nearly 57 percent of women with children under age one are in the workforce. We remain a country in denial. FMLA [Family Medical Leave Act], sadly, is all we've got, and it barely begins to address the needs of new moms, dads, and kids in this most critical and vulnerable phase of human development.

—"Rocking Cradle to Career with Paid Family Leave," *Huffington Post*

Children are, at once, deeply familiar and profoundly alien. . . . Their minds seem drastically limited; they know so much less than we do. And yet long before they can read and write, they have extraordinary powers of imagination and creativity, and long before they go to school, they have remarkable learning abilities.

—Alison Gopnik, *The Philosophical Baby*

For a ringside seat at the miracle of babies' minds, you might try the Institute for Learning and Brain Sciences at the University of Washington. The husband-and-wife team of Patricia Kuhl and Andrew Meltzoff presides over I-LABS, where an eight-ton machine, through a process with the tongue-twisting name of magnetoencephalography (MEG), churns out dazzling images of cerebral action in infants, tracking the birth of language. These researchers are riding the latest wave of neuroscience, which has pushed early child development and education into the gray matter of parents, economists, corporate CEOs, philanthropists, policymakers, and educators.

As the second decade of the 21st century got under way, the pre-K brain hit prime time at NBC's annual education summit, a visual tour provided by I-LABS's Kuhl.[1] American viewers learned of babies' hundred billion neurons and the pruning of synapses to strengthen neural connections. They heard of the 116 different areas in the infant brain and the fiber tracks that connect to the corpus callosum—a bundle of neural fibers, a super highway that links the right and left sides. They saw an adorable nine-month-old, with helmet and rattle, listening and babbling as the MEG machine scanned every second of activity. The ultimate reality show.

"The next time you're engaged in a conversation with a baby, and anything or anyone tries to interrupt that activity, I want you to say: 'Stop, I'm building a brain here,'" Kuhl told her national audience. "It's the most important thing in the world."[2] Her presentation was riveting. But this construction project is not high priority.

GROWING THE GARDEN OF HUMAN CAPITAL

In the autumn of America's discontent, the populace buffeted by income inequality, *Capital in the 21st Century* made its way to our shores. By the following spring, author Thomas Piketty, an unassuming French economist, had achieved rock-star status. His 700-page opus on the unequal accumulation and distribution of wealth since the 18th century was securely ensconced on the *New York Times* bestseller list.[3] Ooh-la-la! Still, not everyone was captivated. Economist James K. Galbraith delivered a critique in *Dissent* magazine, "a pillar of leftist intellectual provocation," taking Piketty to task for his quantification of capital as "an agglomeration of physical objects."[4]

Economists have been talking about human capital—or skills, creativity, and enterprise—since the 17th century, when a man named William Petty made one of the first attempts to estimate the monetary value of a human being.[5] Hundreds of years later, Petty's professional descendants have continued his line of work, developing and quantifying the concept of human capital, which, by some estimates, creates two-thirds of our modern economy's wealth.[6]

I'm not crazy about this rationalistic framework—it evokes human trafficking, a colleague once said—but pragmatism trumps fuzzy, warm morality in the United States, the world's foremost exporter of capitalism. "The mere thought of investment in human beings is offensive to some among us," Theodore W. Schultz told his audience, in 1961, at the seventy-third annual meeting of the American Economic Association, in St. Louis. But, he added, "Investment in human capital accounts for most of the impressive rise in the real earnings per worker."[7]

In recent years, another Petty descendant, Nobel laureate James Heckman, has taken human-capital creation mainstream, right into the minds, if not the hearts, of Capitol decisionmakers. A longtime professor at the University of Chicago, Heckman has become quite the crusader, working with psychologists, sociologists, and neuroscientists on what he calls life-cycle skill formation. His mantra—"skills beget skills"—captures two esoteric phenomena, called static and dynamic complementarity. In regular English: The benefits from investment in human capital depend, in part, on existing levels of skills, with investments today enhancing the stock of future skills and increasing the ultimate returns to society.[8]

"Human capital is and always has been one of our country's greatest natural resources," Heckman wrote in a letter to the National Commission on Fiscal Responsibility and Budget Reform, during one of the debates about deficit reduction that habitually tear the nation asunder.[9] He's a regular at the meetings of all the august bodies that hold children's lives in the balance—including a White House Summit on Early Education, where he laid out a path for "going forward wisely."[10] The administration had gotten on board—replete with the hashtag, #investinus—uniting country and children and pledging a billion dollars in funding.[11]

TOWARD A SOCIALLY JUST ECONOMY

A billion dollars is no small change, of course, unless you do a little comparative budget analysis. "Cost of Military Jet Could House Every Homeless Person in U.S. with $600,000 Home," headlined a short piece in the *Huffington Post* soon after Piketty's transatlantic trip. Author Robbie Couch was reporting on a project, seven years behind schedule due to chronic incompetence, to create a fleet of F-35 Joint Strike Fighter jets. The $400 billion committed to the military, he revealed, using data from an outfit called Think Progress, was enough to fund the National School Lunch Program, now serving about 31 million students annually, for nearly a quarter of a century.[12]

The competition between guns and butter is as American as apple pie, global policing a symptom of our bipolar disorder, ever at the mercy of the changing geopolitical winds. One lugubrious July, ZERO TO THREE, a national organization with a core constituency barely talking, much less conversant in the art of advocacy, announced in the *Federal Policy Baby Blog* that spending on children was on a downward slide. The House Appropriations Committee, the post explained, had "crept forward" on investment in key programs for children and families; their total of $150 billion a $6.3 billion cut from the previous year. Ah, but hark! A small patch of light appeared on the crawling infant's floor: Funds for the Maternal, Infant, and Early Childhood Home Visiting program—for the moment, at least—had been spared.[13]

The big picture, however, was another story, captured in exhaustive detail by the Urban Institute's annual *Kids' Share* report. Federal spending on children had fallen to $2 billion from 2010 to 2011, the first such decline in nearly 30 years. The children's share was reduced to about 10 percent of the budget pie, with spending as a share of total economic output (aka Gross Domestic Product) also shrinking, to 2.5 percent. The forecast for the future couldn't be bleaker: By 2022, the children's portion of the budget was expected to drop to 8 percent, and their share of GDP, to 1.9 percent, with significant cuts in early care and education.[14]

In a later accounting, the Institute duly noted that federal spending had declined by $34 billion between 2011 and 2012 just as temporary relief from the American Recovery and Reinvestment Act was drying up. State and local governments, they conceded, were having difficulty making up the shortfall. The bottom line: Expenditures on America's precious human capital in 2013 totaled $464 billion, up just a few billion from the year before but significantly lower than the peak of $499 billion in 2010.[15]

"Billions here, billions there—we're talking real money," Grover Russell Whitehurst, formerly of the Institute of Education Sciences, told policymakers, discouraging preschool for all.[16] The world has noticed our anxiety. Insights from the Social Expenditure Database from the Organisation for Economic Co-operation and Development (OECD)—purveyors of the PISA tests on academic achievement—are hardly reassuring. America's preference for private, cost-effective, market-based solutions with the illusion of choice translates into a low ranking, on the cusp of the bottom third of public social spending as percentage of GDP. Nor do we shine on the OECD's Social Justice Index.[17]

"I'm beginning to feel like Talthybius, a Greek character and bearer of bad news," Michael Morrison wrote at his blog *Decisions Based on Evidence*, in response to the embarrassing cross-national comparison. Then I must be Cassandra, who predicted the fall of Troy only to be banned from prophesizing by her father, Priam, who declared her mad and locked her up.

In the six categories that contribute to a socially just market economy—poverty prevention, access to education, labor market inclusion, social cohesion and nondiscrimination, health, and intergenerational justice—the United States ranked near the bottom of the 31 nations surveyed. Our alarming poverty rate—roughly one in every four children under the age of six—placed us just above Mexico and the organization's newest member, Chile.[18]

This is a problem, particularly if you happen to believe that children are public goods, not pets—an argument that has made economist and MacArthur fellow Nancy Folbre hoarse since the late 20th century.[19] Joining her, among a growing cadre of critics of the status quo, have been Janet Gornick, the prime mover of the Luxembourg Income Study, and Marcia Meyers, director of the West Coast Poverty Center at the University of Washington. In *Families That Work*, the two connect the dots between the nurturing of human capabilities—dryly dubbed "positive externalities" by the experts who study society's resources and production—and gender equality, child well-being, and a viable economy.

Yet, Gornick and Meyers harbor no illusions. In comparison with most of Europe, they wrote that the United States is a "reluctant, residual, or only partial welfare state." What we have is a lightweight quilt of means-tested, time-limited cash assistance for the poor, modest child credits for families with tax liabilities, and a refundable Earned Income Tax Credit (EITC) for low-income, employed parents. There are efforts afoot to better pack the quilt, but they remain a tough sell.[20]

The United States is afflicted by an inputs-outputs complex, complicated by our penchant for competition. Stuck with conventional metrics, we stint on the resources, expect stellar outcomes, and remain oblivious to the disconnect. The country has abandoned the care paradigm, Anne-Marie Slaughter, CEO of the New America foundation, wrote in *A Woman's Nation Pushes Back from the Brink*, an expose of the financial insecurity of American families. "Our progress as a species flows from our identity as social animals, connected to one another through ties of love, kinship, and clanship."[21] But care, education, and health read as consumption, not investment, in our national accounting; production of the next generation has become a luxury item.[22]

Lately, an alternative framework has emerged, a stealth movement to radically reformulate economics, derived—wouldn't you know?—from the Greek word *okonomia*, for managing the household. Leading the charge is Riane Eisler, a social scientist, attorney, and cultural critic. Her biography notes that she is the only woman among 20 great thinkers, including G.W. F. Hegel, Adam Smith, Karl Marx, and Arnold Toynbee, to be included in *Macrohistory and Macrohistorians*, perspectives on "an eclectic and civilizationally rich theory of grand social change." Civilizationally? Never heard of that adverb. But I'll take that theory of grand social change any day.

While the woman's nation was pushing back, Eisler's Center for Partnership Studies released a series of Social Wealth Economic Indicators (SWEI) to fill in the egregious gaps of the GDP. Using data from the OECD, the World Health Organization, and the United Nations, she and Indradeep Ghosh, an economics professor at Haverford, set forth new measures that would capture the value of care work in producing high-quality human capital. As is done these days, they spread the word in a Google+ hangout hosted by Carol Evans, founder of Working Mother Media, and promptly designed a series of webinars for further enlightenment.[23]

The world had already begun to look at a slew of new economic indicators focused on outputs, including poverty rates and educational attainment. But the critical inputs were missing. Based on findings from neuroscience, the SWEIs measure human capacity much more broadly, adding to the traditional outputs time spent on unpaid care work, long-term care wages, the gender gap in earnings, and a global gender-gap index.

The poor, orphaned inputs find their home in the Care Investment Indicators—has a nice ring to it, doesn't it?—with creation of human capacity number one. Next up are public spending on family benefits, percentage of GDP for public funding of child care and early education, paid family leave, long-term care, employer support for child care, GDP share for environmental protection, and the costs of education and prison. Which reminds me of Marian Wright Edelman's time-honored meme about sending a child to prison for what it would cost us to send him to Yale.[24]

THE DANCE OF DEVELOPMENT

In 1935, as President Franklin Delano Roosevelt offered yet another new deal to a Depression-scarred citizenry, the U.S. Department of Labor released *Infant Care*, Children's Bureau Publication No. 8.[25] The ten-cent pamphlet urged John and Jane Doe to register their babies within 36 hours after birth to prove age and citizenship and claim the fundamental rights granted by same: education, work, marriage, inheritance of property, and a pension for mother, if she'd had the misfortune to be widowed. Laid out in the table of contents were all the key concerns of new parents. First up, child development, including a daily time card with a rigorous schedule for breastfeeding. Next, hints for keeping the baby well and, most importantly, preventing disease and accidents.

Following was advice on a wide array of topics, among them, selecting the infant's room and clothing, care of special organs (eyes, mouth, ears, nose, and genitals), sleep, outdoor life, and play, as well as the cultivation of the essential, elusive habits, training, and discipline. The publication also weighed in on the interplay of nature and nurture. "Every child carries in his inherited make-up many qualities," the anonymous authors wrote. "Which ones predominate in his future life will depend largely on his surroundings." Decades before the dazzling pyrotechnics of magnetoencephalography, they knew the score: "From the hour of birth he learns from everything around him."[26]

Our knowledge of babies and how they develop has taken quantum leaps, making the earliest conceptions of childhood look positively Pleistocene.

Remember John Locke (baby as "blank slate") and Jean-Jacques Rousseau?[27] My own graduate school days coincided with the awesome forays of developmental psychologists into the minds of babies. I was intoxicated by the findings of this new frontier, whose pioneers—Elizabeth Spelke, Alison Gopnik, Meltzoff and Kuhl, among others—provided nutritious juice as I waded into the evidence-crazed waters of public policy.[28]

Even our youngest citizens, it turns out, have basic knowledge about other people, language, the physical world, and the objects around them, which they explore like "scientists in the crib," testing hypotheses about how the world works.[29] Gopnik affectionately refers to babies, our little aliens, as the "R&D department of the human species—the blue-sky guys, the brainstormers." The role of adults: production and marketing. "Babies make the discoveries," she says, "and we implement them."[30]

While the world turns, changing at unprecedented speed, babies' needs remain fixed. As members of the human species, theirs is a long period of dependence, at turns, exhilarating, exasperating, exhausting, overwhelming. Having reared a couple of infants to adulthood, I look back on that period with nostalgia—and relief that it's over. The acuteness of my absorption and anxiety was like an albatross. "How on earth can I bring a child into the world," Anne Lamott asked in *Operating Instructions: A Journal of My Son's First Year*, "knowing that such sorrow lies ahead, that it is such a large part of what it means to be human?"[31] Now grandma to a growing brood, the product of a blended family, I've watched, in awe, as the older ones have jumped on to the tightrope. How on earth do they do it? How did I do that? How does *anyone* manage?

The task is daunting. From the get-go, children's interactions with sensitive and stimulating caregivers fuel their social, emotional, and intellectual development, with enduring effects on their future capacities.[32] The process of bonding, or attunement, is the first order of business, as parents and babies begin the dance of development.[33] The choreography is delicate, and nuanced, babies building basic trust—a sense of security and optimism that nurtures their desire to engage in the world and take on challenging tasks with persistence and pleasure.[34] Just think of that creature in the crib, pulling herself up and down like a jack-in-the-box. She's obsessed, so delighted with herself. Look at me, I'm brilliant!

In development-speak, the phenomenon of applying nose to the grindstone is called "mastery motivation," a process by which children acquire a sense of competence and control.[35] It's that perseverance that keeps them going. Their insatiable curiosity and formidable new learning skills form the foundation for the students, not to mention the human beings and citizens that they will become. We've taken to calling this "grit," a social skill, also known as character, with which we think we can inoculate children long after the damage has been done.[36]

When your environment is stable and nurturing, the odds for success are good. But they change dramatically when home is chaotic, even dangerous. Or if you happen, say, to be among the one in ten children whose mothers are depressed. A major public health problem in the United States—although we don't like to talk about it.[37] Basic trust, needless to say, is hard to come by when you're carrying the weight of poverty, separation, divorce, unemployment, and financial difficulties, the lot of a growing number of citizens in the nation.

This interplay of nature, what babies bring to the table, and nurture, the environmental contribution, has preoccupied observers of humans for centuries.[38] Modern developmental scientists are aided by finer tools and opportunities than their predecessors could ever have imagined. We know now that the two can't be separated, that neither provides the answer. Still, the plot thickens as assumptions about universal, predetermined patterns fall by the wayside, along with the theorists who set them forth, and practitioners.

Psychologist and pediatrician Arnold Gesell (whose books on what to expect at every age I confess to having consulted in my early parenting years) recently came under withering attack from Anne Fausto-Sterling, a professor emerita of biology and gender studies at Brown. "Maybe the idea that there are fixed standard patterns is . . . wrong," she wrote in "Letting Go of Normal," in the notoriously iconoclastic *Boston Review*.[39] Cocky-locky, the sky is falling!

HOMELAND INSECURITY WITH MAXIMUM STRESS

Survivor is the brainchild of Griffin Technology, a privately held company headquartered in Nashville, Tennessee. Designed to meet or exceed U.S. military standards for protection, the iPad cover is made with sealable ports that keep out sand, dust, and rain and with a polycarbonate shell that minimizes impacts. "Griffintech," the corporation's Twitter handle, claims to back its products with the best customer support in the business. You can order the device online, or call an 800 number, where a live human being provides the dish on this exemplar of American ingenuity. Military standards are high in our country—the Department of Defense child care system has long been the gold standard for quality. Guarding the homeland and its citizens is our first order of business. But what about the millions of civilians under five, those whom we've dubbed "too small to fail"?[40]

"Why won't the U.S. ratify the U.N.'s child rights treaty?" Karen Attiah asked at the *Washington Post*—a quarter of a century after 190 members of the General Assembly adopted resolution 44/25, otherwise known as the Convention on the Rights of the Child.[41] Why, indeed? The ninth clause of the preamble could not be more clear: "The child, by reason of his physical and mental immaturity, needs special safeguards and care, including appropriate legal protection, before as well as after birth."[42]

At least Amnesty International is on the case, summarizing those rights in Frequently Asked Questions, posted on its website. Freedom from violence, abuse, exploitation, hazardous employment, abduction, or sale leads the call to action. Free compulsory education is wedged between adequate nutrition and health care. Next up: equal treatment regardless of gender, race, or culture, followed by the right to freedom of expression and safe access to leisure, play, culture, and art. So sensible, and comprehensive.

As for America's procrastination problem, well, "International treaties undergo extensive examination and scrutiny before they are ratified in the United States," the third FAQ tells us.[43] (Apparently, 30 years passed before we ratified the Convention on the Prevention and Punishment of the Crime of Genocide.) Not least of the impediments has been the opposition, led for a time by Jesse Helms. The five-time senator from North Carolina and conservative gadfly, who died on Independence Day in 2008, pronounced the agreement "incompatible with the God-given right and responsibility of parents to raise their children."[44]

Such hubris to think about encroaching on divine gifts. But what about that niggling issue of unequal child development? Even the World Health Organization, which regards social justice as a matter of life and death, has tempered its expectations: They're calling the goal of closing the gap in a generation "an aspiration not a prediction."[45]

Deconstruction of the discrepancies, which emerge in the first years of life, fueled the work of the late Clyde Hertzman, a prime mover of the Human Early Learning Partnership, at the University of British Columbia, and something of a cult figure among young pediatricians concerned about the social determinants of health.[46] The factors that influence outcomes are the object of endless scientific inquiry: family income, parental education, parenting style, neighborhood safety and cohesion, community socioeconomic status, access to high-quality child care, health care. The list goes on and on.

Here in the land of rugged individualism, Jack Shonkoff, of Harvard's Center for the Developing Child, has had his work cut out for him, translating the evidence into theories of change.[47] *From Neurons to Neighborhoods,* the new-millennial bible he edited with Deborah Phillips, then executive director of the Board on Children, Youth, and Families of the National

Research Council, took the nature-nurture bull by the horns. He's the go-to guy for everything you've always wanted to know about toxic stress, the underbelly of Hertzman's inequality factors. This phenomenon—a neurobiological tsunami generated by inadequate adult support in the face of adversity—has become the ultimate signifier for America's uncomfortable conversation about the deteriorating state of our children.

Physical abuse, mental illness, violence—at home and in the community—and the burdens of family economic hardship. Such a cringe-inducing litany of stressors.[48] The National Child Traumatic Stress Network offers an infinitely rich typology for all to see online, including natural disasters, neglect, refugee and war zone trauma, school violence, sexual abuse, terrorism, and traumatic grief. Forced separation of parents and children, the fate of 72,410 deported immigrants when last recorded, must fit into that final category.[49] Along with children of incarcerated parents, who find themselves in "challenging circumstances," as FindYouthInfo.gov calls them, offering resources on their "overlapping problems."[50]

While certain kinds of stress are good for children—they build resilience, or that all-important grit—the toxic kind, if prolonged, can do considerable damage. At a forum in Harlem some years ago, hosted by Irwin Redlener, an expert on disaster preparedness, Shonkoff channeled a legislator in Kansas: "It's like having an adrenaline rush 24/7," he said, as a PowerPoint graphically drove home the wear and tear on the burgeoning infant brain.[51] Most importantly, toxic stress diverts energy from the prefrontal cortex, the center of executive function, or the heart of babies' capacity to plan, focus, and learn.

The outcomes, both immediate and long term, include developmental delays, learning challenges, and physical and mental illness that can extend all the way into adulthood.[52] We know this, having spent decades tracking the effects of adverse childhood experiences (ACE) in a longitudinal study, begun in the mid-1990s, a collaboration of Kaiser Permanente and the Centers for Disease Control.[53] "What's an ACE score?" the study's website asks on a page with calculators in English, French, German, Icelandic, Norwegian, Spanish, and Swedish. The answer: "Use the ACE Score Calculator to find out!"

We Americans like knowing where we stand and we like our sports metaphors. "Iowa, let's kick some ACEs," pediatrician Nadine Burke Harris roared at a conference in Des Moines, having changed the title of her PowerPoint, she confessed, to capture that irrepressible spirit. The founder and CEO of the Center for Youth Wellness in San Francisco, she's a star quarterback for the team.[54]

A MALNOURISHED HUMAN ECOSYSTEM

The work of the pediatricians lies squarely in the tradition of Cornell child psychologist Urie Bronfenbrenner, whose bioecological theory of human development undergirds the most progressive, if starved, strain of American social policy, including Head Start, Community Schools, and Promise Neighborhoods. Children, he argued, don't develop in isolation but, rather, in relation to the institutions in which they are nested: home, school, community, workplace, and the larger society.

In a human ecosystem, development depends upon the interactions among these environments and the constellation of relationships that bind them. "Whether parents can perform effectively in their child-rearing roles within the family," Bronfenbrenner wrote in *The Ecology of Human Development,* "depends on . . . demands, stresses, and supports emanating from other settings,"[55] By way of clarification for the likes of Jesse Helms and his ilk, he went on to cite the specifics—such "external factors" as flexible job schedules, adequate child care arrangements, the quality of health and social services, as well as friends and neighbors ready to help out in case of emergency.[56]

Portia Kennel knows this inside out. A senior vice president at the Ounce of Prevention Fund, she was raised in East St. Louis, Illinois, by a mother who did her best to provide for her children on a maid's income. But when Kennel was seven, her mother realized she couldn't do it alone and turned to public assistance. "I remember the visits by the public aid worker, and how she treated my mother," she said. "I thought 'how can she talk to my mother like that?' I'm going to be a social worker. I can do it better." Kennel's early experience informed the philosophy that's guided her career: You can only create real change in children's lives by respecting and partnering with their parents.

One November, before the nation celebrated its bounty, the eponymous Perryman Group, an economic and financial analysis firm in Waco, Texas, released *Suffer the Little Children.* An assessment of the economic cost of child maltreatment, the report opens with the often-cited, but unheeded, quote from Nelson Mandela: "The true character of a society is revealed in how it treats its children."[57] Like purveyors of ideology everywhere, CEO M. Ray Perryman took to the opinion pages of his local paper, the *Midland Reporter-Telegram,* to spread the news.

He did not bury the lead. "As horrific and unimaginable as it sounds, child maltreatment is pervasive in the United States," he wrote, declaring it a pressing public health issue of utmost social concern. Perryman attested to the persistent physical and emotional consequences to victims, which, he conceded, were "truly incalculable."[58]

You've got to give the man credit. He would not be put off by "Images That Dare You to Turn Away," depicted in Stephanie Wang-Breal's *Tough Love*, a documentary about the child welfare system that premiered at the DOC NYC festival about the same time as his report's publication.[59] Perryman was also right in line with two Associated Press investigative reporters who would release their findings just before Christmas. A survey of 50 states, the District of Columbia, and branches of the military revealed that 800 children had died of abuse or neglect in a six-year period, "many of them beaten, starved or left alone to drown while agencies had good reason to know they were in danger."[60]

Incalculable devastation, indeed. But that doesn't stop us from crunching those numbers to figure out the tab. When Perryman did his estimates, based on the 3.3 million cases of first-time child maltreatment in 2014, he found a gold mine. The tally for the total economic cost of abuse in a year included $5.9 trillion in lifetime spending on health, social welfare, and crime; $2.7 trillion in lost gross domestic product; and nearly 28 million "person-years" of employment—such a humane term—or nine years of lost work for each individual unlucky enough to have suffered such a tragedy.[61]

Perryman also applied his formidable analytical skills to hunger, which afflicted one in seven households in 2013, nearly seven million of them in the most severe category of what we prefer to call "food insecurity."[62] An infographic on his website is cluttered with eye-popping numbers, none rounded up for effect. We learn of health costs: $461.9 billion in increased annual spending due to higher incidence and severity of disease, $221.9 billion loss in gross domestic product, and reduced lifetime earnings to the tune of 15.9 million person-years of employment. Education appears in the cost column, too—in the form of additional expenses to compensate for "issues" related to empty bellies and reduced lifetime earnings due to lower levels of schooling. Here, we're looking at an annual deficit of $146.7 billion over a lifetime in personal income.[63]

So what's the solution? Perryman, honored by the Democracy Foundation for promoting capitalism in mainland China, proposes expansion of food banks and other forms of distribution to meet the current need and reduce costs. But the charities are working overtime, mapping the meal gap—the translation of the food budget shortfall into number of meals—using something called "hungry calculus."

According to Feeding America's survey of 3,143 county and congressional districts across the nation, food-insecure individuals reported a daily budget shortfall of $2.26 per person, or $68.74 monthly.[64] In the organization's county-level food cost index—compiled with Nielsen of television ratings fame—those figures trended upward in the places where food is more expensive, such as Los Angeles and New York. The organization had also done due diligence on the incidence of the problem among different races and ethnicities. Of the 101 counties where African Americans constitute the majority of residents, 94 rate high on the food-insecurity scale—including Humphrey's County, Mississippi. The nation's winner in this dubious ranking, the county posted unemployment at 16 percent and poverty at 41 percent.[65]

Ah, yes, those small, confounding factors in mapping the meal gap. Parents who are especially adroit navigators of the social service system might avoid the minimal impact of transient adult food insecurity on their toddlers' development. Persistent hunger, on the other hand, is another matter altogether.

Buried on page 15 of the survey are a brief history and mild critique of the poverty guidelines, established by Social Security Administration economist Mollie Orshansky in 1963, the year of Martin Luther King's dream. The poverty threshold, an eternal sore spot for those who rue America's tight-fisted approach to social welfare, was set by multiplying by three the food costs for a "bare-bones" meal plan.[66] Feeding America notes, as others have done ad nauseam, that the figures have barely changed in the more than half a century since the original calculations. But however you slice it, or don't—as in homes where the bread box is empty—almost 50 million people, 16 million of them children, are going to bed hungry each night, here in the land of plenty.[67]

Why does no one mention the Special Supplemental Nutrition Program for Women, Infants, and Children (WIC), which sustains nine million? Good food, counseling on healthy eating, and health care referrals to low-income and postpartum women and their babies. Such solid inputs. The outcomes are not bad, either: healthier births, higher intake of key nutrients, less consumption of sugar and fats, and better preventive care. No wonder the Center on Budget and Policy Priorities described it as highly effective.[68]

Of course, WIC has weathered its share of battering by funding uncertainty, as the Center noted in a policy brief on the impact of sequestration—a term that only a wonk could love. Merriam-Webster's definition mimics the cold, redundant jargon of bureaucracy: the practice of imposing automatic government spending reductions by withholding appropriations by a fixed percentage that applies uniformly to all government programs except those exempted.

"Will WIC be able to serve all eligible low-income women and young children who apply?" authors Zoe Neuberger and Bob Greenstein asked, plaintively. While $7.046 billion had been appropriated the previous year for fiscal year 2013, the final legislation had also included one of those across-the-board cuts, of about two and a half percent, which would reduce funding available to the program by $177 million. On top of that, WIC stood to lose another $14 million, courtesy of the Office of Management and Budget, forced to bring "aggregate non-security spending down to the pre-sequestration funding cap required under the Budget Control Act."[69]

Ah, but wait, they had not finished documenting the damage. The coup de grace was an additional loss of $333 million, part of a 5-percent reduction in nondefense discretionary programs. WIC participation was already waning, having declined to 8.9 million in 2012 from a peak of 9.2 million in 2010, in the midst of the Great Recession. Enrollment was continuing to edge down, the threat of far deeper cuts looming. State and local WIC agencies were in cost-reduction mode, laying off staff and leaving openings unfilled.[70] The outlook was bleak, the larder bare.

FAILING OUR FAMILIES, THE NATION'S WEALTH PRODUCERS

How did we get into this mess? There are no easy answers. An ersatz want ad, drafted by economist Shirley Burggraf, may help illuminate the path.

> Parents willing to bear, rear, and educate children for the next generation of social security taxpayers and to carry on the American culture of learning and progress. Quality parenting preferred. Large commitments of time and money required. At least one parent must work a double shift and/or sacrifice tenure and upward mobility in the job market. Salary: 0. Pension benefits: 0. Profits and dividends: 0.[71]

"Would anyone be answering this ad in the twenty-first century?" Burggraf asked the readers of her treatise on the feminine economy and economic man.[72] What a crass take on parenthood, such a distortion of that rosy vision of mother and apple pie. And let's not forget the hearth, in the house behind the white picket fence, off limits to the two and a half million children now homeless in America. That's one in thirty sons and daughters, in families mostly headed by single, working women, inhabitants of a growing matriarchal Third World.[73]

These days, the newest crop of middle-class progenitors is asking Burggraf's question, in stitches over an account of a fictional study, conducted by the Pew Research Center, on the latest trends in procreation. More Americans are putting off children until companies are ready, the *Onion* announced. "Raising a child nowadays," the satirical news outlet noted, "requires parents' employers to sacrifice a tremendous amount of time and resources."[74]

Of course, this dilemma might easily be construed as a First World problem, the province of the relatively small percentage of the labor force that toils in the corporate sector. Low-wage workers hovering around the outdated poverty line are really up a creek without a paddle. But the support deficit is universal, the degree of impact varying across the socioeconomic spectrum. Former U.S. treasury secretary Lawrence Summers may have told Ann Crittenden, author of *The Price of Motherhood*, that childrearing is the most important job in the world, but our ledger sheets say otherwise.[75] The United States remains an outlier, cited by Human Rights Watch for failing its families, the nation's major wealth producers.[76]

Here, parents are left in the lurch, pining for Finland's baby boxes, a tradition since the 1930s, while hordes of Americans were battling the dust storms that damaged the ecology and agriculture of the prairies.[77] A gift to all Finns, the box, with a mattress, duvet cover, and quilt, serves as the infant's first bed, its contents a sight for new parents' sore, tired eyes. Among the goodies are a snowsuit, hats, and insulated mittens and booties, the better to guard against the frigid Nordic temperatures. Onesies and leggings are also included—in unisex patterns—as well as a hooded bath towel, nail scissors, toothbrush, and a wash cloth. They throw in a picture book, teething toy, and bra pads. How thoughtful of them to think of mother's leaky milk ducts.

The box had claimed prime space in the BBC's *News Magazine*, the grateful voices of parents punctuating the story. "This felt to me like evidence that someone cared, someone wants our baby to have a good start in life," Helsinki resident Mark Bosworth said.[78] A graph of the descending infant mortality rate and a timeline of the maternity pack's history were also included. In the 1970s, with more women in the workforce, easy-to-wash stretch cotton and colorful patterns had replaced the white, stiffer baby garments, vestiges of an earlier era with ample time for laundry and ironing—or so those who delegated these tasks to others might think.

Meanwhile, American babies born at Ohio State's Wexner Medical Center hospital during football season spend their first hours in the nursery swathed in bright red "Beat Alabama" blankets—a special "bowl gift," designed to nurture diehard fans for the home team.[79]

Sociologist Arlie Hochschild's "second shift," carefully documented in time diaries of late-20th-century working parents, is still in effect.[80] The work-balance juggling act is as frenzied as ever, embodied today in the "iconic image of the economically insecure American . . . a working mother rushing to get ready in the morning, brushing her kid's hair with one hand and doling out medication to her aging mother with the other."[81] The rest of the developed world has been paying close attention to these seismic shifts. But in the United States, early care and education have long been an afterthought, pushed aside like toddlers in the sandbox by the competing priorities of others.

PAID LEAVE: CHIMERA OR POLICY WHOSE TIME HAS COME?

Harold Levy, executive director of the Jack Kent Cooke Foundation, has the look of the Oxford don he might have been had he never left that English university. He served as New York City's public schools chancellor from 1999 to 2002—a brief detour from a career spent mostly in finance. A decade later, in preparation for a forum promoting paid family leave, hosted by the National Center for Children in Poverty, I invited him to make the case for a policy whose time had come. Then a managing partner at Palm Ventures, a company that invests in businesses that have a transformative impact, Levy's first words were blunt: "I admire what you're doing," he said, "but I don't think you're going to see this happen any time soon."

If only he could have seen the future. "New Dads Likely to Take Paternity Leave If Paid Time is Offered," the *Wall Street Journal* headline would read—just two years later.[82] A recent study at the Boston College Center for Work and Family had found 70 percent of full salary to be the winning threshold for uptake. Men's failure to be active parents in the first few months of life, to the detriment of maternal well-being, sets a pattern that is difficult to change, the authors had observed.

Backstage was just not an option for this "new man," the vast majority of whom rated children as their top priority in life. They saw caregiving as a 50/50 proposition—gender equity right from the start.[83] I'd heard the same rap from my firstborn, their generational peer. A new father, he called me from the east, as I stepped out of a Children's Institute event at the Portland Museum of Art, to tell me he had to extend his leave. Four weeks was not enough, he told me; his partner was not yet back to normal. Of course, she would never be there again, irrevocably changed by the process at hand.

Still, Levy agreed to do the deed. Over lunch at the Ford Foundation headquarters, preaching to the converted, he invoked the biblical injunction, from Proverbs, declaring parents as first teachers. "Listen, my son, to your father's instruction and do not forsake your mother's teaching," the Old Testament urges. "We have to put parenting ahead of work," Levy said.

"We need to offer time to foster cognitive development. The source of our economic growth is intellectual capacity."[84]

Just days before the former schools chancellor would deliver his wisdom, Koa Beck vented on the blog at Mommyish.com. "There is a reason American women should be bitterly resentful over their measly maternity leave," she wrote. "We're the only industrialized country that asks mothers to make the completely unrealistic decisions that they do."[85] Beck had interviewed Liisa, a Finnish mother of three who had kept a diary for a week of her paid leave, granted exclusively to mothers for the first four months, with the option to share an additional 154 days with their partners.

Liisa was far from rich, she reported, yet her diary read "like a woman of pronounced privilege." Why, just think, she was able to collect her older son from preschool and prepare nutritious, home-cooked meals, fostering healthy eating habits and keeping weight in check. While not on par with a visit to a luxury spa, neither was it "fraught with pressures to keep up with professional responsibilities while lugging around a breast pump."[86]

Signs of progress are in evidence, although you have to stick very close to the ground, high-powered magnifying glass in hand, to see them. California and New Jersey, the states that pioneered paid family leave, have been joined by Rhode Island. Connecticut, Vermont, and New Hampshire have ventured into task-force mode, ready to consider the options. A few brave cities are slowly patching together the quilt—made in the USA, not in Finland—adding paid sick leave to the list of workers' rights. The District of Columbia's added a line in the budget for eight weeks of paid family leave, to be used upon the birth or placement of a new child, or for care of another relative.[87]

A handful of states have been grappling as well with the sticky question of "pregnancy-related limitations," resolving to provide "reasonable workplace accommodations."[88] Such benevolent legislation makes it possible for women to stay on the job—the goal of Peggy Young, a United Parcel Service truck driver, who sought temporary relief from heavy lifting when she was pregnant with her daughter. Unfortunately, her request sent the nation's trusty carrier into a tizzy, consigning Young to the remainder heap, unemployed without health insurance. "Many nights I didn't sleep so well," she announced on National Public Radio, after taking her case to the highest court in the land.[89]

As for the federal government, it's coming along, slowly. The Department of Labor organized a road show, hosting regional forums that hit all the right chords: higher wages, pay equity, sick days, paid family leave, affordable child care.[90] Labor Secretary Thomas Perez, who lost his own father at the tender age of 12, had elevated time around the dining room table to the lofty level of family value—a sentiment I tweeted giddily. It must have been the heat, at that June summit on work and family in Washington in 2014.

The men at the helm of the government were letting it all hang out, including the Father-in-Chief. He had abandoned multitasking for the moment, taking off his commander and executive hats. The time has come for us to move out of the mid-20th century, he told the mostly female gathering, by now swooning in ecstasy. He had called for the nation to leave the "*Mad Men* era," his workforce cabinet czar responding in a joyous, jazzy riff, with a reference to *Leave It to Beaver*.[91]

The following January, on the eve of Obama's State of the Union address, his trusted advisor, Valerie Jarrett, would take her boss's case to LinkedIn, the popular online forum for the nation's professionals. "This is the very first place we're breaking this news," she wrote, "because you're in the best position to drive change." Paid family leave is not a privilege, she argued; it's a worker's right. It was finally time to birth this baby. The president was calling on Congress to pass the Healthy Families Act, offering succor to the states. He'd even throw in some funding from the Department of Labor, for program design and implementation. The Father-in-Chief was leading the way, signing a memorandum that would ensure at least six weeks of paid leave for federal employees. Why, he was even hoping that Congress might tack on another six weeks of administrative leave.[92]

Still, the ghosts of Jesse Helms hover on Capitol Hill, squelching any inclination to intervene in that sacred realm of the family. The United States remains exiled from civilization, with Liberia, Suriname, and Papua New Guinea. And we are still left "expecting better"—a bitter play on words chosen by the National Partnership for Women and Families for its annual report card on the progress of the nation's humanity. California took home an A minus. Not a single state merited an "A," and 17 were rated "F," blackened on the national map.[93]

LET'S BLAME IT ON THE PARENTS

On the leafy campus of the University of Virginia, brainchild of Thomas Jefferson, the Institute for Advanced Studies in Culture is preoccupied with human flourishing—in the spirit of the paterfamilias. The scholars take an interdisciplinary approach to the question. Their work is divided into three areas: the person, the community, and the constitutive elements of meaning, whatever they may be. Among their many projects is one on the moral lives of children.

A new period of childhood has emerged, they proclaim, one that is not easily understood, and calls for further scrutiny. To be sure, children have problems, including divorce, violent computer games, and obesity. But the immediate and measurable impact of these issues pales by comparison to recent social transformations that have "altered and destabilized the conditions of childhood with enduring questions of character, maturation, stability, moral coherence, self-knowledge, and identity."[94] More than the usual nurturance and guidance are required in this time of radical transformation. Children's very souls are at stake.

Poverty was the theme of a recent issue of the *Hedgehog Review*, the institute's forum for critical reflections on contemporary culture. "Commentary on the Great War" (the First, *not* the centerpiece of the Great Society) by Wilfred McClay, the G. T. and Libby Blankenship Chair in the History of Liberty at the University of Oklahoma, was followed by "Post-Prozac Pathology," a review of books about "dysfunction and disaster, illnesses and pratfalls, failed marriages and failed careers, alcoholism and breakdowns and outrageous conduct."[95] A social order gone to hell in a hand basket.

If truth be told, I had trouble connecting to the content; it just wasn't resonating. But I plowed on, encouraged to find "Picturing the Poor: Photographs of Poverty in America." A click on the link to the essay placed me on pages 40 and 41, a spread with images of Jacob Riis's "Street Arab," a New York institution with a bohemian instinct, a vagabond "acknowledging no authority, and owing no allegiance to anybody or anything, with his grimy fist raised against society."[96]

To see more, I could have subscribed to the digital or print version. Instead, I made a mad dash for my bookshelf, and a copy of *The Moral Intelligence of Children*, one of the many works of Robert Coles, born at the beginning of the Great Depression. A child psychiatrist, he found his life's calling during a stint in the Air Force at a Mississippi hospital, beyond which lay a deeply segregated society. In collaboration with his wife, Jane Hallowell Coles, he began what would be an ongoing ethnographic exploration of children fielding the most challenging, complex social and economic problems—among them, first-grader Ruby Bridges, who desegregated William Frantz Elementary School in New Orleans in 1960. I exhaled, relieved to be, finally, in the company of a sane social critic.[97]

"Not much has shifted in our public sensibilities from the religious moralism of the 1800s," Valerie Polakow wrote, alluding to single mothers and children in late 20th-century America, inhabiting "lives on the edge."[98] Back in the 19th century, those in poverty were seen as depraved, and undeserving, their questionable conduct the subject of vituperative discourse. Their families were isolated, domestic islands governed by the doctrine of *parens patriae*, English law that permitted public intervention in the case of inadequate parenting—a means of regulating "'defective' families in order to protect children."[99] The spirit, if not the letter, of the law is flourishing today, although the same cannot be said of the humans to which it applies. On the brink, on the edge—choose your metaphor—women are still on the margins.

Neither are they alone. As Kenneth Braswell reminds us, mothers don't have the monopoly on child well-being. Paternal behavior is a significant factor. We're not addressing the issue holistically, the leader in the expanding field of responsible fatherhood told me, as he awaited the release in New York and Los Angeles of *Spit'in Anger*, a documentary about the toll of fatherlessness on Black men. "How can we have this conversation without thinking that this population *wants* to be poor?" he asked. The frame is too narrow. We conceive of giving as a handout—such a drain on that precious Gross Domestic Product. "There's no scarcity of resources in this country," Braswell said. "Joblessness, health and deep racial disparities; it's not all their fault."

Yet it's so much easier to blame the victim. In one of those delicious twists of fate, that task has fallen to Richard Reeves, an émigré from the United Kingdom, home of George III, the great father against whom the United States staged the ultimate rebellion in 1776. He and his colleague at the Brookings Institute, Kimberly Howard, joined America's metric scientists in their favorite pastime, measuring "the Parenting Gap." A pithy quote from John Locke introduces us to the subject: "The well educating of children is so much the duty and concern of parents, and the welfare and prosperity of the nation so much depends on it."[100]

But their hearts belong to Amitai Etzioni: "Parents have a moral responsibility to invest themselves in the proper upbringing of their children," the Israeli-American sociologist wrote, his wisdom the frame for this status report on the state of the nation's wealth producers.[101] Who could argue with that? Caregivers are the key players, developing that prime real estate, the infant brain. Still, there are practical and moral limits to the reach of public policy. In a free society, the authors contend, families operate as private institutions. "Except in extreme cases of neglect or abuse," Reeves and Howard wrote, "Parents are at liberty to do things their own way—even when their own way is hopeless."[102] There goes that street urchin, the bohemian nomad.

To best fulfill their mission, the authors relied on the Social Genome Model of the life cycle, a handy little tool that tracks the academic, social, and economic experiences from conception through middle age. Such illuminating findings, with strong links between parenting quality and income, race, education, and family type. And who were the unfortunate in the weakest category—winners of the booby prize—you're dying to know? Low-income parents, of course, who were poorly educated, Black, or unmarried.

Whenever would they learn? Reeves and Howard need to take a social mobility memo from Isabel Sawhill, the author of *Generation Unbound: Drifting into Sex and Parenthood Without Marriage*, whose resume includes a brief stint at the Office of Management and Budget in the early 1990s. "Humans are bad at self-control," she said. Long-acting reversible contraception (LARCs) might be just the solution.[103]

TAKE THE LOAD OFF FAMILIES

"It's come to this: the dentist chair as vacation for the harried American parent," I tweeted, with a link to a piece at the *Motherlode* by Erica Reischer, blissed out by repairs on a cracked tooth. She was surprised to find this oasis of calm in her breakneck schedule. Of course, this child psychologist knows she's lucky to have a career and family, demanding though they may be.[104]

In 1995, taking a page from Silicon Valley, the Commonwealth Fund tried its hand at a startup. Christened Healthy Steps for Young Children, the model promised preventive pediatric care for children from birth to age three, with a focus on child behavior and development and support for parents. Fifteen years later, Michael Barth, the program's founding director, reflected on the program's past and future. "Innovative," he called it.[105] Healthy Steps had been wildly successful, replicated at scores of sites across the country, where managers offered flexible implementation in keeping with local needs. The sites that were forced to close were universally disappointed, lamenting the loss of the positive outcomes adoption had brought. But finances were tight, the government's funding streams always threatening to dry up.

One blindingly bright morning, I boarded New York City's Number 6 Lexington Avenue subway, bound for Healthy Steps at Montefiore's Family Comprehensive Center in the Bronx. The elevated train wends its way north through some of the most vulnerable districts in the nation, belied by the bucolic English names of the stops: Parkchester, Castle Hill Avenue, Westchester Square, and Williamsbridge Road. The demographics of Healthy Steps tell a different story, one of diverse people, decidedly unprivileged. Fifty percent of the families are of Hispanic origin, and 35 percent are Black; the others, Irish, Italian, Eastern European, Albanian, and Bangladeshi.

Healthy Steps director Rahil Briggs, an associate professor of clinical pediatrics at Albert Einstein College of Medicine, had mesmerized me earlier with a rapid-fire recitation of the findings of a survey of toxic stress. From 2005 to 2010, she and her team had tracked more than 3,000 children from six to thirty-six months, using the Ages and Stages questionnaire, which identifies early social-emotional problems.[106] From six to eighteen months, she reported, the infants and toddlers looked okay. By the time they had reached 24 months, the risk factors—child abuse, domestic violence, maternal depression—were compromising their ability to cope.

The model, first set up as a research program in 2006, has blossomed on Briggs's careful watch. In four clinics, which serve 15,000 babies to five-year-olds, physicians, psychologists, social workers, obstetricians, and gynecologists work side by side, offering a full complement of services. Here, parents can combine well-baby visits with on-site therapy sessions that bolster their mental health, while bringing them up to speed on the behavior and social development of their infants. "The landscape has changed profoundly since we started universal screening," she told me. "There's vastly increased recognition of the good fit between primary care and the kind of work we do." Unfortunately, the landscape for funding has barely changed.

Mental illness is always top of mind here. The hospital's initiative has made a dent, reducing mothers' depression and anxiety, offering low-income parents the support that their peers down the subway line in Manhattan's Silk Stocking district take for granted. Briggs laments how the problem gets pushed under the rug in the larger society—not because pediatricians aren't aware, but because they don't have any solutions. They've been working on this issue for a long time at Montefiore, home to one of the oldest social pediatric residencies. "When you say 'have you heard of attachment?'" Briggs told me, "they don't give you a blank stare."

At a "Baby and Me" class, just after Halloween, a 14-week-old was dressed as a Twizzler, his mother clicking away with her smartphone camera. Around them, infants gathered for a game of peek-a-boo. One little guy, in a giraffe suit, was next. "Where's Caleb?" his mom asked.

"Super baby," crooned the group's facilitator, who had combined early childhood education and social work in a master's program to prepare her for her job. The class, which meets in 12-week sessions with a break for holidays and August, is low key, a mixture of parenting tips and cheerleading. Like all infants whose moods may alter from moment to moment, Super baby was now unsettled and had dissolved into tears. "You can never spoil your baby too much," the group's leader reminded the parents. "They feel safe to explore."

Twizzler's parents were taking a feeding break. "We're alternating nights," his father said. "Last night was mine." They looked remarkably happy and relaxed for parents barely out of the newborn stage, their tenderness and collaboration a model for all. The baby's mother was feeding him, cooing and talking in perfect "parentese." Meanwhile, the toddlers in the group were learning the ropes. "You're doing such a nice job cleaning up," the facilitator told the children, as they put the blocks back in their neon-orange buckets. One of them was not cooperating. "It's hard to get them to clean up," she told the mother. "Do you sing the clean-up song?" she asked.

For the final activity, she brought out a parachute. Soon, all the babies were supine, looking up at this wonder. "Red and yellow, green and blue, these are the colors over you," she sang, quickly moving on to "The Wheels on the Bus." The parachute swirled. Barely skipping a beat, the leader launched into "London Bridge Is Falling Down," preparing the parents to swing the babies in the parachute. The boy in the giraffe suit kicked his legs in joy.

Soon it was time to leave. The leader took one last group shot and started everyone on goodbyes. The father of Twizzler held his baby, readying him for the transition. "What's wrong, Dooodoo?" he asked his son, speaking in perfect parentese. "You're tired."

CHANGEMAKER: TERRIE ROSE

Through the Eyes of Babes

In her book, *Emotional Readiness*, Terrie Rose prefaces one of the chapters with a quote from William Doherty, director of a project called Minnesota Couples on the Brink: "We reinvented family life in the 20th century but never wrote a user's model." A child psychologist and pioneering social entrepreneur, Rose has dedicated herself to writing the manual and applying its wisdom—pulling parents and their children back from the precipice.

From her dissertation on the impact of foster care on infants and toddlers, to the founding in 2002 of Baby's Space to serve the Little Earth Native community in Minneapolis, she's nurtured attachment and sensitive, stimulating relationships between infants and parents—the sine qua non of healthy development. "Presence, consistency, and stability" is Rose's guiding mantra, the foundation for the program's service model, premised on the idea of child care as a catalyst for collective impact in the neighborhood.

"We designed the model before we even had a space," Rose told me. "What did families need? That was the driving force." All of Baby's Space children—most are Native American, the others Black, Hispanic, and White—are eligible for free or reduced-price lunch. Many of the families began with a teen pregnancy, amid great financial instability. Homelessness is not rare, and community violence is a fact of life.

Rose's theory of change had its roots in her early work as a statistician for Minnesota's landmark longitudinal study of parents and children, begun in 1975. Balancing a growing family with a blossoming career, she launched her other baby at the University of Minnesota, taking the rich evidence base at her disposal and translating it into practice and policy. Soon, she had left academia and was raising hundreds of thousands of dollars, honing her mission, and pondering the thorny issue of full-scale replication—efforts that brought her to the attention of George Askew, the founder of Docs for Tots, who nominated her for an Ashoka Changemaker fellowship.

Working with McKinsey Social Venture Partners and Ashoka, Rose proved to be a quick study. "I learned that people are attached to their local model of child care," she told me. "The financial and policy landscapes had changed so significantly that full-scale replication was impossible." Also challenging was the outlier status of early childhood, and misconceptions about its value.

"I was sitting at a gathering at the National Press Club, filled with a table of innovative people," she said. "They were having trouble seeing how they could leverage early childhood in the way that they'd leveraged K–12. After we all spoke, the head of New Profit Inc. said 'I still don't understand.'" Rose attributes the disconnect to the field's inability to articulate a national vision, echoing many of her colleagues in a profession long on the margins of influence.

Still, she clung tenaciously to her mission. "I feel really deeply about the value of place-based, predictable service," she said. "Baby's Space is always thinking about fairness, while accounting for individual differences." On family night, leftover food goes home with everyone, regardless of need, building trust with the whole community. Even as Rose stepped back from her creation, passing the baton to Deb Lund, the new executive director, she was grappling with the tension inherent between the impulse to rescue and equity—the impetus for her life's work.

"How do I maintain my sense of balance, and provide consistency for each family?" she asked. "People will hear a tragic story, and want to take that child home." The program strategies seem to be working. Ninety-four percent of infants and toddlers and 90 percent of preschoolers are on track developmentally, and those who are struggling are supported by special education and family services. Eight of the early childhood teachers in Baby's Space are parents with children in the program, a bridge between the intimate space of the home and practice in the classroom. All of the children are ready for kindergarten.

In her drive for consistency—and continuity—Rose pushed the boundaries of Baby's Space beyond the earliest years, founding Tatanka Academy, a public school for children from five to eight years old. "We followed the lead of the families," she said. A bridge had collapsed one summer, many children had witnessed two shootings in the neighborhood, and six were leaving for kindergarten. "They began in September," Rose said. "One of the six was suspended, two were running away from their teachers, and one never registered. So we started a kindergarten program."

The transition to the primary grades is perilous. "All of our second-graders have three or more adverse childhood experiences," Rose said, "and the majority of kids have five or more. We're seeing the learning and behavioral impact of the stresses on kids." When teachers don't see a child in school, they call home. Keeping communication open is critical. While the faculty works hard to ensure close collaboration, striving for a hundred percent participation in parent-teacher conferences, they don't automatically assume that absence is a sign of disinterest or lack of care.

"It's a total shift from practice and perceptions in the K–12 world," Rose said. Meetings to discuss goals and progress for children with disabilities are held at the parents' convenience, on site, at Baby's Space, or at the school, which has morphed into TEAL Elementary Academy for Learning, serving students through the sixth grade. "We're trying to infiltrate the system, but it's painful, and if it's painful for us, imagine how it is for kids and families. Eighty percent of our children are, or will be, involved in child protective services at some point in their lives, and half of them have a parent who has been incarcerated."

While all of the teachers at the elementary school are licensed by the state of Minnesota, they're newcomers to the field, and their knowledge of early child development is sketchy. "We think every licensed teacher should work with toddlers first," Rose said. "They don't have enough practical training and understanding of behavior to be confident, competent elementary school teachers." Words of wisdom from the woman who wrote the book on how early experience and mental health predict school success.

CHAPTER 2

Elusive Equity and the American Dream

In New York City, the fault lines of educational equity are most visible in early childhood, with preschool admissions the crucible for liberal, white, middle class parents, whose aspirations, anxiety and guilt collide in a combustible mix. While they pay lip service to equality, equity and diversity, and spend time telling you how much they love their community for its abundance of all of the above, when push comes to shove . . . "my kid" comes first.

—"That Ever-Elusive Equity," *Huffington Post*

The United States must shift course if it is to survive and prosper as a First World nation in the 21st century. . . . Our future will be increasingly determined by our capacity and will to educate all children well—a challenge we have very little time to meet if the United States is not to enact the modern equivalent of the fall of Rome.

—Linda Darling-Hammond, *The Flat World and Education*

The United States has long looked covetously at the educational outcomes of Finland—they of the enviable PISA (Programme for International Student Assessment) scores. How does this tiny Nordic nation at the top of the world do so well on those international tests of academic mastery? It's a mystery that continues to confound us. For one thing, the Finns revere children and see early childhood as a time for play, exploration, and the foundation for citizenship in a democracy.[1] But there's something deeper here, captured in an article in the *Atlantic*, one of America's oldest forums for discussion of subjects of national interest, dating back to the young life of our republic.

Parse the language of a brief interview with Krista Kiuru, Finland's minister of education, and some clues emerge. Strewn with references to equality, equity, individual potential, and quality education, the document is a study in contrasting perspectives, a message in a bottle, lost in the waters of the cold Atlantic. "Equal means that we support everyone and we're not going to waste anyone's skills," Kiuru said. "We can't know if one first-grader will become a famous composer, or another a famous scientist. Regardless of a person's gender, background, or social welfare status, everyone should have an equal chance to make the most of their skills."[2] For the Finns, human capital is a precious natural resource.

A DREAM MORPHS INTO A NIGHTMARE

As America climbed out of the worst economic slump since the Great Depression, inequality surfaced in the national conversation. "We the people understand that our country cannot succeed when a shrinking few do very well and a growing many barely make it," the nation's first African American president declared in his second inaugural address. "We are true to our creed when a little girl born into the bleakest poverty knows that she has the same chance to succeed as anybody, because she is an American, she is free, and she is equal, not just in the eyes of God but also in our own."[3]

The subject of U.S. income inequality—now on par with that of El Salvador—is incendiary in the land of the American Dream. Here, we pull ourselves up by our bootstraps and go for the gold with impunity—*E pluribus unum* be damned.[4] "Obama Proudly Declares Class War" screamed the headline of a piece by Deroy Murdock—a columnist at the *National Review*—mercilessly skewered by Jon Stewart in his "Slumdogs vs. Millionaires" segment of *The Daily Show*. "They don't like welfare cheats, the moocher's class," said one of a parade of Fox News commentators on screens behind Stewart's head. Among them was Charles Krauthammer, a Harvard- and Oxford-educated political pundit and physician, who ruefully remarked, "There's a lot more people who want to suck on the teat of the state."[5]

He neglected to mention the 22 percent of children under six in the "moocher class"—including those in households living on two dollars per day, per person, a condition dubbed extreme poverty by the World Bank. As of 2011, researchers Kathryn Edin and H. Luke Shaefer had discovered almost one and a half million of them in the United States, home to nearly three million children. From 1996, when welfare reform ushered in a long, painful decline of government benefits, to the aftermath of the Great Recession, the prevalence of extreme poverty had risen sharply.[6]

Not, mind you, that it has been a picnic for those living in regular poverty, unmodified by the adjective we use to describe death-defying sport. According to UNICEF's *Innocenti* report, the U.S. child poverty rate had earned us the place of second among developed nations, surpassed only by Romania, whose status as an advanced economy is, indisputably, embryonic.[7] The teat of the state in our First World nation has run dry.

WHITHER THOU GOEST, OPPORTUNITY?

In our ascent up the ladder, bootstraps in tow, we tussle with the ethos of our founding document, which declared equality a self-evident truth, along with the inalienable rights of life, liberty, and the pursuit of happiness.[8] Seeking our own private utopias, we butt up against the dreams of others. But economic catastrophe has a way of turning our heads in a different direction. It has hit us hard in the early 21st century—affecting all "races, colors, and creeds," as Tavis Smiley and Cornel West observed in their scathing poverty manifesto, *The Rich and the Rest of Us*.[9] From 2009 to 2012, incomes in the top 1 percent of the population grew by 31 percent, while the bottom 99 percent virtually stagnated, the nation's top earners capturing a staggering 95 percent of the income gains in the first three years of what some optimistically proclaimed "the recovery."[10]

Comparison with El Salvador is all well and good. Still, shaming has its limits in the Age of Irony, political polarization, and the penchant for a quick, results-driven fix. I cling to the moral outrage of Children's Defense Fund founder Marian Wright Edelman, who has devoted her life to documenting "The State of America's Children," a harrowing litany of offenses against our youngest citizens: death, abuse, impoverishment, prison, malnourishment, mediocre child care, limited access to preschool, and subpar literacy and numeracy.[11]

I pine for the unreconstructed wisdom of Jonathan Kozol. He bravely boarded a tiny plane in Boston in the wake of cataract surgery to spread the gospel at a poverty forum at the Schuyler Center for Analysis and Advocacy in Albany, New York's state capital. "I'm an old-fashioned guy," the author of *Savage Inequalities* said, frail but unvanquished in red high-top sneakers, his sight as clear as ever. "I believe that Martin Luther King was right, that racial segregation is a sin. . . . We can't talk about poverty if we ignore the elephant in the china shop."[12]

The bandwidth of social change is broader than ever. Moral outrage persists, but activism has a different cast these days, energized, but also trivialized, by social media, where 140-character tweets promote causes of all stripes.[13] In the American tradition of reinvention, the focus of the conversation has returned to our country's idealistic narrative of "opportunity"—within a context of strict accountability and market-based strategies. We talk of points of leverage, coaching for equity, paying for success.[14]

The Low-Income Investment Fund announces a "first-of-its-kind" Social Impact Calculator at a meeting of the Clinton Global Initiative—the better to assess how its work is improving the lives of low-income children and families.[15] Even the Center for Law and Social Policy, a nonprofit founded at the tail end of the 1960s, and a hotbed of advocates for initiatives that help the poor, has adopted corporate lingo. Announcing the launch of its new online commentary, "What's Next? The Agenda for Reducing Poverty and Expanding Opportunity," the center mentions that primary author, executive director Olivia Golden, "has delivered results as a leader in federal, state, and local government."[16]

Where is the land of opportunity? Ask Harvard's Raj Chetty, and Berkeley's Emannuel Saez, economists who have been tracking recent trends in intergenerational mobility, or the lack thereof. Their penchant for statistics, charts, and arcane language is impressive, their work tough going for the uninitiated.[17] Terms of art like *log-log intergenerational elasticities* (IGE), *Gini coefficients*, and the *copula* of the distribution routinely pop up in their papers, obscuring the human cost. So what have they found?

In the spirit of our digital age, Chetty and his colleagues created a website, The Equality of Opportunity Project, where nongeeks can finally get the dish.[18] "Contrary to popular perception," they argue, economic mobility in the United States has not changed significantly over time; the American Dream is still possible for many. Still, they concede, intergenerational mobility is significantly lower in the United States than in most other developed countries—a trend that has been well documented by the Organisation for Economic Co-operation and Development, which, by the way, cites the positive effect of early childhood education on the process of climbing the proverbial ladder of success.[19]

With the help of a flashy interactive map, Chetty et al. show that mobility varies substantially depending upon where you live. The numbers cast a harsh light on income inequality, which has increased exponentially over the period of study. The odds of reaching the top fifth of the income spectrum from the bottom fifth in the nation's 50 largest cities range from a meager 4.4 percent in Charlotte, North Carolina, to a paltry 12.9 percent in San Jose.[20] Never mind rural and suburban poverty, growing like weeds, or the nation's original families barely eking out a living on the reservations. One in four Native Americans are now living in poverty, including the 43 percent—nearly triple the national average—on North Dakota's Standing Rock Reservation.[21]

The bottom line, as the scientists dispassionately note, is that "the consequences of the 'birth lottery'—the parents to whom a child is born—are larger today than in the past."[22] Areas that are less segregated, and have lower levels of income inequality, better schools, greater social capital, and more stable families are fertile ground for American dream weaving.

Ah, yes, there's the rub. That little girl born into bleakest poverty—the president's standard-bearer—is hardly a random statistic. She is, increasingly, the object of great scrutiny by the U.S. Department of Education (DOE), whose own website makes explicit the categories ignored by the economists. Opportunities to learn and achieve, the DOE proclaims, must be available to all, regardless of wealth, home language, zip code, gender, sexual orientation, race, or disability.[23] Disparities in these categories, our ever-expanding taxonomy of inequality, are out in plain sight, acknowledged in the dry prose of a government document.

IN THE GAP: A REALITY CHECK

In the shadow of the Great Recession, the Educational Testing Service (ETS) began investigating the "Black-White Achievement Gap"—a "whodunit detective story," they described it, "without a clear whodunit ending."[24] While the magnitude of achievement gaps has waxed and waned since the National Assessment of Educational Progress introduced the "nation's report card" in 1969, the disparities in outcomes continue to confound data-gatherers like the ETS, and keep DOE officials up at night.

Linda Darling-Hammond, a Stanford professor who has carefully deconstructed the anatomy of inequality, sees a nation in denial. In *The Flat World and Education*, she offers up stomach-turning details of the Luther Burbank School, a plaintiff in a California lawsuit filed on behalf of low-income students of color in 2002. More than half a century after *Brown v. Board of Education* outlawed segregation, guaranteeing an equal education for all, Burbank was infested with vermin, cockroaches, and mice. Bathrooms were locked, there were no computers, and not a librarian was in sight. The institution, funded by ever-dwindling public money, "represents a growing number of 'apartheid schools' across the United States."[25]

How brave of Darling-Hammond to tell it like it is, joining former president Jimmy Carter, who used the "A" word in his book about the peace process in Palestine.[26] Most ordinary Americans, she insists, are unaware of the disparities. They're under the mistaken impression that schools must be equitably funded in the United States and that the schools their children attend are the norm. We're shocked to learn that less than a third of Native

Americans graduate high school in South Dakota. We're startled to discover that 63 percent of Latino children don't attend preschool.[27]

Our comfort with profound inequality is nothing less than "the Achilles heel of American education," Darling-Hammond wrote, "older than the country itself."[28] Or, in the words of Cherie Craft, founder of Smart from the Start and the product of a Boston housing project: "I was bussed to a suburban school district—moving from cold and bare bricks to watching the scenery of beautiful homes, trees, and lawns," she told me. "I couldn't understand why I lived *there* and others got to live *here*."

When the Educational Testing Service returned to their whodunit detective story, two years after the earlier investigation, they had finally solved the mystery. Suddenly, the nonprofit that "drives innovation in educational measurement" had awakened. Their document, *Poverty and Education: Finding the Way Forward*, reads like a social justice manifesto. Noting the disturbing prevalence of extreme poverty in the United States, the ETS issued a report card on the fairness and progressivity of state education funding, including declining financial support for preschool programs. Broadening access to preschool came in third on their list of recommendations, after raising awareness of the incidence of poverty and its consequences, and equitably and adequately funding schools.[29]

They had apparently gotten wind of Helen Ladd's speech to the Association for Public Policy Analysis and Management. An economist at Duke University and a cofounder of the Broader, Bolder Approach to Education, Ladd hit it out of the park with a data-packed indictment of current education policy, which reflects a deep disregard for the impact of poverty on student outcomes, leaving educators to pick up the slack.[30] She anticipated the elevation of inequality to the national agenda in the wake of the Occupy movement, warning that our failure to pay attention would lead to greater achievement gaps in the future.

Educational equity continues to rear its ugly head in our national conversation, meriting a tsunami of entries on Google and a hashtag of its very own (#equity) on Twitter, where it shares the list with the private kind. Meanwhile, the Department of Education's Office of Civil Rights had been getting up to speed on its inimitable bureaucratic timeline. Just as the spring equinox arrived, the office released a survey, the first in nearly 15 years, of 97,000 American public schools. "U.S. Schools Plagued By Inequality Along Racial Lines" topped an article by Lalita Clozel, reverberating over the newswire of the *Los Angeles Times* and piercing the shells of Darling-Hammond's ordinary Americans in denial across the nation.[31]

The federal agency's spin was gentle, pointing to "troubling racial disparities," among them access to preschool and the high rate of suspension of boys of color, who represent 18 percent of preschool enrollment but 42 percent of students suspended once.[32] "This rich information allows us to identify gaps and cases of discrimination to partner with states and districts to ensure equal access to educational opportunities," said Catherine E. Lhamon, assistant secretary for civil rights, in the agency's carefully crafted press release, "From Native American tribal nations to inner city barrios, all of our children deserve a high quality education."[33]

TECTONIC SHIFTS IN THE AMERICAN LANDSCAPE

At a Starbucks on Riverside Avenue in Minneapolis, a group of Somali men clustered around the tables. On this June day, as Twin Cities parents pushed baby strollers, exulting in a belated burst of warmth, I waited in line for a latte, en route to visit Baby's Space, an early childhood program. The scene was strange, and riveting—a new American village, hanging on tenuously to the routines of a life left behind.

The men's heated discussions have earned them the nickname "Starbucks dads" in the Somali community, the largest such group in the United States. A perfect metaphor, some say, "for absent parents too mired in the affairs of their home country to pay attention to their children," many of whom are inexorably drawn to jihad.[34] Where were the women, I wondered? imagining them in lonely apartments and houses, isolated and depressed. Seventy percent of Somali households are headed by women living in poverty, as compared to 26 percent of their peers in Minnesota's general population. Those lucky enough might be found at Isuroon, an organization "seeking health and empowerment for Somali women."[35]

Alas, "accepting immigrants into our nation places a heavy strain on already tight financial and social resources," as the eponymous ThirdEyeMom noted at her blog.[36] A self-described writer and social good advocate living in Minneapolis, she has been observing the changes in the local geography. This wife of the heartland, and mother of two children, argues for substantial investment in immigrants, some of whom, she says, "do truly amazing and achieve the American Dream." Not lost on her is the importance of the example she sets for her children, whose classmates are Somali, Asian, and Mexican: "It is critical I teach them cultural understanding and sensitivity as well as acceptance and love for their world"—and the world of their children, which will be even more diverse than the one they inhabit today.[37]

The universe of "all our children" in 21st-century America is expanding exponentially, families morphing into a multitude of forms, colors, and identities. As the first decade closed, the majority of babies born in the United States were ethnic and racial minorities.[38] The United States had also surpassed all nations as a destination for immigrants, taking in a record 40.4 million—11 million, undocumented—who were moving from Mexico and Central America across the continents to Asia and Europe, and Africa.[39] More than half of the 18 million children of these immigrant families are non-White. By 2018, the majority of the U.S. workforce will be people of color, and by midcentury—if not sooner—no single racial group will dominate the population.[40]

What about that heavy strain on resources cited by ThirdEyeMom? We have barely begun to talk about children with special needs, a population growing by the moment and long on the margins of equal opportunity.[41] Or youngsters living with parents of the same gender. Like all children, their well-being rests on support from consistent, loving, healthy adults, which resoundingly trumps sexual orientation—as the American Academy of Pediatrics affirmed after an extensive research review.[42]

And how about the school-to-prison pipeline, the destiny of too many African American boys? Or the burgeoning population of Latino children, stranded between two languages? Not to mention the youngest members of the country's ancestral tribal nations with their legacy of forced separation, isolation, and impoverishment—a fate shared by the children of undocumented immigrants.[43] The pieces of the pie, and the stakeholders, are multiplying. These tectonic shifts are transforming the landscape of early childhood, forcing a collective reckoning with the impact of poverty, race, culture, and identity on children's development, learning, and outcomes.

RACING TO ADVANCE RACIAL EQUITY

"Today's kids are the thinkers, artists, parents, entrepreneurs, leaders and workers of tomorrow," a report on the status of Washington State's children optimistically declares. "When they have the opportunity to reach their full potential in life, all of us benefit."[44] These children, as a map of race and ethnicity depicts, represent unprecedented diversity, the official census survey straining to encompass it all. Filipino and Pacific Islander, Polynesian, Samoan, Bangladeshi, Chinese, Vietnamese, Cherokee, Blackfoot, Aleut, Pueblo, Yakima, Indonesian, Laotian, African American, Somali, Guinean Nigerian, Eritrean, South African, Kenyan—a world of rich and limitless possibility.

Yet the data are bleak. More than 620,000 of Washington's children are living in families that cannot meet their basic needs, including 440,000 who are what we have taken to calling "food insecure," a euphemism that cannot conceal the magnitude of the sin. One in three third-graders cannot meet the reading standards, and one in four will not graduate from high school on time.[45] While children of color are rapidly becoming the majority, the current information barely illuminates the resources they bring or the barriers to opportunity they face. As Washington was creating an Early Learning Plan in 2010, the state had yet to fully reckon with the incomplete picture. Imbued with the West's inimitable can-do spirit, advocates started a movement to eliminate race as a predictor of progress and success for children from birth to the age of eight.

Thrive Washington, a public-private partnership, took the lead, calling together dozens of stakeholders for a conversation to develop a racial equity theory of change. "We didn't know what we were doing," Thrive's president and CEO Nina Auerbach told me, on a typical cool, wet day in Seattle, not long before she left to lead the Washington Association for Infant Mental Health. To get up to speed, they consulted the National Equity Project, one of a growing number of results-driven sources of social transformation. "It's almost impossible to change alone," the organization's website claimed, promoting an annual Coaching for Equity Institute. The event, open to all who could afford the $1,200 registration fee, draws a wide range of customers—principals, administrators, teachers, nonprofit leaders—who learn how to lead productive conversations about race and bias in the workplace.

For Auerbach, the question was clear: How do you change policy to make children of color a high priority? Using a model from the Aspen Institute, Thrive mapped out a theory of change in a series of visually gorgeous graphics, reaching for universal metaphors to convey the goals. A house, two trees, and a couple wheeling an old-fashioned pram fill a quadrant dedicated to increasing the voice and influence of those furthest from opportunity. Two cows and a farmer on a red tractor inhabit the quadrant labeled "Inform practice with diverse measures and diverse stories." The third quadrant, which references decisionmaking that genuinely meets the needs of communities of color, features a lone lighthouse. The fourth—the design and implementation of responsive systems—shows a woman and a child in a kayak on a deep blue sea, dotted with whales, a nod to Marian Wright Edelman's logo, a registered trademark, for the Children's Defense Fund: "Dear Lord, be good to me, the sea is so wide and my boat is so small."

All of this looks great on paper, but like all human endeavors, the path is strewn with obstacles. "We have been able to build a lot of strong partnerships," Thrive's Lauren Hipp told me, after Washington had put the finishing touches on its theory of change. "It's not an easy conversation. In King County, people have been thinking about equity for decades. Other parts of the state are not as well versed." Nor are all stakeholders engaged; some question the focus on race, rather than income—a leitmotif in the national dialogue about inequality and social mobility.

"We have a lot of work ahead of us," Hipp said, "and we're not naïve." Since her involvement with the project, she has moved on to another cause, joining MomsRising, dedicated—heaven help them—to building a family-friendly America. But Washington had made progress since the project's inception, Auerbach reported two years down the line. The state had gotten the hang of the racial equity tool: a living, breathing document that promised the gold ring of collective impact.

FREE TO BE YOU AND ME, AND SUCCEED IN THE USA

Talk is good, but it is just an aperture; we get stuck on the language, so clinical, insufficient, and freighted with unintended consequences. And then there's that age-old deficit theory, which devalues the strengths that the marginalized bring to the table. With distance, a new generation of researchers is putting the politics of popular expression and educational inequality under the microscope, demystifying loaded terms that have long dominated the conversation about children, poverty, race, and class.

Researchers Sylvia Martinez and John Rury take us on a tour of the terms *culturally deprived* and *disadvantaged*, from the 1960s onward, noting how they engendered controversy while frustration with educational change grew. They report on a group of sociologists at the University of Chicago, who convened a meeting to obsess about the nation's slow progress. In the report that emerged from their deliberations, they traced the "problem" to children's experiences in the home, "which do not transmit the cultural patterns necessary for the types of learning characteristic of the schools and the larger society."[46] Into the breach leapt the term *at risk*, another loaded descriptor, soon to be followed by *social and cultural capital*, which are all the rage these days.

Nearly half a century after the sociologists grappled with cultural deprivation, the National Black Child Development Institute declared they had had enough. It was finally time to take a strengths-based approach, one of celebration and appreciation. In *Being Black Is Not a Risk Factor*, a manifesto of equal parts rage and hope, Barbara Bowman, an editor of *Eager to Learn*, a seminal tome on early childhood pedagogy and one of the field's elder stateswomen, launched a frontal attack on the deficit model. She highlighted the ongoing legacy of segregation and discrimination, which feeds a poverty of the body and spirit that carries significant and mental dangers.[47]

Bowman wrote of poorly resourced communities, with lousy schools and housing, meager employment opportunities, and a hostile world. She also robustly defended Black families, who against all odds are supporting their children's healthy development. "They walk, talk, love, make categories, represent ideas, use symbols, etc.," she concluded, "even though they may do these things in different ways than White children."[48]

The report's "Points of Proof," models of social change across the nation, provided glimmers of an encouraging evidence base. Still, they are scarcely nourished. As Smart from the Start's Cherie Craft ruefully observed, "We work under the radar and we've been left out of the conversation." Funding in the race for outcomes is tough to get; private philanthropy has more causes than you can shake a stick at, and Promise Neighborhoods, the closest thing we have to a holistic antipoverty initiative, is a mere blip on the government's Excel spreadsheet.[49]

The United States has a long, blighted history of blaming the poor, the foundation of the deficit model that continues to haunt us. It is easier to pin blame than to understand and fix the problem, as Sasha Abramsky points out in *The American Way of Poverty*: The Republicans have taken this "sleight of hand" to a new level, "turning verbal denigration of the poor into something of an art form."[50] By delinking nature and nurture, and putting the onus on the environment, we thought we had neutralized the problem. Young children labeled "disadvantaged" or "at risk" would emerge unscathed, the better for the attention paid.

But how wrong could we be? The stew has inexorably thickened, a morass of race, class, ethnicity, and the growing list of variables defining our identities and cultures. "Poverty is seen for a lot of kids as a trait, not a state," Brooke Richie-Babbage, a Harvard-trained lawyer, told me. The founder and executive director of the Resilience Advocacy Project, she and her team train youth, primarily those of color, as leaders in their communities in the fight against poverty. "Gandhi has this quote—about throw-away children. We don't say it, we don't admit it, but we treat poor kids like they're throw-aways."

As No Child Left Behind (NCLB) was signed into law to level the playing field, sociologist Annette Lareau jumped into the fray with *Unequal Childhoods: Class, Race, and Family Life,* an ethnographic study of the impact of parents' social class on their life experiences.[51] A classic in the field, the book takes us into homes and communities, where she and her research team observed the everyday interactions and activities of low- and middle-income families across the racial divide.

Middle-class parents, they found, practiced concerted cultivation, based on a set of principles to ensure that their offspring were impeccably trained in the rules of the game. They put a premium on challenging conversation and hyperarticulate speech. They developed their children's interests, master-minding family schedules, playing an active role in schooling, and routinely tapping into their own social and professional networks. Self-assertion, at home, and in the community, with other adults, was highly prized, a comfortable place in the world and a sense of entitlement among its byproducts. Yet their schedules were so packed that unstructured time—for quiet, play, and daydreaming—had disappeared. The tradeoff: These kids had that all-important social capital, which oils the wheels of what passes for civilization in 21st-century America.

In working-class and poor households, life had a distinctly different pace and ambience, the rhythms of a childhood of accomplishment of natural growth. While parents were protective and caring, they granted their children more autonomy in leisure activities, which often included spending time—after school and on weekends—with extended kin. Missing were the professional and domestic treadmills so common in middle-class homes. These children appeared to enjoy their playtime. They tended to show more creativity, spontaneity, and initiative than their middle-class peers, learning to collaborate and negotiate conflict.

So there you have it: constraint versus entitlement, a yawning opportunity gap. A collision of race, class, and the rules of the game—or dominant norms and values.

EXPANDING THE EXPECTATIONS WE HOLD

Linda Espinosa, who has spent her professional life working with young children, grew up in a large Hispanic family in mid-20th-century America, the heyday of the deficit model. "There are pockets of excellence," she told me, "but the conditions have hardened for those who have grown up in very deprived circumstances." Espinosa bears witness to the consequences of misguided practice, neglect, misunderstanding, and bigotry, which extinguish the life force of bright, curious children.[52] Her blunt assessment echoes that of Felicia Delaney, CEO of the National Black Child Development Institute: "The words we use, the expectations we hold; the beliefs in our hearts—all these things matter."[53]

Espinosa recounted her early experiences with Mexican immigrants in California, who then constituted 25 percent of the population—and were on their way to passing the majority mark by 2014.[54] She cited the work of Robert Crosnoe, at the University of Texas, who has studied Mexican immigrant families. "The children who came in were so delightful," she said.

"There were real cultural differences around interpersonal relationships. When they came into the classroom, they would listen. They didn't have behavioral and management issues." These children had social-emotional skills that are important for school readiness.[55]

But their language abilities were limited—out of synch with the values of the school. Espinosa is an impassioned advocate for dual-language learning, although she notes that even early childhood educators have been hesitant to embrace the research that supports it. The United States has long been insular, a monolingual culture, which we have exported with our irrepressible spirit of exceptionalism. As Espinosa pointed out, the advantage that Mexican youngsters showed in their earliest years disappeared by third grade, a casualty of acculturation into a system with different values, including the dominance of the English language.[56]

Whatever happened to the best interests of the child? We've become a society in which parental incarceration is the stuff of *Sesame Street*, updated for the digital age—an attempt to explain "life's difficulties" to preschoolers. Little Black boys are being expelled from preschool at an unprecedented rate.[57] Reimagining a language to replace "at risk" and "culturally disadvantaged" is just the beginning. Richie-Babbage argues that our language varies along the income spectrum. "We tend to talk about opportunities in a narrow way for kids in poverty. We need as a society to redefine what we think they're capable of."

A NOBLE EXPERIMENT IN A TALE OF TWO CITIES

As the Dow Jones Industrial Average ascended, Bill de Blasio, New York City's public advocate, ran for mayor. Universal prekindergarten topped his agenda. Stealing a trope from Charles Dickens—*A Tale of Two Cities*—he identified early childhood as the locus of the battle against economic inequality.[58]

An avowed progressive, with a youthful stint at the Quixote Center, a social justice organization, on his resume, de Blasio sought to fund his ambitious plan by increasing the income tax on those fortunate enough to be earning more than $500,000.[59] Such hubris, whispered the hedge fund titans behind closed doors. Who was this man, tilting at windmills? They were hardly quaking in their Prada boots, as the *International Business Times* confirmed: The city has retained its title as the favorite home of billionaires across the globe, claiming 96 of their ilk—former mayor Michael Bloomberg among them.[60]

Yet in the world's top financial center, the poverty rate continues to rise and the gap between rich and poor is cavernous. Or in the words of Laird Bergad, a professor at the City University of New York and author of *The Comparative Histories of Slavery in Brazil, Cuba, and the United States*, "The Gini index of inequality in household income increased from .44 in 1990 to .50 in 2010, a certain statistical measure of rising income inequality."[61]

The bottom line: We've left 0, or full equality, and we're edging up, inexorably, toward 1—a massive concentration of wealth in the city at large, among racial and ethnic groups, as well as among the 2.4 million Hispanics, the largest number of any city in the nation. In its density of millionaires—just over four and a half percent of the population, or one out of 22 residents—New York is first among American metropolises.[62]

Upon de Blasio's election, he welcomed New Yorkers to his *camino*—or Sherwood Forest, home of another iconoclast, to whom Tod Newcombe alluded in his commentary "Can Mayors Really Be Robin Hood?"[63] Politicians frequently get thwarted as they move from campaign mode to governing. The mayor's new deputy for housing, a former Goldman Sachs executive, no less, crunched the numbers. The tax increase was equivalent, she said, to the cost of a small latte at Starbucks, or $3.50 a day.[64]

The mayor persevered. Roadmap and IOU in hand from the Campaign for Educational Equity—nearly half of $4 billion owed to the state's school children, after years of litigation—he set to work to make good on his promise. But Andrew Cuomo, the governor up in Albany, was having none of this noblesse oblige. By spring, de Blasio had left his tax plan behind, and $300 million—almost 90 percent of the state's funding for prekindergarten—was on its way to the nation's largest school district.[65]

The task, delegated to Richard Buery, another new deputy mayor, and Sophia Papas, the head of the city's office of early childhood education, was herculean. The skeptics gathered. De Blasio had pledged full-day public preschool to more than 53,000 four-year-olds by September—just months away—more than doubling current enrollment.[66] The model promised instruction in synch with the state's early learning standards, as well as recruitment and retention of teachers with early childhood certification. Also part of the package was increased support for youngsters whose native language is not English—the case with nearly 20 percent of kindergartners—and greater attunement to parents in what policymakers generically define as "high-need" districts.[67]

The need, of course, could not be less generic. Four years after a national economic recovery had been declared, one in every ten children in the city was living in a community with a poverty rate above 40 percent. Some were in Bedford Stuyvesant, Brooklyn—designees of Category IV, the highest in the Census Bureau's taxonomy of family economic insecurity *in extremis*. Others made their home in the South Bronx neighborhoods of Hunts Point and Mott Haven, where almost three-quarters of all youngsters could claim that dubious distinction.[68] "This is a big lift," Buery told the audience at a prekindergarten forum on Manhattan's Upper West Side. "There are going to be lots of things we won't have solved."[69]

One of those things is Jonathan's Kozol's elephant, still standing, defiantly, in the china shop. "New York, famously liberal and proudly diverse, has the most racially segregated public school system in America," wrote journalist Errol Louis, an anchor of *NY1 News*, as the new administration was getting up to speed.[70] His data came from the Civil Rights Project at UCLA, which had just released a damning report on inequality in the Empire State.

Predicting a "damaged future" for the city's students, the investigators noted that in 19 of New York's 32 community school districts—including all in the Bronx, and two-thirds in Brooklyn—White children comprised 10 percent or less of the student body. In charter schools, White students were scarce (less than 1 percent of enrollment), members of the league of apartheid institutions.[71] Louis placed some of the blame on real estate—at a premium in the city, and a driver of gentrification—taking to task local agencies, including the Human Rights Commission, for lax enforcement of discrimination laws. "New York's famous diversity . . . masks the startling fact that the vast majority of residents retreat every night to blocks where our neighbors look like us."[72]

The evidence base to which we look for validation—forged in the smithy of the deficit model—confirms that poor children gain more from preschool when they are in close proximity to youngsters with greater resources.[73] Their language skills improve, and they pick up behavioral cues from their peers.[74] But benefits of integration go both ways. When Amy Rothschild, an early childhood educator, taught in a public prekindergarten class in Bridgeport, Connecticut, she was electrified by the mingling of parents of all income levels. She saw a family on public assistance bring frozen lasagna to affluent suburbanites, easing the burden of a child's illness. During the morning drop-off, she watched as college-educated parents talked about summer-enrichment options with seasonal day laborers.[75] Social capital, organically made.

On a warm day in late spring, as de Blasio's team was training teachers and ramping up outreach to families across the city, I took the A train to Bedford Stuyvesant. I made my way through the quiet streets to the Breevort

Children's Center, one of five programs run by the Brooklyn Kindergarten Society, whose efforts to stimulate the youngest minds in the borough's most vulnerable communities preceded the mayor's by more than a century. But like other nonprofit organizations across the city, they were worried about survival, their fundraising capabilities stretched thin and resources meager.

The arrival of universal prekindergarten—welcome in the abstract, and over the long term—poses an existential threat. "Who's going to stay here if they can go across the street?" is the plaintive cry, a reference to the local public school, where salaries are higher, the work year is shorter, and the burdens lighter. When we sat down to talk in the staff lounge, with its soothing dark green walls, director of curriculum and instruction Takiema Bunche Smith expressed concern about the staff. "The teachers have a lot on their plates," she told me.

She was still thinking about a recent conference at Brooklyn College on approaches to early childhood education in Sweden, where everyone was White, and she was the bridge between worlds. Taking a page from de Blasio, Bunche Smith told me a "Tale of Two Brooklyns," divided by the variety of experiences that children have before the age of five. "In day care centers, in nursery and preschools, and in public prekindergarten, it's so bound by class," she said. "No one's talking about this. There are all these paths that children take. We have the same expectations for them; we have the standards, benchmarks, but they're so out of synch with child development and teacher preparation."

As in other neighborhoods plagued by extreme poverty, toxic stress— intense and prolonged adversity without the protective love of adults—is ubiquitous in Bedford Stuyvesant. Emotional abuse, chronic neglect, mental illness, domestic and neighborhood violence, economic fragility: The list is long, the damage potentially great to children's developing brains and future health. "They don't have a soft place to land," Bunche Smith said.

But the youngsters are not the only victims. Many of the Breevort Center's early childhood teachers are also living under difficult circumstances, while moonlighting at other jobs to make ends meet on their subpar salaries. To reach the wage levels of their colleagues in the public schools who teach four-year-olds, further education and credentialing will have to be added to their calendars, already filled to capacity, the list of burdens growing.[76]

On the way into the prekindergarten classroom—to be funded, in part, by the city's new initiative—Bunche Smith led me to one of the center's garden patches, where she worried about the vulnerable seedlings. "Jim needs to bring some covers for the garden," she mentioned to a colleague, who had planted habanero peppers, hoping to keep the squirrels away. During a quick chat with another teacher about the conference, she talked about expanding the network. "We're forming a partnership with the Swedish teachers," she said, adding that she hoped to collaborate with educators from other countries in the future. Bunche Smith, herself, would soon leave the center to head up the Education Leadership Institute at FirstStepNYC, an early childhood initiative that had taken root in Brownsville, another Brooklyn neighborhood in need.

Inside, the children had gathered, offering a prayer of thanks for all their gifts: mommy, friends, daddy, and finally, themselves. Suddenly, the energy shifted. Within moments, led by an African dance teacher, perched on two sculptural marvels of wedge sandals, they began to move to the beat of the music, slowly at first, then picking up speed, their bodies wriggling on the tiny dance floor, ecstatic.

CHANGEMAKER: TALINA JONES
Loving Him in His Difference

In 2004, Talina Jones gave birth to Kareim, a beautiful baby boy. The occasion, one of delight and transformation for parents, was a nightmare. Alone in her room, Jones listened to the doctor deliver a litany of things that were wrong with him; the infant she had just brought into the world had Down syndrome.

"It was mostly horrible, and all I wanted to know was 'can I feed him?'" she said. Yes, she could, one nurse told her, affirming Kareim as "the sweetest baby ever." There was nothing wrong with him; she should take him home and love him. Jones, now chair of New York State's Early Intervention Coordination Council, which oversees services for children from birth to three, still remembers that parting wisdom—a source of light amid the sadness, transmuted into her life's work as an advocate for children with special needs.

Jones talked of the first months of her son's life with startling immediacy. At the time of Kareim's birth, she and her partner lived in East New York, one of Brooklyn's most underserved communities. There were a hundred appointments set up, people coming and going—a surreal blur, in which the needs of the new mother and child were often second to protocol and fear. One of the therapists refused to come to the neighborhood after four in the afternoon, arriving at nine in the morning, after Jones had been up all night nursing. No one had prepped the new mother on breastfeeding, and there was no lactation specialist, forcing her to travel to Park Slope, an upper-middle-class enclave an hour's bus ride away to rent an electric pump for $300 a month.

By the time Kareim had celebrated his first birthday, Jones had married and joined her husband in Syracuse, where she found a more welcoming early intervention community. "Everyone was participating, everyone was coming to my home," Jones said. "During assessments, they were always mindful of me, listening when I told them about things he could do." As her son moved out of toddlerhood, Jones was invited to take part in the Early Intervention Partner Training Project, a three-month immersion in the history of disability rights and advocacy, sponsored by the New York State Department of Health. She had found her niche.

Advocacy came naturally. But Jones decided her critical skills needed an upgrade. The product of an all-girls boarding school in Maryland, she headed over to Syracuse University to inquire about applying for placement as an undergraduate. "Here I am, in the administrative office, with my son on my lap, with my sister-in-law, who has a master's from the University of Buffalo," she told me. "The woman said, 'I don't know if you're ready for this. It's pretty rigorous.'" Jones graciously insists the rejection was a gift: "I will show her one day, I thought." She began at Onondaga Community College, went on to Empire State, and years later applied, and was admitted, to graduate school at Syracuse, which has a strong disability rights program. "So it's come full circle," she said.

Perceptions of disability, and the language we use to describe it, have changed, but practice, and the attitudes that inform it, haven't caught up with the research. Fear of otherness, or differentness, also dies hard. "As a child, I was considered intellectually gifted," Jones said. "I based how I knew people on their intelligence." But after discovering Howard Gardner's theory of multiple intelligences, her thinking changed. "Kareim can hear a tune and hum it, and he has social and emotional intelligence that you couldn't pay people to have," she told me.

"I cannot look at his inability to do things; I must be looking at what he can do. The total sum of who he is." Still, as the mother of a child of color and special needs, Jones lives with her own particular brand of anxiety. "When I realized that my son wasn't speaking, I went to sleep and cried," she said. "He is a tall boy, a Black boy, and in this world, he's a target of people who should be protecting him." Jones has grown to embrace her son's singularity.

"In my own identity as a Black woman from East New York, I always rejected the melting pot," she told me. "Outsiders would see poverty, and despair, but I found a lot of richness, brilliance, music, and I didn't want to assimilate. My family's from New Orleans. I like the gumbo metaphor. Why can't I love him in his difference?"

Labels and classification constrict, as Jones saw all too well in Kareim's transition to kindergarten. She and his early intervention team had decided to push for an inclusive setting—a class mixing children of all abilities—in their first meeting with the Syracuse public school system. "I'm not easily intimidated, but it felt like us versus them," she said. The chairwoman balked at Jones's request, then backed down, claiming, "We're going to give it to you, because he's going to be classified as mentally retarded in three years anyway." Jones's husband grabbed her leg to keep her from jumping over the table. "'I know he has an intellectual disability, but you're not going to label him,'" Jones told the chair. "How is that going to tell you about his outcomes?"

Jones's passion for her son and his well-being infuses her work with families across the state. Although her own pursuit of higher education has connected her to the larger policy conversation, she insists that families don't require a degree to claim their seat at the table. They have the expertise— rearing a child with a disability is the prime credential. "What we *do* need is the development of leadership," Jones said. In partnership with Bonnie Keilty, past-president of the Council on Exceptional Children, she has been collecting stories from families, whom she sees as prime movers for change.

"We need to talk about IDEA [Individuals with Disabilities Education Act], the children are getting older, and we need to take this canon of history to the policy tables," she said. While she praises New York's financial commitment to early intervention—at a little under $6 million, it's a "huge number for a non-constituent group," she says—Jones still sees a chasm between families' needs and the systems they rely on for sustenance. "How can I be a player if I don't have enough information?" Jones asks. She continues to fill in those gaps.

CHAPTER 3

CHAPTER 3

Adrift in the Age of
Teacher Effectiveness

On the eve of the . . . primary . . . the *New York Times* offered up "Years
of Despair Add to Uncertainty in Florida Race." Among the afflicted,
leading the pack, was a preschool teacher. With her home in foreclosure, her
accountant husband laid off, and two children to support, she has taken to
hawking homemade chili, at $5 a jar, off the interstate. Something is really
wrong with this picture.

—"Preschool Teacher Sells Chili to Make Ends Meet," *Huffington Post*

People themselves are not commodities—we do not permit them to be
bought and sold. Therefore, it's hardly surprising that the work we put
into developing and taking care of people is difficult to commodify. The
quantity and quality of care work depends heavily on cultural values of love,
obligation, and reciprocity—values that are seldom adequately rewarded in
the marketplace.

—Nancy Folbre, *The Invisible Heart*

What does it take to be an effective early childhood educator? So asked
Laura Colker, a curriculum developer and teacher trainer in Washington, DC, in *Young Children,* the flagship publication of the National Association for the Education of Young Children. The question had "long gnawed
at reflective teacher educators, idealistic teachers . . . and worried families,"
she wrote.[1] Yet practitioners' voices were missing from the conversation,
their perceptions unsolicited.

The current literature proved unsatisfying with its focus on educators
beyond the primary years. One of two exceptions, a study conducted at Ball
State University in 1980, had produced data from authentic sources, a list of
four key characteristics floating to the surface: sound knowledge of subject
matter, personal interest in each student, a lovely and warm atmosphere, and

enthusiasm. To begin to address the gaps, Colker initiated her own, admittedly unscientific investigation, interviewing 43 early childhood practitioners. Twelve characteristics emerged. Passion, perseverance, and willingness to take risks topped the list, followed by pragmatism, patience, and flexibility. Respect, creativity, and authenticity came next, followed by love of learning, high energy, and a sense of humor. A Rorschach test of professional identity.

Early childhood educators are infinitely resourceful, doing the most challenging work in the world, but they have struggled mightily to define themselves and their role. Just months after this healthy bout of reflection, Barack Obama would appoint Arne Duncan secretary of education of the United States, ushering in an age of early learning, with strict accountability. The spotlight would be harsh, the demands great, forcing unprecedented recalibration.

A WORKFORCE UNDER SIEGE

One morning before Election Day, America's educators woke up to find themselves on the cover of *Time* magazine. "Rotten Apples, It's Hard to Fire Bad Teachers," the headline read.[2] Randi Weingarten, president of the American Federation of Teachers, immediately got to work, demanding a swift apology and delivering a petition, with 100,000 signatures, to the publication's headquarters in New York City. This old-media stalwart, still sold in supermarket check-out lines, had pinched a nerve, the pain radiating through the collective corpus of the teaching workforce.[3]

Written by Haley Sweetland Edwards, the story highlighted Silicon Valley entrepreneur David Welsh, who had made his first fortune on the $41-billion merger of two fiber-optics companies. Lately, he had brought his skill set to another arena, master-minding the legal strategy behind *Vergara v. California*, an incendiary court case, which ruled that tenure protects failing teachers, violating the civil rights of students.[4] Along the way, Welsh and some of his well-heeled peers had discovered value-added measurement (VAM), a controversial method for evaluating educators' effectiveness based on student test scores.

No doubt they had all scanned a study which found that replacing a classroom teacher with a VAM score in the bottom 5th percentile with merely an "average" educator would increase students' lifetime earnings by more than $250,000. Never mind all those serious questions about validity.[5] Herein lay the fix for the stewards of the nation's future, perceived to be dismally inept.

We're always looking for that silver bullet, our admiration unbridled for those who possess one. Patience for the long, slow process of change is limited, not to mention the resources for making it happen. It's so much easier to throw out the old, bad crop and bring in the new. But continuity may have its virtues, as a business reporter noted at *The Verge*, musing about "Why Twitter's new head of product could be the one to fix it."[6] The company, which had lost a number of high-level executives in just a year, had promoted Kevin Weill, an insider who had worked there for five years and was popular among his co-workers. The longevity, homegrown expertise, and collegial spirit that Weill's promotion would seem to honor are rare today in any industry. But they are in especially short supply in education, whose "products"—human capital and those who nurture it—are vastly undervalued.

THE UNCHARTED SEAS OF EFFECTIVENESS

On January 3, 2001, at 5:51 A.M., the temperature in Washington, DC, hovered just under 20 degrees Fahrenheit, the wind-chill factor pushing the mercury down toward the single digits. Later that day, at the first session of the 107th Congress, the Senate and House of Representatives enacted legislation "to close the achievement gap with accountability, flexibility, and choice, so that no child is left behind."[7] The first two mandates of this crucible of 21st-century education reform signal the wind's direction: improving the academic achievement of the disadvantaged and preparing, training, and recruiting high-quality teachers and principals.

To succeed in the former, or so some thought, the nation would have to get going on the latter, but what about those "serious labor market obstacles," as one report called them? Inequities in school funding, wildly different student needs and costs, the local nature of teacher employment, and the glaring differential in staff salaries and working conditions. The last impediment was not least, affecting as it would the supply to "hard-to-staff" schools serving "poor, minority and low-achieving children."[8] There was little time to waste.

In "No Child Left Behind FAQ," Charles Coble, executive director of the Teaching Quality Policy Center at the Education Commission of the States, grappled with the vexing issue of how states would define this breed of "highly qualified" teachers.[9] By the first day of the 2002–2003 academic year, all teachers in programs supported by Title I funds—in those hard-to-staff schools—were expected to be up to snuff. When classroom doors closed for the summer of 2006, all teachers would need to be highly qualified in their area of specialization, one of the core academic subjects.

Under the provisions of NCLB, Coble noted, a teacher with a bachelor's degree, certification, and competence in their subject of specialization could claim the much-coveted compound adjective for his or her very own.[10] Decisions awaited on a long list of questions—ten in all. How would the current workforce, including educators with provisional licenses, fit into this schema? Should the definition be refined, or tweaked? What about substitute teachers, or those working with children with special needs and English language learners?

The subject of how states and local school districts might deliver the professional development to ensure compliance lay way down near the bottom of the list. Lisa Delpit, the author of *Other People's Children*, had recently called for a reconceptualization of teacher education to "lessen the 'modern prejudice' that pervades our society, alienating and disempowering large segments of our population."[11] But Coble was more interested in the logistics of the operation. While he gave a nod to the challenges of bilingual teacher preparation—scarce in many states—the other serious labor market obstacles were nowhere to be seen. Not a word do we find about the least-qualified teachers and untrained aids charged with leaving no child behind in the nation's most vulnerable communities. Among them, in the shadows, stood the early childhood workforce.

How quaint this discussion, with its focus on defining a new construct. "Highly qualified" had not yet morphed into "highly effective," suggestive of a new, even better machine. Credentials and formal training, it had now been determined, were all well and good, but they were no guarantee of high-quality teaching in the classroom. "The education of teachers in the United States needs to be turned upside down," a blue ribbon panel commissioned by the National Council for Accreditation of Teacher Education (NCATE) declared. Academic coursework "loosely linked to school-based experiences" was insufficient.[12] Clinical experience, along the lines of hospital interns and residents—an idea long embraced by experts in teacher preparation, but sketchily adopted—would be the new model.

Guidance for this massive undertaking would come from Sir William Osler, a key figure in professionalizing medical education. "He who studies medicine without books," the good doctor said, "sails an uncharted sea, but he who studies medicine without patients does not go to sea at all."[13] Although, as Jal Mehta, a professor at the Harvard Graduate School of Education, noted in his critique of American education in the journal *Foreign Affairs*, "The medical profession places less emphasis on setting targets and making sure physicians meet them—there is no such thing as No Patient Left Behind."[14] Doctors, of course, might argue otherwise, sharing as they do the burden of corporatization with the other developers of human capital.

The country's teacher preparation institutions, alas, were poor gymnasts, caught off balance under the new regime. They have a "serious and profound" perception problem, the National Council on Teacher Quality asserted, in its first consumer guide. "Many in the field do not believe that training will arm novice teachers with skills that might make them more effective," the authors wrote, employing the analogy du jour, referencing mastery of surgical methods by medical students.[15]

Criteria for ratings ranged from selectivity to coursework and opportunities for development of teaching skills. Unfortunately, the methodology was flawed, inaccuracy of the data, "shocking," a mere paper review of published course requirements and syllabi checked against a list that conveniently ignored the quality of instruction, evidence of student learning, and—the billion-dollar question—"whether graduates can actually teach."[16]

But there was no turning back. The paradigm had shifted, hurried along by Bill and Melinda Gates. Between 2009 and 2012, as NCLB's heir, Race to the Top, plied the nation with standards-based accountability, a cadre of researchers from the Measures of Effective Teaching (MET) project fanned out across the country collecting data on some 100,000 students from 3,000 teachers in six urban districts. Using a variety of measures—student survey responses, scores of lesson videos from classroom observations, student achievement on high-stakes tests and "more cognitively challenging assessments"—the zealous investigators developed new instruments and technology, the better to serve the burgeoning number of state teacher evaluation systems.[17]

In the introduction to the 616-page tome documenting this "massive engineering feat" funded by the spoils of Microsoft, the authors urged readers to "keep in mind the ultimate objective of closing the gap between teaching as it currently exists in our nation's classrooms and teaching as it needs to be to maximize every student's chances of graduating high school equipped to succeed in college and beyond."[18] The apples were rotting. By the standards of the MET project, preschool teachers lay at the bottom of the barrel.

JUST BABYSITTING

The *Early Years* journal, home to global research on the field's latest obsessions, is a hotbed of self-reflection, analysis, and brainstorming. Within its pages, masters of teacher preparation investigate the role and identity of Icelandic preschool educators through the lenses of symbolic interactionism and democratic professionalism. No aspect of practice escapes scrutiny, including the quality of interactive conversations with low-income three- and four-year-olds during small- and large-group activities. An article entitled "'It's More than Care'" poses the urgent questions of the moment, highlighting the tired refrain of teachers of young children, forever justifying the value of their work.[19]

What does it mean to be an early childhood educator? Do they perceive themselves as professionals? As Stephanie Feeney, a professor emerita at the University of Hawaii, observed in a heated conversation on BAM! Radio, connecting the "education village" online: "We must behave as professionals, whether or not we are regarded by society as professionals."[20] While today's early childhood teachers behave "as if," cognitive dissonance is rampant. "In the world of education," Amber King, a professional-development specialist, commented in one of the online LinkedIn groups where the field's ongoing identity crisis rears its ugly head, "ECE is at the bottom of the totem pole, and even looked down on by other educators."[21]

Meanwhile, our Canadian neighbor, Rachel Langford, was exploring the dominant discourse within early childhood teacher preparation programs. A professor at Toronto's Ryerson University, she sought to define the "qualities, disposition, and responsibilities of a good early childhood educator"—a task that has confounded the field for years, although not for lack of trying.[22] To achieve her goal, she adopted a three-prong strategy: analysis of ten North American early childhood textbooks published from 1971 to 2003, interviews with instructors at a community college in Ontario, and 204 assignments in which students recorded their views on the good early childhood educator.

Langford compared her data analysis to block building, evoking those rapidly vanishing staples of the kindergarten classroom. From the depths of this constructivist project, the "B" word emerged. "Society still sees ECEs [early childhood educators] as 'babysitters,'" one of the students observed, "but . . . they don't realize . . . we prepare children for the world. We are enriching their early development, and help them to grow into individuals." She noted, too, that her four field placements had boosted her confidence in making the case for the importance of early childhood education to those outside the field.[23] Sir William Osler's clinical practice model in action.

Still, changing the conversation is not easy; the American polity is polarized and perceptions are deeply entrenched. Consider the battle between Chris Christie and incumbent Jon Corzine for the governor's seat in New Jersey, waged in the tender aftermath of the Great Recession. "He's still putting in money for universal pre-K, because he's decided that the *government* should babysit for children?" the Republican challenger barked, captured for posterity in a Corzine advertisement on YouTube.[24] The former Goldman

Sachs executive with a progressive bent lost his seat. Christie moved right on into the state's executive chair, with visions of the highest policymaking position in the land dancing in his head.

Babysitting, or caring in any of its myriad forms, has no cachet—and no market value. It's not a coincidence that family practitioners and pediatricians are the lowest earners among physicians. Economist Nancy Folbre blames Adam Smith. His *Wealth of Nations*, the "first systematic explanation of the 'trickle-down theory,'" anticipated Reaganomics by two centuries, a bible for champions of the pursuit of self-interest.[25] Smith's "invisible hand" operated in the impersonal market, a kingdom of avarice and unbridled ambition. Moral sentiments belonged in the domestic realm, the haven of services to other people, deemed unproductive by this prime mover of the Scottish Enlightenment. Folbre warned of the consequences in *The Invisible Heart*: "No society oriented exclusively toward individual success—to exclusion of care for the next generation—can reproduce itself."[26]

While Aristotle may have perceived human capability as the "chief good," the "working of the soul in the way of excellence," we remain distracted by the long, and growing, list of other threats to the species.[27] Our eyes are on Wall Street and the Gross Domestic Product, neither of which has any truck with the work that Smith maligned.

But all is not bleak. In a case of great American ingenuity, the Caring Economy Campaign is pressing forward—17 million and counting when I last checked—with the huge task of shifting the capitalist behemoth to a "humane and prosperous economy"—one (just imagine!) that "recognizes the enormous return on investment in the most important, yet undervalued, human work," that of "caring for and educating people starting in early childhood."[28]

MOTHER-TEACHERS ON A WORTHY MISSION

In "An Essay on the Education of Female Teachers," Catharine Beecher, the 19th-century normal school pioneer, pondered the role of what we now call human-service providers. "Woman, whatever are her relations in life," she wrote, "is necessarily the guardian of the nursery, the companion of childhood, and the constant model of imitation." Beecher saw home and school as inextricably linked, "two naturally feminine realms in which women could nurture the next generation."[29]

Her "mother-teachers" are having something of a renaissance today, carrying on the tradition in the precincts of evangelical homeschooling, where they seek to cultivate in their children, through contemplation of scripture and classical works, the virtues of truth, goodness, and beauty.[30] As Dana Goldstein wrote in *The Teacher Wars*, Beecher and Horace Mann, the newly elected secretary of education in Massachusetts, "would define public education as America's new, more gentle church, and female teachers as the ministers of American morality."[31]

Who better to pursue this great mission, thought Mann, than a woman, "head encircled with a halo of heavenly light . . . and the celestial radiance of her benignity making vice begin its work of repentance through very envy of the beauty of virtue"?[32] Ah, but how would these missionaries, keepers of the Aristotelian soul, be remunerated? On Mann's watch, his state's corps of educators underwent a radical revamping along gender lines. By the 1840s, females outnumbered males four to one—a move, as Mann noted in his 11th annual report, that saved the state $11,000. The women had been willing to work for half of what the less virtuous sex demanded.[33]

Down in New York, however, teacher and women's rights activist Susan B. Anthony wasn't having any of it. Divinely she might come—but with resentment, her halo of heavenly light illuminating the injustice. From Canajoharie Academy in Palatine Bridge, she gave vent to her frustration: "That salary business runs in my head . . . ," she wrote in a letter to her mother. While the parents of her students appreciated her good work, and she had increased enrollment, Anthony would not receive a raise.[34]

Nearly two and a half centuries later, Marcy Whitebook, a researcher at Berkeley's Institute for Research on Labor and Employment, and Rory Darrah, an early childhood consultant, would take to the pages of one of the industry magazines to reminisce about rights, raises, and respect. These second-wave feminists, then teachers of young children, had founded the Child Care Employment Project, in the twilight of Berkeley's free-speech movement. In partnership with other teacher-activists, they spawned the Worthy Wage campaign, "central to women's liberation, racial equality, and economic equity."[35] Much work awaited these warriors, who found a welcome in the nutritious soil of Berkeley, Ann Arbor, Boston, Madison, Minneapolis, and New Haven. But the workforce was still in the shadows. Who were these people anyway? What and how were they doing in this netherworld of care and education?

In 1989, the year my daughter was born, the National Child Care Staffing Study was published, the first of its kind. Child care workers—as they were commonly known before neuroscientists and a Noble Prize–winning economist elevated them to shepherds of human capital—were pulling in an average hourly wage of $5.35, or an annual income of $9,363 for year-round, full-time employment. Nearly 60 percent of the study sample earned under $5 an hour, with 28 percent earning less than $4. The poverty threshold for a family of three was $9,341, and yearly cost-of-living adjustments or merit increases were not part of the equation.[36]

Wages, the investigators discovered, were linked to two significant quality indicators—developmentally appropriate practice and ratios of adults to children—which in turn, predicted better teacher-child interactions, those stimulating, sensitive, engaging behaviors that light the fire of teaching and learning. Teachers were leaving in droves, directors reporting an average annual turnover rate of 41 percent, up from 15 percent in the previous decade. High turnover is a problem for any organization; the cost of training new hires is considerable. But stability and continuity are integral to the quality of the institutions and people that nurture precious human capital, and they're especially important for our most vulnerable children.[37]

"Why can't we move this?" Whitebook asked me, yet another two and a half decades later, as she, Georgetown's Deborah Phillips, and UCLA's Carollee Howes returned to the confounding issue of compensation in *Worthy Work, STILL Unlivable Wages.* The median hourly wage of center-based teachers working with children from birth through five years old had now inched up to $10.60. But disparities in salaries across the variegated early childhood landscape were gaping. Child care workers had seen no increase in real earnings since 1997. Colleagues in Head Start–funded prekindergarten were making $11.90 an hour, and those in school-sponsored prekindergarten programs—a growing trend across the country—clocked in at $16. Teachers of children three years old, or younger, fared the worst, earning about 70 percent of the wages of their peers working at the older end of the spectrum, excluding those in kindergarten classrooms.[38]

Millennial "child care workers"—a category to which they have long been banished by the Bureau of Labor Statistics—earn less than animal trainers, embalmers, and barely a hair above preparers of fast food.[39] Many are worried about "economic insecurity," the latest term of art to describe a family's precarious state, and 46 percent of these child care workers, compared to 25 percent the U.S. workforce overall, had been forced by their circumstances to draw on public support from America's ever-eroding social safety net.[40]

The Worthy Wage campaign's shining moment has never seemed so distant. After a day of parades, walkouts, and demonstrations across the country, the paltry compensation of the early childhood workforce had hit the CBS Evening News. "Why did the child care worker cross the road?" Dan Rather asked, riffing on the well-worn riddle, "to get to her second job."[41]

THE VERY MODEL OF THE PERFECT,
MODERN EARLY CHILDHOOD EDUCATOR

What about that first job? In the race to build educators for the new knowledge economy, early childhood has a shaky foundation. There's always The New Teacher Project (TNTP)—brainchild of former Washington, DC, schools chancellor and Students First CEO Michelle Rhee. The organization claims to train "better teachers faster, with focus, practice, and feedback" in the service of ending the injustice of educational inequality.[42] Theory has been thrown out the window, deemed nonessential. "Drill and kill" for adult learners, TNTP's sessions pummel neophytes with a battery of skills for successful implementation: clear lesson delivery, maintenance of high academic and behavioral standards, and maximization of instructional time.

In *Fast Start*, a slick promotional brochure disguised as report cum evaluation, TNTP reported that early results from five-week summer sessions held in 14 sites across the country were promising, if inconclusive. The organization remained guardedly optimistic; a formal assessment of the work had not yet been done, and how unseemly it would be to take credit before the fact. Buoyed by 32 hours of one-on-one coaching, those who performed better during the training elicited higher ratings from their principals and did better on districtwide evaluations. That was enough to proclaim partial victory. The model, if not perfect, had improved.

How, indeed, do we get those guardians of the health, intellectual development, and social competence of the nation's youngest children up to speed? "In all honesty, we can't afford for every teacher to have a coach, we have to be smart and more efficient," Pamela Winton said. A senior research scientist at the Frank Porter Graham Child Development Institute, at the University of North Carolina, Winton directs one national center on inclusion, supporting early childhood educators working with young children with disabilities, and another called—wishfully—CONNECT, dedicated to bridging the ever-widening gap between the evidence base and the teacher in the classroom.

Those scientific data are just not trickling down into the places where early childhood educators are trained, with courses on child development characterized by more breadth than depth and scant attention paid to working with families, who are key partners.[43] Fragmentation across the key early childhood sectors—child care, Head Start, pre-K, early intervention, family support—is the order of the day. "I feel like a broken record," Winton said. "We have a multitude of standards, sets of competencies, practices for each little silo."

The malaise is even more pervasive: This is a field that has yet to decide upon the basics. In the era of *The Widget Effect*, TNTP's report on

America's abject failure to distinguish among the different levels of teacher effectiveness, Georgetown University and ZERO TO THREE, a national organization that advocates for infants, toddlers, and their families, convened a summit. Teachers matter a great deal, I wrote in a report on the proceedings, which addressed the science of professional development, but "exactly which skills, competencies, qualifications, and modes of professional development produce the best outcomes for children remains an urgent question."[44]

Exactitude is elusive, pulling the players in different directions—including practice-oriented training, now high on the federal research agenda. Martha Zaslow, a senior scholar at Child Trends, a research organization, proclaimed the latest conceptual shift. Echoing NCATE's blue ribbon panel, determined to turn teacher preparation upside down, she conceded that professional development focused on coursework alone was inadequate to the task. "We're standing it on its head now, and beginning to say . . . if you want to change practice and quality, you need to begin by directly intervening with practice.[45]

What happens in the sphere inhabited by teacher and learner is alchemy, defying our best efforts at deconstruction. You would think a little theoretical grounding, higher order thinking, and analytical skills might come in handy for this monumental undertaking. Even aspiring doctors are urged to pick up those goodies—along with Solo cups for beer pong—during their undergraduate careers, majoring outside of biology and organic chemistry. Not to mention the legions of students across the United States in whom we seek to inculcate these cherished components of a high-quality education. But the early childhood field has long been stuck, debating the merits of a bachelor's degree.[46]

In the mid-2000s, the Economic Policy Institute took its turn weighing in on the status of the workforce. "Losing ground in early childhood education," they reported.[47] Among teachers and administrators across center-based early childhood programs—excluding public school prekindergarten—the share of those with a four-year college degree had declined, from 43 percent in the mid-1980s to only 30 percent as NCLB was getting up to speed. Education levels for home-based child care providers, only one in nine of whom had a college degree, were even lower. Fewer than half had any education beyond high school—sub-baccalaureate, as the economists described it—a decline, they observed, that was "all the more remarkable," compared to the increase in education levels of American workers at large.[48]

While this downward trend in educational attainment has abated in recent years, the question of the baseline credential is still unsettled.[49] Never mind that 93 percent of public elementary and middle school teachers have a BA, with nearly half among them holding a master's degree or higher.[50] Never mind the robust evidence for the BA's utility—including *Eager to Learn,* a seminal work of the National Academy of Science.[51] Some among the punditry have called for busting the "monopoly on the awarding of recognized postsecondary credentials for early childhood educators."[52] Let them eat cake—or alternative paths to certification.

CHALLENGED TO CARE

We pay a lot of attention to empathy and emotional intelligence, prime ingredients in our quest for greater civility—and productivity. Ashoka Changemakers, a global network of social entrepreneurs, has launched an initiative to enhance the ability to understand what other people are feeling, the better to solve problems, lead effectively, and drive change. The Institute for Health and Human Potential offers a "Free EQ Quiz," citing research from the Harvard Business School: Highly intelligent people whose emotional quotient is low, they claim, are consistent underperformers. After you've filled in the bubbles and tallied up your score on defensiveness when criticized, staying calm under pressure, and managing anxiety, stress, anger, and fear, the organization invites you to contact them to "improve your ability to manage your emotions and connect more skillfully with others."[53]

We will not be thwarted in our pursuit of equilibrium, undeterred by irrational, inherently human tendencies. Andy Hargreaves, a professor at Boston College's school of education, and the coauthor of *Professional Capital,* has been slogging through the muck. Disturbed by the neglect of emotions "in the increasingly rationalized world of educational reform," he embarked on a project to tease out the effects of worry, hope, boredom, despondence, and frustration on the process of teaching, learning, and change. Why, any one of those pesky feelings might trip you up in managing a classroom, foiling attempts at student achievement.[54]

In interviews with 53 Canadian elementary and high school teachers, Hargreaves mined the rich lode of emotional labor, drawing heavily on Berkeley sociologist Arlie Hochschild's classic text on the subject.[55] How did teachers perceive their interactions with students, and how were they managing? Hargreaves wanted to know. Warning against the embrace of indulgent emotion, he argued that it might be "helpful or harmful, raising classroom standards or lowering them"—or otherwise detrimental to the educator operating in today's chilly, rational climes.[56]

Hargreaves's investigation excluded teachers of two-year-olds, whose tempestuous repertoire has been known to challenge even the most sensitive of souls. Their tantrums are just the beginning, a prelude to more fireworks along the developmental spectrum. Four-year-olds, and even children as young as three, are facing expulsion and suspension from preschool for "behavior problems," the amorphous phrase we employ these days to categorize the unmanageable.[57] You might melt down, too, if you hadn't had breakfast, you had witnessed a shooting in your neighborhood, or if you just hadn't gotten around to regulating all the chaos in that frontal cortex, something that boys tend to get around to later than girls—I hear it's not fully in gear until age 25—to their detriment in the new, rigorous environments of the early childhood classroom.[58]

For those on these tempestuous frontlines, the going can get rough. In a study of nearly 4,000 state-funded prekindergartens across the United States, conducted by William Gilliam, of Yale's Child Study Center, 10.4 percent of teachers reported at least one expulsion during the past 12 months, with rates higher for older children and African Americans. Boys were more than four and a half times more likely to be expelled than girls. Number four on Gilliam's list of recommendations for reducing what he called a "severe response to challenging behaviors" speaks to the question of burnout: "Like truck drivers and hospital staff, PK [prekindergarten] teachers need reasonable hours and regular breaks in order to do their best work."[59]

In an effort to help new teachers do their best work, professors of early childhood education Lisa Goldstein, of the University of Texas in Austin, and Debra Freedman, of Penn State, pored over electronic student journals, assigned for a course in classroom organization and management. They hoped to glean a better understanding of the role of caring in teaching and learning, with Nel Noddings as their guide.[60] A former Stanford professor, mother of ten, and grandmother of multitudes, her work has endeared her to generations of educators looking for alternatives to traditional pedagogy and the rationalized world of education reform.

Noddings returns to the original dyad—a template for the relationship between student and teacher. The infant responds to the mother with a heartwarming display of wriggles, smiles, attentive stares, and cuddles. But when the baby is unresponsive and the process is short-circuited, the caregiver is depleted by the "constant outward flow of energy," an occupational hazard for emotional laborers.[61] When all goes well, the process is bi-directional, a harmonious balance promoting optimal conditions for growth and learning.

Goldstein and Freedman worked hard with their apprentices, modeling the kind of tender, loving care they hoped the student teachers would bestow upon their children. But ethnographic forays have a way of confounding expectations. "Like all of the skills, attitudes, and dispositions required to teach well," they wrote in the *Journal of Teacher Education*, "caring is not always as easy as it may look to novices."[62] One of their teachers—immersed in work with predominately poor, African American, and Hispanic first-graders—was hitting the wall on classroom management. "I feel Green Oaks students require a firm hand because they come from dysfunctional homes where there is no element of structured discipline," she wrote in her journal.[63]

How unsettling to see a student equate dysfunction with families of color of low socioeconomic status. Why, she wasn't yet a mother and hadn't even met the families. Worse, her judgment that parents were derelict in their duty was shared by her peers—a disturbing discovery for these educators of the next generation of early childhood teachers, so dedicated to culturally responsive practice. The deficit theory lives on—amid the collision of class, race, good intentions, and emotional turbulence.

Yet wouldn't you know that the "firm hand" has its proponents among the teaching corps of color. In another ethnographic study, published in the journal of *Urban Education*, Franita Ware mourns the loss of a historical model of Black teaching, highlighting two practitioners of warm demander pedagogy. Rooted in an ethic of caring and responsiveness, these educators "provide a tough-minded, no-nonsense, structured and disciplined classroom environment for kids whom society had psychologically and physically abandoned."[64]

Here, authority is sanctioned, the extension of parental customs in the home. "Sometimes I mean-talk them in varying degrees of severity," one of the teachers said. "Sometimes when you do yell, it is not always right. . . . Sometimes you have to go back and say—"what was really going on with you . . . ? I'm just so sorry."[65] This veteran of a high-needs school district saw herself as an "other-mother," protecting her students against low expectations with firm, loving care, and hoping they would pay it forward in their communities and in the society at large.

LEADERS AT THE CONFERENCE TABLE

Connections may be the heartbeat of learning, as former Spanish teacher Tyler Thigpen wrote in "Taking a Relationship-Centered Approach to Education," but sustaining them is tough.[66] Still, the *Stanford Social Innovation Review* busily documents best practice. In "The Missing Link in School Reform," Carrie Leana, a professor of organizations and management at the University of Pittsburgh, pondered the obsession with the highly skilled individual teacher. Her research, conducted over a decade in urban school districts, suggested that the exclusive emphasis on human capital—experience, subject knowledge, and pedagogical skills—was misguided, dwarfing the more important social kind of capital, or "the patterns of interactions among teachers."[67]

In a survey of more than 1,200 New York City teachers ranging from kindergarten through fifth grade, Leana and her colleagues asked them to weigh in on their sense of competence, or lack thereof, with regard to math. Educators in the early grades were most uncomfortable, but three out of ten fifth-grade teachers also expressed low levels of confidence—math-phobes, the district's coach described them. The investigators dug deeper. To whom did the teachers talk when they had questions or needed advice? In most cases, they sought advice from one another, nearly twice as likely to consult their peers than outside experts and four times more likely to consult their peers than the principal of their school. "It's dangerous to express vulnerability to experts or administrators," one teacher said; "they will take your professional status away."[68]

Such status is precarious these days, the path toward a solid professional identity and leadership, strewn with obstacles. "I can see how people can be deterred. It's incredibly hard work with none of the glamour," Cristina Mendonca, a graduate student in early childhood education at the Bank Street College of Education, told me. "The most skilled ones should be teaching the youngest, but the salaries don't support it."

The daughter of immigrants from Argentina and Ecuador, Mendonca majored in psychology and education as an undergraduate at Mt. Holyoke and then embarked on a career as a marine animal trainer, working at the New York Aquarium. When Hurricane Sandy struck in 2012, her future seemed to be slipping away. She had enjoyed interacting with young student visitors transfixed by the Pacific walruses and California sea otters. Someone told her she would make a great special education itinerant teacher. "Infancy is where it all starts," she said. "I began to think about what I could do to advocate for that age group."

Bank Street is the ancestral home of the developmental-interaction theory. Rooted in "interconnected spheres of thought and emotion," this philosophy spawns teaching that puts a high premium on meeting children at their particular stage of growth and engagement with people, the environment, and the community.[69] "Our focus is relationship based," Marjorie Brickley said of the college's brand of teacher preparation, as I sat with her and a colleague, Alanna Navitski, in an office overlooking a rooftop playground. "They're not learning by rote, they're learning in an affect-laden way."

Brickley is codirector with Navitski of Bank Street's infancy program. She also organizes the school's annual Infancy Institute—where participants had flocked to a session called "'Don't Get So Upset!' Help Young Children Manage Their Feelings by Understanding Your Own." She's followed a path similar to her peers in the larger early childhood workforce, starting out at a community college and moving on to a four-year institution for her undergraduate degree. Equity and the value of different perspectives are bred in the bone.

"Conflict is an opportunity to learn about another point of view, what is driving somebody else," Brickley said. "We're always wondering about the experience of the family, of the child, and of our coteachers." The crucible is the conference group, the college's centerpiece of advisement, a process that also includes one-on-one sessions with a mentor, who observes students at their sites in the field. Here, the students come together, setting the agenda, opening up the conversation to policy issues and social justice, and flexing their leadership muscles.

On a raw, rainy evening in late fall, I returned to this sanctuary for neophytes, the scene of my own baptism into a new professional identity. I settled into a small chair, joining Mendonca and her peers in a classroom for nine- and ten-year-olds, day workers in Bank Street's laboratory school for children. "There's a mutual understanding of everybody being in the same place," Mendonca said of the group. "I know I'm getting nonjudgmental feedback. I'm developing a philosophy, and in a very practical sense, they give me ideas to think outside the box."

Flooded with sense memories, I began to watch as the women went through their paces, deconstructing the delicate choreography of emotional labor. Navitski, who had recently given birth to her first child, opened with some housekeeping details. "I have one other thing," she said, after dispensing with the logistics, "*The Child with Special Needs*, by this guy named Stanley Greenspan."[70] They should take a look at it, she said, explaining the different approaches for working with children with special needs. I remembered this child psychiatrist whose play-based approach to intervention—"floortime," he called it—I had used with my own children, sitting with them on the hard parquet wood into late childhood. Greenspan, who died shortly after finishing *The Learning Tree* in 2010, has left his clinical expertise online, offering home workshops in meltdowns and tantrums, regulatory sensory processing disorders, and a lifespan approach to autism.[71]

But "this guy," as I learned in my return to graduate school, is out of fashion among the policymaking set, proponents of applied behavior analysis (ABA) in ascendance. Used in the course of everyday activities, ABA is designed to decrease maladaptive behaviors—including aggression—and foster those that make children, well, less challenging. Among those pro-gram components deemed "effective" is antecedent manipulation, or "the modification of situational events that precede the target behavior" through "prompt/fading procedures, behavioral momentum, contrived motivational operations, and inter-trial intervals."[72] Most important is the reliance on ob-jective information that tracks the progress of these maladapted little ones—indispensable in our quest to perfect data-driven systems and practices for continuous program quality improvement.[73]

After breaking the ice with the recitation of their favorite comfort foods—including cheese with guava jelly and ice cream, a native Cuban dish—the group got down to work. Today, the focus was on the trials of toddlers separating from parents. "In my work with twos, it's totally day by day," one of the women said. But they were acclimating, she reported, taking that great leap from parent to other caregiver. "Now, they want you to hold them in your arms." Another student teacher was struggling with a scientist, worried about rising cortisol levels in her child's brain. The mother refused to leave, lest his stress increase, and was micromanaging the staff of the child care center, down to their facial expressions in inter-actions with her son.

"You're supposed to stress them out," the daughter of a psychotherapist told the group; "that's how they grow." Navitski weighed in, acknowledg-ing the different perspectives and bodies of expertise in the parent-teacher relationship and reminding them of the "third space," an idea she had float-ed a few weeks earlier. "The mom is over here, and you're over there, but both of you are okay," she said. "The question is, how are we going to work together?"

The clock was running down. There's so much to talk about, Navitski said, glancing around the table. "I was thinking about trial and error this week," Mendonca said when her turn came. "With the kids who don't do eye contact, I'm trying to figure out what's going on in their head, what can I physically do." That day, she had moved toward her goal of helping a child on the autism spectrum to use an item purposefully. "We played with the piano for a little while," she told the group. "I just started tapping the keys and he tapped them, and then I swooped all the keys, and he imitated me."

Mendonca was still figuring out the child's cues, critical to establishing a trusting relationship. Sometimes he would emit a high-pitched sound, fluc-tuating in level and tone, and she had no idea what it meant. Having worked in a Montessori school, where student initiative is prized, she found it hard to repeatedly explain how everything was done; she felt odd and vague-ly apologetic. But, later, at circle time, when Mendonca was attending to another child, he approached her, touched her arm, and made eye contact. "I get it now," she told the group. Connections in the making.

CHANGEMAKER: JESSICA SAGER

Telling Their Stories

"All the world's a stage," Jacques observed in Shakespeare's *As You Like It*, "and all the men and women merely players . . ." We're actors, bound together on the path of human development—from infancy to old age. Jessica Sager's path began in the theater, her passion as an undergraduate at Barnard College. But she was soon diverted from the boards, falling in love with the students she worked with at the Teachers and Writers Collaborative, whose futures seemed less than assured.

Sager headed to Yale Law School just as Bill Clinton's revamp of welfare reform took hold, sending low-income mothers back into the workforce within months of giving birth. "I got really concerned about what was going to happen to the babies," she said, "and I came up with the idea for a lab school for parents to train them to be early childhood educators, inspired by best practices around the country." Launched in a housing project in New Haven, in partnership with Janna Wagner, the project served as the prototype for All Our Kin, an organization that trains family child care providers, ranging in age from 18 to 70, which they founded in 1999. "We've come to admire these women who do the work out of love, are so mission driven, underresourced, and stressed," Sager said. "We're equally passionate about women's equality and justice."

For many parents with children under the age of three, home care is the preferred choice, serving nearly 30 percent of infants and 25 percent of toddlers whose families receive child care subsidies across the nation. The quality of this kind of care is variable, often mediocre, but it's inexpensive and flexible—two requirements for low-income and non-English-speaking families, many of whom work nontraditional hours and are in dire financial straits. The women who sustain them, and whom All Our Kin supports, are their demographic twins. The majority are poor and Latina, but they also serve a substantial African American population—links in a delicate chain of caregiving in the Connecticut communities of New Haven, Bridgeport, Norwalk, and Northern Fairfield County.

Sager looks carefully for the leverage points. She asks the chicken-and-egg questions that have haunted the field for decades: "In the absence of economic incentives, do we look at competency-based education? Do we achieve professionalization and then look for compensation?" There are no easy answers.

All Our Kin addressed child care quality first, creating a licensing tool kit to help providers meet the state's health and safety requirements and providing mentors during the process. They collaborated with the Connecticut Children's Museum and the city of New Haven, sending more than 300 mothers into the workforce. Every dollar spent on the project yielded dividends of roughly $15 to $20, a significant boost to the gross regional product. Graduates of the program earned between $20,000 and $25,000, or an average annual income of $23,000—more than 10 percent above the going wage for their counterparts in the early care and education industry.

Such gains are impressive, but the women still live on the margins, keeping Sager up at night. The path to higher education is a tough one. The Child Development Associate (CDA), long recognized as a valid baseline credential in the field, is insufficient. "The CDA is an amazing idea, a really rich credential, but it's not enough," Sager said. "I see this moving further, with certification, requiring degrees." She talks of the need for better articulation, agreements between two- and four-year colleges that smooth the path for providers, whose credits and coursework too often don't move along with them.

Subsidies are also critical. Long workdays and precarious finances make this journey nearly impossible for most of All Our Kin's clientele. Sager hopes that Connecticut will include her clients when they finally get around to implementing a quality rating and improvement system. Many of these initiatives around the country provide incentives for climbing the career ladder. "But right now," she said, "teachers of infants and toddlers are out in the cold."

In the meantime, Sager and her staff focus their energies on professionalizing the workforce, fertilizing the soil. "One critical factor in preparing children for school is their social-emotional development," she said. "They need basic skills, like listening, and paying attention, one place where family child care providers have a lot of strength." Bimonthly consultation and coaching—offered in English and Spanish—from All Our Kin's master teachers break the isolation of novices. "They mentor providers, to set goals and figure out where they are, classic executive function stuff," Sager said. The organization also connects providers to family child care networks, opportunities to further hone their skills, build their businesses, and boost their social capital.

They bring content as well, curriculum covered in six to eight weekly sessions on infant development, early literacy and numeracy, and children's physical health and the outside world—among other subjects that constitute the field's core knowledge. "In Bridgeport and New Haven, providers have organic gardens," Sager told me. "We're using them as teaching tools, and within all these streams is always the question: What do we think is a high-quality relationship?"

Replication, or expanding the reach of the model, is the gold ring of collective impact. All Our Kin has worked with Wellspring Innovative Solutions to conceptualize growth more broadly. The organization is looking at policy shaping as an integral part of the picture. "We've redefined our own work as it's dawned on us how important it is to tell the story," Sager said. "We've taken a slow, grassroots, one-person-at-a-time approach, but there are other ways." The organization has established an annual policy fellowship, attracting energetic college graduates to lift up providers' voices, amplified by social media and exercised in site visits from policymakers.

Sager continues to lead the troops, getting the message out. "The early childhood workforce is underpaid, underresourced and disrespected," she wrote in an opinion piece in the *Connecticut Mirror*, sharing the byline with Wagner, now the organization's chief knowledge and learning officer, and Anna Rader, a former policy fellow. All Our Kin's profile and visibility are expanding. The Aspen Institute and Harvard's Center on the Developing Child have highlighted the organization, one of a number of promising two-generation initiatives to move vulnerable young children and their parents toward educational success and economic security.

Now it's time for the main protagonists to take the stage. "I think we can go a lot further—we're just at the beginning," Sager said. "We're trying to give family child care providers opportunities to tell and share their stories."

CHAPTER 4

The Yin and Yang
of Education Reform

At the turn of the 21st century, Jeanne Shaheen put early learning on the
map of the Education Commission of the States. . . . Pre-K had finally entered
the big boys' club. Still, we worried. Where was child care . . . Infants and
toddlers? Supports for parents? What about academic pushdown? Beggars,
we took this small and tasty morsel, a wedge . . . into the sacred realm . . .
of the American family. A baby step . . . but we weren't going backwards . . .
we'd push back up, transforming K–12 with the wonders of developmentally
appropriate practice. Talk about denial.

—"Developmentally Inappropriate," *ECE Policy Matters*

The imaginative play that we so early abandon, the attention to children's
nascent friendships, these are . . . the precursors of what Piaget called
intellectual "decentering," . . . the ability to imagine the world without
oneself at its center. As we stint on one, we injure the other. As we eliminate
from our schools and from our children's . . . lives the time and space for
exercising their creative imagination and building personal ties, we've
cheated our children and our society in a far more critical way than we're
inclined to understand.

—Deborah Meier, *The Power of Their Ideas*

Adults have always argued about the course of a proper education—a
hair-raising drama in which children have been silent actors. The play-
wrights were men born of the revolutions that rocked Europe in the 17th
and 18th centuries. Among them was Johann Amos Comenius, a Moravian
bishop upset by the violence of the Thirty Years' War. His own brand of
pedagogy originated in God and nature: a vision of "gardens of delight,"
in which "large numbers of children were to grow, play, and learn together joyfully and harmoniously."[1] Scorning formal schooling for children

younger than six, Comenius, nonetheless, prescribed a detailed syllabus for mothers of progeny from birth on up in *The School of Infancy*, published in English in 1650.

Nearly four centuries later, we are still at it. "Early Schooling Damaging Children's Wellbeing, Say Experts," read the headline in a recent issue of the *Guardian*, "the world's leading liberal voice." More than a hundred teachers, writers, and academics—including Lord Layard, director of the well-being program at the London School of Economics—had written to the secretary of state, to protest Great Britain's education policies. The quest for school readiness, they asserted, had gotten terribly out of hand, foisting "the tests and targets which dominate primary education' upon four-year-olds."[2]

TINKERING TOWARD UTOPIA

Arne Duncan's *annus horribilus* had reached its nadir. Amid growing protest against high-stakes testing, the U.S. secretary of education had launched a frontal assault on White suburban moms. How dare they suggest that the latest Common Core standards for math and language arts were wreaking havoc with their children's love of learning? "All of a sudden, their child isn't as brilliant as they thought they were," our chief education officer said, referring to the decline in test scores occasioned by the adoption of the new policy by a growing number of states.[3]

Duncan's glib assessment, rattling maternal sensibilities, helped secure his place as one of the villains in the ancient drama of human development— or tragic hero, in the eyes of early childhood educators. This is the man, after all, who had propelled the years from birth through five to the highest reaches of the federal policy agenda, promising a cool $10 billion for early learning, through his signature Race to the Top initiative.[4]

Meanwhile, as tensions simmered between the populace and the policymaker, the latest strategies to improve education outcomes came under review. "Could Falling Test Scores Be a Good Thing?" Scott Gillum, a voice from gyro, a global ideas shop that ignites decisions in a numb world, wondered in *Forbes* magazine.[5] The test scores in question—the bane of the education secretary's existence—are those of America's high school students, whose competence in math, reading, and science is measured each year, along with that of their peers from more than 50 countries, by the Programme for International Student Assessment (PISA).

Each December, upon the scores' release, the United States has a full-scale panic attack, watching the inexorable shift downward, a prosperous future slipping away. But these much-maligned results, Gillum reassured us, might not portend the loss of America's competitive edge. He cited Yong Zhao, author of *World Class Learners*, who had compared the PISA math scores with those of the Global Entrepreneurship Monitor, which assesses the activities, aspirations, and attitudes of individuals in more than 50 countries, 23 of them PISA participants.[6]

Wouldn't you know that Zhao found an inverse correlation between test scores and perceived entrepreneurial moxie? The top performers on the PISA tests—Korea, Singapore, Taiwan, and Japan—were hardly stellar on the innovation front. As Sir Ken Robinson, a former British academic turned proselytizer for the vanishing imagination, has suggested, in one of his eviscerating attacks on the American way of learning, we may be educating ourselves out of creativity.[7]

Across the world, the leaders of developed nations are tearing their hair out in a quest to ensure preeminence. The United States is leading the way, applying disruptive innovation—a popular business strategy—to human development, learning, and teaching.[8] Data collectors on Ritalin, we measure every indicator in the book. Our children are on their treadmills, each milestone anxiously awaited, and progress dutifully recorded. "Gesturing Predicts Children's Future School Success" headlined a post by Susan Sirigatti, former school principal and editor of *Human Milk*, which spilled into my overflowing inbox. One of many from a blog dedicated to fostering "A Smarter Beginning," the piece highlighted a study, conducted at the University of Chicago, which found a gap among infants' gesturing across socioeconomic classes—a harbinger of stunted language acquisition.[9]

Even the subconscious has not escaped scrutiny. We now have Sleep'n Sync, a noninvasive, patent-pending product designed to "revolutionize a child's outlook while they sleep." For just 20 dollars a download or 36 for a CD/book, this series of audiotapes, available at iTunes and Amazon, and based on principles of neuroscience, promises a multifaceted brain lift, alleviating the stress of bullying and test-taking, fostering flexibility, dispelling anger, and enhancing reading and communication skills.[10]

Nothing is off limits in our pursuit of cognitive complexity. And money follows the quest—if not those who most need it. Thus did Megan McClelland, an associate professor of health and child development at Oregon State University, find herself the recipient of a $1.6 million grant from the U.S. Department of Education to track the outcomes of 400 preschoolers who had played a tweaked version of the classic children's game "Head, Shoulders, Knees, and Toes."[11] In the original game, the directives match the body part; in McClelland's experiment, she required the children to do the opposite, touching toes, for example, when she asks them to touch their heads. Never mind that some of her undergraduates had trouble executing the task. The four-year-olds who finessed it delivered to McClelland a rich lode of data. They were more likely to pay attention in class or keep nose to the grindstone in specific activities—key signs of a well-functioning prefrontal cortex, the locus of school readiness and academic success.[12]

Children are the youngest, most fragile casualties on the battlefield. But they are hardly alone. In the modern era of high-stakes accountability—enshrined in No Child Left Behind and Race to the Top—the fate of public schools and educators has hinged on metrics of adequate yearly progress, annual professional performance reviews, and the hotly contested value-added model, which rates teachers based on their students' test-score gains from fall to spring of the academic year.[13]

Such policies have continued to provoke the ire of teachers and their representatives in recent years. As education historian and activist Diane Ravitch announced one Independence Day in her eponymous, well-read blog: "Breaking News: NEA Delegates Pass Resolution Calling for Arne Duncan's Resignation."[14] By the time page views had passed the 14-million mark, the education secretary was having a delayed epiphany, noting, in a post on the DOE's *Homeroom* blog, that testing was "sucking the oxygen out of the room," robbing "school buildings of joy," and causing "unnecessary stress."[15]

Our madness—an obsessive-compulsive disorder—may seem aberrant, but it is merely a blip in the long history of education reform. "Tinkering toward utopia," as Stanford emeritus professors David Tyack and Larry Cuban describe the process in their book so named, is torturous.[16] Citizens always "have sought to perfect the future by debating how to improve the young through education," they wrote, but "actual reforms in schools have rarely matched such aspirations."[17] Fierce ideological strife is woven into our DNA, along with a healthy appetite for capital creation, of the greenback variety. Between improving the young (and saving the poor among them), and feeding the maw of the U.S. economy, it is a wonder that any reforms ever live up to their promise.

READY OR NOT, HERE THEY COME

Just before my initiation into parenthood, Terrel H. Bell, one of Arne Duncan's predecessors, ordered a blue ribbon panel to examine the quality of the American education system. Released in 1983, the report highlighted a perceived crisis of monumental proportions, laying out the dilemma in the first two sentences: "Our nation is at risk. Our once unchallenged preeminence in commerce, industry, science, and technological innovation is being over-taken by competitors throughout the world."[18] Not a word was uttered about early education, the reference points trending upward: the absence of higher-order thinking skills in 17-year-olds, the College Board, the SAT, remedial mathematics courses in four-year colleges.

Among the bullet points of abject failure was the decline in standardized test scores of high school students since the launch of Sputnik. The National Aeronautics and Space Administration offers a geeky account of the orbit of the world's first artificial satellite in 1957, whimsically noting that its four "whip-like antennas . . . looked like long 'whiskers' pointing to one side."[19] No meteoroids were detected, and the rocket scientists provide not a hint of repercussions for America's future. Wikipedia, our digital-age successor to the *World Book* and *Encyclopedia Britannica*—staples of Sputnik-era home libraries—describes the launch as a crisis marked by fear and uncertainty, a key Cold War event that set off a "Space Race" between the United States and what was then the Soviet Union, in response to "a perceived technolog-ical gap between the two superpowers."[20]

Clearly, we Americans were not up to snuff—and it was high time we did something about it. As the 20th century sped along, Sputnik receding in the rearview mirror, President George H. W. Bush gathered with governors from all 50 states to brainstorm ideas for reforming education. School read-iness floated to the top of the agenda. The objectives, listed in the 260-page *Data for the National Education Goals Report*, were lofty.[21] All children would have access to high-quality and developmentally appropriate pre-school programs. Parents would be trained, the better to support the nation's youngest students. The final objective aimed the highest, acknowledging the complex interplay of ecological factors that influence learning—home and neighborhood, or those beyond educators' direct control, routinely ignored by policymakers, the guardians of accountability, and fierce protectors of John Doe taxpayer.

The American public was on board, as the 22nd annual Gallup Poll would attest, and the deal was sealed in the Goals 2000: Educate America Act of 1994.[22] The first Bush, grandfather of No Child Left Behind, legis-lation for the new millennium, had officially welcomed preschool to the beleaguered precincts of K–12 education reform.

I polished my analytical skills on Goals 2000. Fresh out of graduate school, at the now-defunct Child Care Action Campaign, I jumped right into that systems merge, managing a project designed to document effec-tive partnerships in 68 low-income communities across the nation between early childhood programs—Head Start, child care programs, and state prekindergarten—and public school districts. "Until a vision of American education reform that includes early childhood is widely shared," I wrote, setting the context for the final report, "the goal of universal school readiness will remain elusive."[23]

What were we thinking? The early childhood landscape was a mess: a patchwork of public and private programs plagued by uneven quality, an undereducated, generally impoverished workforce, and anemic investment. How the field was going to bring these youngest students with their variable backgrounds up to standard was anyone's guess. Even in the best of circumstances—and we saw some of those in our inventory—assessing readiness, "a somewhat narrow and artificial construct of questionable merit," would be daunting.[24]

School readiness defies definition. What exactly does it mean? How do you know if a child is prepared—and for what? A classic survey of parents and teachers, conducted on the cusp of the Goals 2000 legislation, highlights the divergence of opinion.[25] The surveyors divided their work into two clusters of behavioral and school-related items. Included in the first category were the ability to verbally communicate needs, wants, and thoughts; take turns and share; display enthusiasm and curiosity in approaching new activities; and sit still and pay attention.

The second listed proficiency with pencils and paintbrushes, counting ability (up to 20 or more), and knowledge of the letters of the alphabet. Both groups converged on the need for well-honed communication skills and positive approaches to learning. But stark disagreement emerged on the question of the academic items: The percentage of parents who rated them very important or essential ranged from six to eight times greater than that of teachers.

The etiology of this disagreement between the stewards of children's development is unclear, the intersection between parental anxiety and education policy hard to locate. Parents have always taken pride in their offspring's precociousness, a tendency against which Jean-Jacques Rousseau railed in *Emile*, the bible of the "New Education," published in mid-18th-century France.[26] The Enlightenment philosopher prescribed experience outside the home, in nature, where children, he thought, should be left to observe, honing their sensory abilities through exploration and games. He advised ample time for play. And he introduced formal reading instruction at the advanced age of 12, eschewing flash cards, as well as other gimmicky learning aids.

Rousseau's a far cry from Amanda Gignac, a Texas mother and blogger at *The Zen Leaf*, who criticized her six-and-a-half-year-old son in an interview with a *New York Times* reporter. While he routinely tackled 80-page chapter books, she called him a "reluctant" reader, noting that "he would still read picture books now if we let him, because he doesn't want to work to read."[27] Work to read? Whatever happened to pleasure? Gignac claimed she was quoted out of context, but no matter: The acceleration of skills acquisition is embedded in contemporary education policy, aided and abetted by parents and educators, caught between conflicting desires for children's well-being and their academic progress.

IN THE QUICKSAND OF EXPECTATIONS

The primacy we stubbornly accord cognitive development is problematic. Emotions matter, as a policy report from the Society for Research in Child Development bluntly declared in the early days of No Child Left Behind.[28] It was clear to the authors that children's emotional and behavioral adjustment was essential for their school success. They rued the emphasis on academic preparedness, overshadowing students' complex inner lives. The brief also sounded a warning for young children exposed to psychosocial stressors—domestic and community violence, maternal depression, parental substance abuse, and extreme poverty—just to name a few of the reasons that James may have trouble sitting still and paying attention in his kindergarten classroom. For such children, especially, emotional skills serve as protectors.

Today, the goal of universal readiness is as inchoate and elusive as ever. Around four million children enter kindergarten each year, many of them unprepared for school.[29] Backpacks hanging off their tiny frames, they bring great expectations and an array of strengths, weaknesses, languages, socioeconomic circumstances, and cultural customs—a significant achievement gap in tow. Those who track this divide have identified sizable differences in cognitive and social-emotional development as well as health status as early as nine months, with disparities growing in the preschool years. One study found a 60-percent gap in average cognitive scores between the nation's most affluent children and their poorer peers. Youngsters from low-income families have also been found less likely to receive positive behavior ratings at nine and 24 months than children in families that are more financially secure.[30]

The descendants of the policymakers who declared the nation at risk keep trying to crack the code. Longitudinal data systems from birth through 12th grade are among their favored strategies. States have embraced the cause with a vengeance, tracking indicators of readiness—or what children need to know and do—and codifying them. By the end of the first decade of the 21st century, 50 states and the District of Columbia had developed Early

Learning Guidelines, or "Readiness Standards," as Wyoming calls them, for preschool children from three to five years of age. Nearly half were working on a set for infants and toddlers.[31] In a nod to the research, all but two states include guidelines for social-emotional development: Self-concept, self-control, social relationships, cooperation, and peer interactions make frequent appearances in the rubrics.

Children who enter kindergarten with so-called prosocial styles tend to make new friends more easily and form warm bonds with their teachers, both of which predict high achievement. Youngsters who are more impulsive and aggressive, on the other hand, have more tempestuous relationships and are less engaged, stymied in their academic progress by a growing dislike of school.[32] One study of "person-oriented patterns of school readiness" in a group of four-and-a-half-year-olds concluded—eureka!—that those with superior social skills and average cognitive skills fared better than their less socially competent peers with equal intellectual prowess.[33] The standards, alas, are often poorly articulated, those that tend to children's social and emotional states vying for dominance with guidelines for math and literacy.

Early childhood's merge with the K–12 system has disturbed the delicate ecology of Rousseau's whole-child approach, in which collaboration, empathy, and creative solutions emerge in the rough-and-tumble terrain of human relationships and exploration proceeds according to an individualized timeline.[34] This collision of cultures has reached new heights of absurdity with the Common Core, as states struggle to map the standards across the spectrum, including history, economic concepts, and civics and government as foundations for two-year-olds' emergent knowledge.[35]

The consequences for children are considerable. "Our protective urges are stymied," Peter Mangione, codirector of WestEd's Center for Child and Family Studies in Sausalito, California, told me. "Our tenderness is critical for their sense of well-being." A child psychologist, he served as a technical advisor to Ohio when the state was crafting its standards for children from birth to age five. The outcome was a document that puts social-emotional development on an equal footing with cognition and general knowledge, with references to play generously sprinkled across the rubric.[36] Still, Mangione worries that we expect infants to act like third-graders. "We're asking the child to do what they're not ready to do, and we're not supporting what they're ready and meant to do," he said.

We're also assessing them out the wazoo—on a rising tide of preschool suspension and expulsion rates. A recent "Data Snapshot" of school discipline, restraint, and seclusion, issued by the U.S. Department of Education Office for Civil Rights, highlighted this egregious, homegrown phenomenon in its first bullet point: Nearly half of the 18 percent of Black children enrolled in preschool already have more than one suspension on their record, with 79 percent of boys claiming that dubious distinction. The school-to-prison pipeline has reached our smallest civilians.[37]

Today, a growing number of states have adopted universal assessment of kindergarten students, grappling with the twin challenges of reliability and validity in their instruments. This is a time- and labor-intensive activity, as Jennifer Stedron and Alexander Berger noted in a technical report for the National Conference of State Legislatures on strategies to promote school readiness.[38] Comprehensiveness and methods vary wildly. "Ideally, evaluation of the complicated set of skills and behaviors that comprise 'school readiness' would use multiple assessment methods," the authors wrote, conceding that valid information about a classroom of kindergartners might not capture aspects, say, of a particular child's language development.[39] Nuance, needless to say, does not come cheap.

But early childhood educators are rising up. "Too Many Tests!" the cover of the magazine of the Maryland State Education Association proclaimed one December, just before Christmas. An early gift. The group had called for immediate suspension of the kindergarten readiness assessment in the wake of a survey of kindergarten teachers. Sixty-three percent of them reported that they had received no meaningful data to inform instruction from administration of the exam. The article featuring the survey quoted Lily Eskelsen Garcia, president of the National Education Association, one of the country's two major labor unions for public school teachers. "The testing fixation has reached the point of insanity," she said.[40]

TAKING THE TEMPERATURE OF TESTING WITH DOOMED RESIGNATION

To quantify is to have the illusion of mastery over all that defies our control, yet the metrics fall short, the ends perverted beyond our wildest imagination. Assessment is necessary, a critical tool for marking human progress, or lack of it. But as the late Asa G. Hilliard III, a professor of educational psychology and early proponent of Afrocentrism, once was reputed to have said: "If you want elephants to grow, you don't weigh the elephant. You feed the elephants."[41] America's youngest students have had the grave misfortune to enter the academic arena in a period of measurement gone berserk.

George Madaus, a professor emeritus of Boston College and the former head of the Council on Measurement Education, has made a career studying the history and vicissitudes of testing. "Deeply ingrained in the American psyche," testing, he and Michael Russell wrote in an essay about its paradoxes, is a technology, "the application of science to satisfy a pressing and immediate need to solve a problem or serve as a means to an end."[42] As a policy tool, high-stakes testing offers reams of data, surfacing the vagaries of student achievement, while sidestepping the underlying causes of the gaps: poverty, cultural and language barriers, chaotic home lives, toxic stress, and hunger.

Testing is also economical. Multiple-choice exams, hailed as the "leading edge of scientific efficiency" upon their introduction after World War II, are scored quickly and inexpensively, out of human hands, promising at least in theory, objectivity.[43] But to what end? "The scientist, in practicing the scientific method, cannot utter a single word about an individual thing or creature insofar as it is an individual," the southern writer Walker Percy observed in "Diagnosing the Modern Malaise," one of a collection of essays in *Signposts in a Strange Land*. "This limitation holds true whether the individual is a molecule of NaCl or an amoeba or a human being.[44]

Like weathermen recording levels of heat, cold, and environmental toxins, Madaus and his colleagues have observed the threat of testing to American students' well-being over time. In the years after World War I, when the repercussions for educators, students, and schools were less punitive, a morning that contained a standardized test was an easy one. Following World War II, and into the 21st century, Madaus and Terence-Lee St. John report "a relentless shift, at first subtle, then dramatic, in the significance of standardized tests in education, culminating in the passage of the NCLB Act of 2001." They observe the ubiquity of test talk—at the dinner table, at the bus stop, during play dates.

These metric scientists concede the difficulty in quantifying the emotional toll on students of the pressure to perform. It's so subjective, isn't it? They've collected numerous examples throughout the literature, citing, among others, A. A. Milne. When the creator of the world of Winnie-the-Pooh presented his father with a lackluster exam result, the author wrote in his autobiography, the man "turned his face to the wall, and abandoned hope"—a "biblical gesture of doomed resignation."[45]

Such was the mood of the National Early Childhood Accountability Task Force, which gathered in the mid-2000s to design a framework for assessing young children. The report of their deliberations is a study in ambivalence, the language cautious, redundant with adjectives (difficult, daunting, challenging, complex, variable)—as if by modifying the nouns, the authors could dim the harsh light of accountability. They spoke directly to the anxiety of their core constituency of early childhood educators, the most recent initiates of No Child Left Behind. Conceding the readers' misgivings, they tried to put them at ease. "When accountability efforts are of high quality," the task force members insisted, "when they safeguard children, and . . . are used in the service of program improvement, they can contribute powerfully to make America's early education fair, just, and equitable, and among the best in the world."[46]

Still, the team was between a rock and a hard place. They knew well the great distance the field would need to travel to get anywhere near the best in the world. Early childhood educators were struggling as accountability efforts had moved into high gear. For so long, children's achievements had been observed and recorded by teachers. Their jottings in notebooks, and digital successors, as well as portfolios of students' work, gave wide berth to the complexity of human development. Progress was not tied to program or teacher evaluation. Bubble tests, for those who could barely hold a pencil and sit still in their seats, much less fully understand instructions, were anathema.

But what about that key to the realm? The task force coveted the potential benefits of a merger with the K–12 community: the concession to early education as a public good, the possibility of predictable financing, and recognition—common in all economically advanced nations—of early childhood as the foundation of the entire enterprise.[47] In any event, the marriage was a *fait accompli*. Determined to work "toward a robust, positive, and rigorous culture for early childhood accountability efforts," they embraced the core assumptions of the latest effort at tinkering toward utopia.[48]

Not everyone fell in line. In an appendix to the report, Joan Lombardi, a former policy advisor in the Clinton and Obama administrations, and Samuel Meisels, an expert on alternative assessment, registered their dissent. Lombardi weighed in on the tremendous variance of development and warned that the lack of attention to ecological factors—health, home and community environment, parenting—would stymie programs' efforts to ensure optimal conditions for learning. She hoisted a red flag for the unintended consequences of aligning assessment across the spectrum from prekindergarten through third grade. "How can we avoid a push down of assessment practices that do not fit the developmental realities of younger children?" she asked.[49]

Meisels, one of the creators of work sampling, a well-regarded performance assessment that documents, through portfolios and other means, children's skills, knowledge, and behavior across time and developmental domains, urged that "no single set of test scores, no single piece of evidence . . . be the basis of decisions to fund or not to fund, to abandon or to replicate a project." He argued for a less punitive approach to accountability, citing Donald Campbell, an expert in program evaluation and quasi-experimental research design, who said, "Evaluate no program until it is proud."[50]

HEAD START'S HIGH-STAKES GAMBIT

Meisels cited precedent for his concern. The field had been badly burned by the roll-out of the National Reporting System (NRS), designed to submit Head Start, a centerpiece of the "War on Poverty," to the rigorous demands of accountability.[51] In the process, the program—which serves less than half of all preschoolers and only 3 percent of infants and toddlers—and notorious for its stranglehold of red tape, would submit to yet another layer of monitoring to determine the fate of future funding.[52]

After nine months of development and a superficial review by a technical work group, George W. Bush went out to sell the new system. The president chose a Virginia Head Start center for his photo op. Hoping to calm the jittery nerves of his audience, he told them, "We would be defeating the purpose of accountability before we even began it if we . . . give standardized tests to four-year-olds."[53] The U.S. Administration for Children and Families sent out a memorandum to Head Start agencies across the country emphasizing that the new assessment and reporting system was by no means intended to "assess the school readiness of individual children."[54]

But the deed, the largest admission of a standardized test, was done. The chair of the NRS technical work group, Craig Ramey, whose research focuses on the development of competence, summed it up. "If you were the head of any industry," he told a reporter, "you would have a quality assurance system in place to determine how your product is faring."[55] By the fall, 450,000 four-year-old widgets were ready for their initiation. Primarily multiple-choice, with a focus on vocabulary, letter naming, and early math skills, the exam was a culture- and class-bound disaster. The Peabody Picture Vocabulary Test included exotic words in the young test-takers' emergent lexicon: *swamp*, *vase*, *awarding*, and *horrified*. Also assumed was children's ability to subtract, use standard metric units, and understand the subjunctive case.[56]

In a scathing critique in *Education Week*, Evelyn Moore, then president of the National Black Child Development Institute, and Raul Yzaguirre, then CEO of the National Council of La Raza, called for a suspension of the NRS, lambasting its poor design, linguistic and cultural inappropriateness, and narrow focus on young children's language and mathematical ability to the exclusion of social development. The test was declared a "flawed experiment," which labeled Black and Latino children failures.[57]

By the time Congress pushed through the Improving Head Start for School Readiness Act in 2007, requiring providers to compete for funding, the test—if not the competition—had been relegated to the archives.[58] The U.S. General Accountability Office had retreated. Offering up a monograph called *Further Development Could Allow Results of New Test to Be Used for Decision Making*, they highlighted the concerns. Among them were the dangers of teaching to the test and narrowing the curriculum. Or, as Meisels described it, a pedagogical model of "passive reception . . . pouring into a vessel knowledge and skills that are needed for competence, rather than recognizing learning as active and teaching as a joint process of interaction between child and adult."[59]

Still, we plod on. In "The Accountability Revolution Comes to Head Start," a remarkably belated acknowledgment of the state of affairs published in the *National Journal* more than a decade after the debacle, Sophie Quinton lamented the enduring poor quality of many Head Start and state-run prekindergartens. The research literature, she wrote, shows that "children spend most of their time playing, eating, and waiting around, and that instructional quality is generally low."[60]

PLAY IS NOT A FOUR-LETTER WORD

We've come a long way from the Enlightenment; the primary engine of human development is vanishing. "It has long been noticed that the smartest mammals—primates, cetaceans, elephants, and carnivores—are the most playful," anthropologist and neuroscientist Melvin Konner wrote in his epic work, *The Evolution of Childhood*. He regards play as the central paradox of evolutionary biology, "combining as it does great energy expenditure and risk with apparent pointlessness."[61] But, oh, what a phenomenon:

> Various adaptive explanations of play include honing of innate motor sequences; getting accustomed to destabilizing movements and unexpected events; establishing or practicing social relationships; safe self-assessment with a view toward future risk taking; and stimulating neuromotor development through neural and synaptic selection, either generally or specifically through the synaptic proliferation of cerebellar purkinje fibers (which may have a sensitive period for permanent experience effects) and the differentiation of muscle fiber types.[62]

Moving beyond the eye-glazing cerebellar Purkinje fibers, we get the drift. The positive emotions evoked by interactions, physical exercise, and mastery of skills in play spurs us toward novelty and more flexible learning—an exquisite and singular means of developing our brains, social selves, and alleviating stress.

Yet across the nation, some of the elders of the species continue to defy science, subjecting children to a misguided experiment. Literacy and numeracy have hijacked the kindergarten curriculum, didactic methods in ascendance. Learning blocks—uninterrupted periods of time dedicated to a particular subject and historically relegated to the upper grades—now dictate the rhythms of the day, and prescriptive curricula linked to standardized tests are routine in many kindergartens.[63]

The contagion has spread to preschool. A trio of studies conducted in low-income, community-based child care centers over two decades, book-ended by the publication of A Nation at Risk and enactment of No Child Left Behind, found time for play among four-and-a-half-year-olds had diminished from 41 percent to 9 percent, children's proto-narrative development and emergent literacy presumably banished to other realms.[64]

Alexandra Papadopoulos is a kindergarten teacher and former grade-level facilitator at the Cutchogue East Elementary School on Long Island's North Fork. Here, kindergarten commands the largest classrooms in the building, and solid, wooden blocks, with which generations of youngsters have played, are abundant. A broad expanse of green space beckons, with an adventure playground and garden. "Play is what I honored," she told me and a group of her colleagues, teachers of five-year-olds. "But even in a place that values play, we have to fight to keep it, like a desperately needed coffee break."

It's hard to get the message out. Early childhood teachers live with the specter of the third-grade benchmarks as well as the standardized tests that measure children's progress toward them and increasingly determine their own professional prospects. Novices are silent; a challenge to the status quo feels daunting, if not impossible, a threat to one's livelihood. Something has gotten lost in translation. To the untrained eye, play remains an enigma. "If someone were to come in," Papadopoulos said, "they wouldn't know we were focusing on literacy if kids were playing or performing."

Even developmental scientists have had trouble defining it, creating a typology with fuzzy boundaries and descriptors that only an academic could love. Is that pretend play, or sociodramatic? Are the kids just engaging in a little rough-and-tumble activity? What about guided play, with adults as directors? Doesn't that cramp their style? Agreement exists on a basic set of characteristics, including pleasure, spontaneity, full absorption, active engagement, and intrinsic motivation. Children at play often create a private reality, in which they assume a wide range of grown-up roles, rehearsing for their performance on society's larger stage. They are, in the deepest sense, at work.

Play's disappearance has awakened an activist streak in some of the field's researchers, who have taken their brief to the pages of staid scientific journals, blurring the lines between advocacy and science.[65] Academics are leaving their ivory towers, clutching copies of *A Mandate for Playful Learning in Preschool*, an evidence-based manifesto. The authors' call to action adopts the tropes of education reform—critical thinking skills, collaboration, innovation—attendant to the precipitous decline in creativity from kindergartners through sixth-graders, recorded by Kyung Hee Kim, a professor of creativity and innovation at the College of William and Mary.[66] "It is time to stop making the false dichotomy between "play" and "education," they wrote. "Children in the 21st century need . . . to go beyond the facts—to synthesize, integrate, create, and evaluate. They also need to collaborate and lead effectively to achieve significant innovation and change."[67]

The research in support of play is robust, as the scientists like to say, and for some, incontrovertible. In this activity deemed frivolous, children sharpen their ability to focus and solve problems; they test their hypotheses about how things work.[68] They learn how to think symbolically, and negotiate conflict with their peers, developing empathy, the bulwark against implosion of our disintegrating civil society. Here, too, as psychologist Jerome Bruner wrote in his classic, *Child's Talk*, "the most complicated grammatical and pragmatic forms of language" appear early on.[69]

One longitudinal study that tracked a group of low-income children through middle school found consistent relationships between these earliest, free-floating conversations and a broad range of skills in oral language and print by the end of kindergarten.[70] Others have confirmed the ease and rapidity with which children learn words embedded in playful contexts, all the while honing emergent reading and writing skills.[71] Nor do numeracy and spatial concepts get short shrift. In a group of four- and five-year-olds videotaped in 15-minute segments of free play, nearly half of that time involved mathematical learning—exploration of patterns and spatial forms, evaluation of relative magnitude, and numerical judgment or quantification.[72]

Even two-and-a-half- and three-year-olds understand the cardinal counting principle, or the idea that the last number represents the amount of a given set. But they keep their competence under wraps in a straight-forward laboratory task, revealing their knowledge only through the plea-sure of games.[73] Children's natural gifts as mathematicians also emerge in play guided by adults, moving them into their zones of proximal develop-ment, or a place where potential is pushed to the limit—a term coined by the Russian psychologist Lev Vygotsky, who saw social interaction as the foundation for learning.

Decades after the trauma of Sputnik, a Harvard graduate student named Deborah Leong discovered Vygotsky's developmental theory. Self-regulation, a product of the prefrontal cortex, the seat of executive function, is a key element. But she was clueless about its practical application. In the early 1990s, now a professor at Metropolitan State College in Denver, Colorado, Leong received an email from a colleague at the University of Wisconsin who wondered if her college had any positions open for Russian professors looking to work in the United States. She told him of her interest in Vygotsky: Did the college know anyone who had used his methods with teachers in the classroom?

"Have I got the person for you," he replied, introducing her to Elena Bodrova, who promptly emigrated to the Rockies, planting the seeds for Tools of the Mind, a preschool curriculum that exercises what Leong calls the "muscle" of executive functions—self-control, working memory, and cognitive flexibility—through play as well as activities with a more academ-ic orientation.[74]

Leong claims that, citing the evidence base, levels of executive function predict academic success better than IQ and social class. In make-believe play, the three components of the muscle fuse. Although recent research has found that direct instruction can limit spontaneous exploration and discov-ery, she's not convinced that they are mutually exclusive, leading a cadre of early childhood educators searching for the middle ground in an increasing-ly hostile policy climate.[75] In Tools of the Mind's 50 minutes of play daily, teachers serve as guides, not purveyors of "drill and kill": They encourage children's play, help them plan, and engage them in games that strengthen cognitive flexibility and self-regulation.

The results have been mixed. In one randomized study of low-income preschoolers in Tools classrooms, youngsters' ability to tamp down their impulses and attentively focus on tasks improved dramatically such that the investigators stopped the experiment so that the control group could reap the benefits.[76] The curriculum fared less well in an evaluation of approach-es for improving preschoolers' social and emotional competence—one in a long line of assessments of the impact of Head Start. When compared with educators who had the benefit of "The Incredible Years Teacher Training

Program" and "Preschool PATHS (Promoting Alternative Thinking Strategies)," the Tools teachers produced an insufficient level of executive function and self-regulation.[77] The curriculum, alas, did not jibe with the theory of change developed by the team for this Head Start CARES demonstration.

IN THE HEIGHTS OF HIGH-STAKES ACCOUNTABILITY

Leong and her ilk are rowing upstream. The window in which they have to work their magic is closing.[78] "If we don't pay attention to the strategies we use to get to the challenging outcomes articulated in current standards, we won't prepare our youth to be creative and critical thinkers," Beverly Falk told me in her light-filled office up at the City College of New York, once known as the "Harvard of the Proletariat."

Editor of *Defending Childhood*—a book with the hopeful subtitle, *Keeping the Promise of Early Education*—Falk navigates this terrain daily with teachers she prepares for the classroom.[79] "Too many educators are introducing inappropriate teaching methods into the youngest grades at the expense of active engagement with hands-on experiences and relationships," she said. "Research tells us that this is the way young children construct understandings, make sense of the world, and develop their interests and desire to learn."

The Oxford English Dictionary defines *crucible* as a place or occasion of severe test or trial, or a situation in which different elements interact to produce something new. Kindergarten has historically been that place for young children. But it is no longer recognizable, the emphasis having shifted to the more painful aspects of the process. This transformation has accelerated in recent years, documented by vigilant, and increasingly alarmed, early childhood educators and advocates. Lately, empirical evidence has been emerging from the academy.

Working with two national data sets, which straddle the implementation of No Child Left Behind, Daphna Bassok and Anna Rorem, at the Frank Batten School of Leadership and Policy at the University of Virginia, have been mapping the landscape. The researchers acknowledge the persistence of tensions, dating back at least a century, between the academic and developmental goals of kindergarten.[80] But even they were struck by the marked alteration of the terrain.

In 2006, they reported, 65 percent of kindergarten teachers—more than double the number in 1998—thought most children should learn to read on their watch. Exposure to social studies, science, music, and art, the staples of a well-rounded early childhood education, had declined, and nearly 20 percent of teachers reported that their kindergartners never had physical education. "The changes we document in our study," the authors concluded, "represent something other than a wholesale shifting of the first grade curriculum down by a year." Kindergarten was now distinct from both kindergarten and *first-grade* classrooms in the late 1990s.[81]

One bright Monday morning, I headed uptown to the Castle Bridge School in Washington Heights, a neighborhood in New York City to which Dominican immigrants have been drawn since the mid-20th century. Leading the weekly community sing, on guitar, was founder and principal, Julie Zuckerman. The scene—parents, teachers, and prekindergarteners through second-graders—was startling, a throwback to the 1960s, with a playlist including "Guantanamera." Here, as Thomas Vorsteg provided translation in Spanish and a version of American Sign Language, and Sally Cleaver pounded enthusiastically on a Yamaha electronic piano, the group started singing: "Each of us is a flower, growing in the garden; Each of us is a flower, we need the sun and rain."

Zuckerman is about as unreconstructed a progressive as you will find in today's inhospitable climate for the species. After teaching for two decades and a stint as principal of the Central Park East elementary school, founded during a kinder, gentler era of education reform, she was ready for a project of her own. Finding that "charters had sucked up all the air in central Harlem," she sought to plant seeds for a public school in Washington Heights. When another spot opened up nearby—at P.S. 128, the Audubon School—Zuckerman grabbed it, commandeering a corridor for her tiny cohort of sixty students in three kindergarten and first-grade classrooms.

In this district, where 91 percent of the children are Latino, a dual-language program maintains diversity, drawing low- and middle-income families of different races, ethnicity, and national origin. Castle Bridge is authorized to extend to fifth grade, but Zuckerman was eyeing expansion upward, to eighth grade—critical, she emphasized, to the success of a bilingual program. "Their language acquisition is amazing," she said of her students, whose playful learning is undergirded by Lesley Koplow's curriculum, designed to foster empathy.[82] In Tatiana Rosa's classroom, a hive of energetic activity, one corner was given over to a bookcase of small stuffed bears. Her four-year-olds had sewn outfits for the animals, with the help of their parents. "During the winter, they worried that the bears would be afraid of the dark," Rosa told me, "so we bought lights."

During Zuckerman's long history with New York City's schools, assessment had reached a fevered pitch, the fallout of No Child Left Behind and its offshoot, Race to the Top. The recent Common Core State Standards were stirring high passions across the political spectrum, making strange bedfellows of the left and the right, including the ultraconservative Tea Party. They had also become an object of fear and, in a growing number of quarters, loathing, by teachers across the education spectrum. "We Need to Talk About the Test," Elizabeth Phillips, the principal of P.S. 321, urged in the opinion pages of the *New York Times*. The parents in her Brooklyn school were not happy.[83]

In the autumn before the spring round of high-stakes standardized tests, Zuckerman got her first glimpse of an exam for her kindergartners. Although it was not aligned with the Common Core, it would be used to establish a baseline score to evaluate all teachers from kindergarten through 12th grade under New York State's controversial evaluation system. "When I saw the test, I said to myself: I'm not going to administer this," she told me as we talked in her cramped, cluttered office, the hub of her fledgling school. "Why would *anyone* give these tests?"

No one at Tweed could justify it, she said, referring to the headquarters of the Department of Education, named after one of the city's most notorious political bosses of the 19th century. "They would turn around to the state, and the whole house of cards would tumble. We were the canary in the mine."

Having assessed the potential collateral damage, Zuckerman then took her brief to the parents. "I said 'we're supposed to give this test—it's pencil and paper, bubbles, and it's inappropriate for kids this age.'" In a meeting with no seats to spare, the Castle Bridge parents had their say. When they hit 80-percent approval, Zuckerman called the whole thing off. Her mandate in hand, Zuckerman opted out, joining a growing number of teachers and parents across the nation in protest.

CHANGEMAKER: ERICKA GUYNES

Plowing a Field of Dreams

Ericka Guynes landed in early childhood in 2008, an interloper from the K–12 universe. As the new principal of the Earl Boyles Elementary School, in Portland, Oregon, her learning curve was steep. But she worked fast, knitting together the disparate strands of a challenging merger.

Within short order, this veteran teacher with more than two decades of experience was battling the odds for Oregon's children. Medicaid only paid for five out of every ten births. Forty percent of children were unprepared for school, their families laid low by financial instability and toxic stress. Thirty-six percent of children were living in poverty, well above the national average. In her southeastern district of Portland, 24 languages—including Dinka, Somali, Vietnamese, Cambodian, Russian, Spanish, and

Pingelapese—were spoken. Twenty-four percent of families, Guynes pointed out, had fewer than ten books in their homes. Working with the Children's Institute of Portland, she strengthened existing partnerships and reached out to others—among them, the SUN Service System, a network of social and support services, the department of parks and recreation, the police bureau, the United Way, and the Multonomah Public Library.

Guynes has always been a stickler for parent involvement. Over the course of her career, she had pushed the boundaries of the home-school relationship, showing up at students' baseball games and *quinceañeras*—the Latin version of the "Sweet 16," if celebrated a year early. But she soon became convinced of the benefits of connecting with families from the time their children are born.

"We welcome parents," she told me. "We've had home-visiting for our preschool families, and our kindergarten teachers said, 'Why don't we do this?' They find parents who are anxious. They build relationships with us. But we learn so much from them." More plans are on the drawing board for the youngest children. Child care providers are beginning to get involved, bringing their wisdom on the benefits of play and other hot topics to trainings at the school. "Baby and Me" classes are also on Guynes's wish list.

The design of Earl Boyles, named for a beloved school custodian, reflects the aspiration toward what early childhood educators like to call a "seamless" continuum, in synch with children's development. "It truly captures what we're trying to achieve," Guynes told me. In the typical school layout, students are segregated by age and grade. Here, preschoolers play next to kindergartners, whose classrooms are adjacent to those of first- and second-graders, all winding around a courtyard, restored by parents, where infants and toddlers play.

The school has also remodeled its lobby, to make room for a family center, with a lending library. "Parents are being trained to be the keepers of that space, training other parents to make it sustainable," Guynes said. Earl Boyles hosts weekly storytime sessions—in English, Vietnamese, Spanish, and Chinese—for children from birth to five, youth librarians serenading infants and toddlers with nursery rhymes.

The *pièce de résistance* is a new wing for early learning, which looks out on an expanse of green transformed into an adventure playground of climbers, tricycle paths, and dirt mounds. A local bond initiative provided half, or $3.5 million, of the project's total cost, with strong support from the district's superintendent, Don Grotting, whom Guynes credits with "a great understanding of early childhood" and who is hoping to import the strategy of early outreach to families to other schools. Boyles's young students watched the construction in awe. "It was like having Bob the Builder on site," she said.

Upon completion of the wing, Guynes could now offer 90 new preschool spots, expanding her capacity to serve four-year-olds in a state stuck at 31 in rankings for access across the nation. She fielded more than 50 candidates to teach in two of the preschool classrooms, which afford opportunities for staff and parents to observe the young students—a much-coveted feature, common in well-endowed laboratory schools. The teachers, who are certified, are paid on par with their peers, working with kindergartners, devoting their first year at the school to further training, securing an endorsement for special education.

What happened inside those classrooms, Guynes insisted, would not "replicate what's going on in K–12." If that were the case, she said, they would not have chosen the Creative Curriculum, which still refers in its literature to the whole child and has not yet banished play, blocks, art, and music, not to mention sand and water tables, to the basement. "I was just talking with our coach about how different instruction looks in a preschool classroom," Guynes said. "We have a lot to learn." Just months before the fall of the wing's opening, Guynes was ecstatic. "Three years ago, we couldn't dream of the possibilities," she said. "I can't describe the feeling of joy."

Along with her staff and community partners, Guynes continues to translate Urie Bronfenbrenner's bioecological theory into practice. The child psychologist, one of the architects of Head Start, placed children and families at the center of the human ecosystem, nourished by neighborhood institutions—including the school. Earl Boyles is intensifying its outreach, moving into the prenatal period, mapping the contours of health and its implications for academic performance. Trained as participatory researchers, parents have served as data collectors for a community health assessment. "The parents are helping to make decisions around the surveys," Guynes said, working with a fellow from the Children's Institute and a professor at Portland State University, where Guynes, who won Oregon's elementary school principal award in 2013, pursued her master's degree in education.

"Our family engagement has increased exponentially, it's growing, it feels authentic," she said. "The work is providing a voice, a forum for our community. Once they have it, they own it." She has already seen the impact: Earl Boyles's attendance rates are the best in the district, the foundation for the outcomes they seek. She proudly shared the data from a PowerPoint presentation by Megan Larsen, a preschool teacher who had previously taught second-graders and who works with the kindergarten teachers to set goals. A video clip showed the children dancing to the letters of the alphabet. "They can interact with each other, write their names, and recognize print," Guynes said. School readiness was beginning to coming into focus.

CHAPTER 5

Profiles in System Building

In May, at the annual conference of Smart Start, North Carolina's public/
private partnership that provides the infrastructure for the state's early
childhood system, Governor Bev Perdue preached the gospel of education,
whipping everyone into a frenzy. . . . She darted back and forth across the
stage. . . . "If you believe in Smart Start, stand up for it!" she exhorted.

—"Prioritizing Early Childhood Education," *Huffington Post*

Systems thinking is a discipline for seeing wholes . . . a framework for seeing
interrelationships rather than things, for seeing patterns of change rather
than static snapshots . . . a sensibility for the subtle interconnectedness that
gives living systems their unique character.

—Peter Senge, *The Fifth Discipline*

On one of our annual days of reckoning for U.S. taxpayers, the *New
Republic* published "The Hell of American Day Care." Written by Jonathan Cohn, a journalist and parent, the article reverberated through the
multidimensional media universe, a painful airing of dirty laundry. Replete
with chilling vignettes of disaster and death, Cohn lamented the nation's
arrested state of development vis-à-vis other advanced economies: "In the
United States, despite the fact that work and family life has changed profoundly in recent decades, we lack anything resembling an actual child care
system."[1] Across the waves of National Public Radio to mommy blogs from
Hawaii to Washington, DC, you could feel the angst.

Within weeks of this bombshell, the U.S. Department of Health and
Human Services announced its intention to improve the safety and quality
of child care. New regulations, it turns out, had been gestating. "Too many
children remain in settings that do not meet minimum standards of health
and safety," noted Secretary of Health Kathleen Sebelius, who already
had her hands full guiding implementation of the hotly contested Affordable Care Act. "These basic rules ensure that providers take necessary
basic steps to shield children from an avoidable tragedy."[2] Fingerprinting,

background checks, and first aid training for providers—the minimal floor for quality—remained unenforced across the land. This prime specimen of a government agency document, 199 pages of redundant legalese, provided the vehicle for a most public, and long-overdue, acknowledgment that America's kids were not all right.[3]

BACK TO THE FUTURE:
STILL CHAOTIC AFTER ALL THESE YEARS?

The proposed regulations, for the Child Care and Development Fund, which serves nearly one and a half million children, highlighted systemic dysfunction on a massive scale. All the states, territories, and the District of Columbia benefit from the fund and are required to be up to speed on their licensing requirements.[4] But the reality was another matter. In the fine print, you could make out the limited power of a federal agency. That big, bad government had better be careful messing with families in the first years of life. Their home is their castle, and intruders are not welcome—especially those who might come bearing suspicious gifts.

To be fair, we've had a couple of notorious departures from this pattern. The last defining battle of U.S. child care reform featured an unlikely warrior. None other than Richard Nixon, not your typical progressive avatar, supported the Child Development Act, which promised a network of federally funded early childhood centers—social welfare policy in the hallowed tradition of European democracies. It seemed too good to be true, and it was, the president, who opened the door to China, caving under pressure from his party's far right.[5] In politics, *plus ça change*. . . . But in the United States, the real policy action is in the states, and in local communities, preserving the right to self-determination that we hold so dear.[6] Here is where early childhood system building has flourished—albeit on a timeline that continues to try the patience of its most tenacious architects.

In 1997, *Not by Chance* hit the pre-digital inboxes of the nation's decisionmakers. Written by Sharon Lynn Kagan and Nancy Cohen, both at Yale's Bush Center in Child Development and Social Policy, the 127-page tome followed four years of collaboration with the field's leading lights. The appendices constituted a Who's Who of 20th-century early childhood cognoscenti.[7] The two had jumped boldly into the void, presenting their "immodest vision" of a high-quality early care and education system for all children from birth to age five. The programs would be supported by a well-funded coherent infrastructure and would be linked to community organizations offering health and family support.

Kagan and Cohen dreamed big. The initiative consciously situated its efforts in the tradition of social reform, highlighting dramatic changes in maternal employment and child care arrangements, the growing number of children unprepared for school, lack of access for the neediest, and the crisis in quality, so "elusive" and demanding of "sustained effort and creativity."[8] Lambasting the erratic, haphazard emergence of programs with different funding streams, regulatory systems, administrative agencies, and legislative mandates, the report issued an all-points bulletin to the village that it takes to raise the children.[9]

Today, 11 million children under the age of five spend their days in a wide—and confusing—array of early childhood settings.[10] They may be the seedbeds of our nation's human capital, but they're far from ideal. Standards, requirements, and funding streams vary enormously across programs. Family child care homes, where nearly a million children spend their days, operate under the radar of regulation.[11] When monitoring and assessment do occur, redundancies and red tape are rampant, an ongoing headache for providers, who toil for some of the lowest wages of any industry.

Turf wars are forever erupting, the parties guarding their funding streams like crown jewels. As for open dialogue and collaboration, they belong in the category of lip service.[12] While the drive for data continues unabated—our very own quest for the Holy Grail—information about children, families, and the early childhood workforce is still sketchy. Pennsylvania is the only state that links child-level data across all early childhood programs and the K–12 system—and even there, not all children are included.[13] Most states are clueless, hard-pressed to provide policymakers with answers to their endless questions about cost-effectiveness, not to mention children's outcomes. How are these programs doing? And are these kids on track?

DETERMINING THE DNA

Before you build, you need a blueprint. You also have to assess the existing pieces: Sometimes a little tinkering will do, but often a gut renovation is necessary. Early childhood education has had to build from the ground up, a process requiring great leaps of imagination, faith, and more than a little pluck. "I looked at it as the foundation of a house," said Marsha Basloe, a veteran of systems efforts in New York and North Carolina and a senior advisor at the U.S. Administration for Children and Families. "A contractor would say: 'Lady, you've got to have the foundation be solid.' It's the part that's not going to show, but it's most important." Finding the right framework is key.

On decisions about where, and on which components, to begin, states are all over the map. As Karen Hill Scott, an architect from California, observed: "the expression of the system varies—just like DNA."[14] In a field as various and diverse as early care and education, in a nation to which those two adjectives also apply, the process is anything but genteel, the components, like rivalrous siblings, screaming, "Me first! How's our data system doing? We need a workforce registry, and wouldn't that career lattice be nice? You think I'm blending my funds with yours? Forget about it." Not to mention the agencies, carefully guarding their meager goods and power in a balkanized world. In the heat of construction, how hard it is to look "beyond the bark and trees" to "the ecology of the early care and education" forest.[15]

System building isn't sexy. Just think about the terms of art: *infrastructure, linkages, coordination, alignment*. The process could not be more fraught. It's not easy wrestling with the field's big issues—equity, quality, sustainability, and accountability—day to day, over time.[16] The work is also messy, a bouillabaisse of values, politics, and culture. Then there's "the vision thing," to quote George W. Bush, creator of No Child Left Behind. He had reportedly dismissed a friend, who had urged him to take some time at Camp David to reflect on, and articulate, his grand plans for the country. What nerve, to press him toward coherence.[17]

Everyone agrees that vision is important: How can you get there if you don't know what "there" looks like? But consensus is hard to get. To call something into being, we must name it. Is it an early care and education system? Or do we use "early learning" as the descriptor, acknowledging the field as the foundation for the big-daddy system, ranging from kindergarten through 12th grade? Ah, but wait. Doesn't "early childhood" system evoke a more complex organism?—one that includes physical and mental health as part of the DNA package.

Even the age range is up for grabs. Take a look at the branding for the burgeoning number of early childhood initiatives and organizations—First Five Years Fund, Thrive by Five, First 5 California, to name just a few. You'd never know that early childhood extended beyond age five. But the National Association for the Education of Young Children, the field's primary professional organization, has long defined this period as birth to age eight. Imagine the repercussions for coherent system building. "States are rapidly jumping on the bandwagon of a birth-to-eight framework," said Kristie Kauerz, an expert on the part of the education spectrum that extends from pre-K through third grade. "Theoretically, it's great, but I wouldn't want to jeopardize all the hard work that we've done over the past 15 years on birth-to-five system building—things like governance, financing, and workforce development."

Such fault lines are par for the course of early childhood system building. Names and age range are just the tip of the iceberg, rapidly melting in the age of climate change. Still, such questions are hardly academic for the field, which has been diagnosed with a severe identity crisis.[18] This is a sector that has yet to come together on some fundamental things, including the nature of the work and those who stand to benefit from it. While children and families are at the heart of the enterprise, too often their needs get lost in the shuffle.

"They don't fit into regression equations very well," said Charles Bruner, one of the grandfathers of system building who founded the first preschool in Iowa. "You're building capacity, but its impact is not always visible. You have to keep your eye on how this all relates back to the children and their families."[19] These vexing issues continue to keep system builders up at night.

A LONG AND WINDING ROAD TO QUALITY

Consensus on the basic nuts and bolts of system building may be tough to get, but the quest for quality is a monumental task. Perception is relative, of course. Some of today's senior architects, burnout hovering at the edges, identify with Sisyphus, pushing his heavy boulder up the mountain. Others, like First Five Years Fund director Kris Perry, see the glass half full, proclaiming the situation much improved. "For one thing, we're describing it as a system," she pointed out, noting the absence of such talk way back in the 1980s, when she worked in child welfare. "People *do* know that there's an early childhood system. We've gotten a little bit of traction in the public mind." While she conceded that the pace seems slow at times, she stuck to her positive scenario: "We know what works, we know what states need, and what kids need."

A new, energetic crop of builders is coming to the fore, weaned on unprecedented support for the work at the highest levels of policymaking. They watched as early childhood became a real player in what the Obama administration dubbed cradle-to-career education reform.[20] This generation has also had the heady experience of hearing the words "universal preschool" in a State of the Union address by the president of the United States, aka POTUS to the fan base, the first to utter them in 50 years.[21] Quality improvement was the top commandment of the Race to the Top–Early Learning Challenge initiative, a potential systems elixir—if prescribed only to the lucky few who made it to the finish line.[22]

Words lose their meaning after endless repetition, detached from their etymological impulse. Such is the case with "quality improvement," a mantra that haunts early childhood system building—and just about every other endeavor. Hundreds of thousands of entries clog Google's trusty search engine. Measurement, evaluation, and regulation—tools of choice in the land of data mania and red tape—attempt to pin it down. But it stays out there, beyond our reach. We've yet to produce a "universally accepted and applied definition," as Patricia Wesley and Virginia Buysse point out in *The Quest for Quality*, a collection they edited of musings on the confounding subject. This, in spite of our ever-burgeoning knowledge about children's cognitive, physical, social-emotional, and academic skills, and the conditions that support their development.[23]

To what end, our Tower of Babel of research, if not to illuminate the path to better outcomes? Still, systems creation continues apace, the architects perched on the wobbly, three-legged stool of research, practice, and the policies that, all too often, leave children's best interests out of the equation.

THE GOOD HOUSEKEEPING SEAL OF APPROVAL

In recent years, quality rating and improvement systems (QRIS) have taken root across the nation—adding yet another ingredient to early childhood's crowded alphabet soup of acronyms. An online posting of a quote from Steven Johnson in the QRIS National Learning Network newsletter attempted to capture the spirit. "The trick to having good ideas is not to sit around in glorious isolation and try to think big thoughts," he wrote. "The trick is to get more parts on the table." How heartwarming to see the continuation of a fine tradition started by Eleanor Duckworth, a beloved professor emerita at the Harvard Graduate School of Education. Her book, *The Having of Wonderful Ideas*, inspired a generation of teachers—a bible, one might say, of innovation.[24]

Quality rating and improvement systems embody Americans' grand illusions of reinvention and "Embetterment," the name—I kid you not—of a full-service Internet and mobile marketing company based in North Pole, Alaska, outside of Fairbanks. The ratings have been compared to those of restaurants and hotels, a kinship that the field has been reluctant to embrace. Needless to say, mentioning children, our most precious natural resource, in the same sentence as, say, "Michelin Star," or "AAA Diamond rating," is distasteful.

Let's set the facts straight. These initiatives rate programs, not children, providing a set of indicators and levels of quality to which stars are attached. They also feed the gaping maw of policymakers and private investors, looking for accountability and healthy returns on their meager investments. Whether or not they help parents is another matter. Quality rating and improvement systems offer a metric, if not the "Good Housekeeping Seal of Approval," for the early childhood industry's anxious, put-upon consumers. For far too long, they've remained clueless about the quality of the settings in which their children spend their earliest, most critical, years of development.[25]

Alas, the systems fall short as change agents, held back by—among others—well-meaning, but painstaking researchers who just haven't kept pace with practice on the ground. They're trapped in their ivory towers, obsessively building that Tower of Babel, insufficiently focused on the "salutary effects of better information on family decision-making."[26]

As an industry, early care and education defies easy understanding. The list of "products" is long: Head Start; Early Head Start; child care; Educare; prekindergarten; nursery schools; nannies; and family, friends, and neighbors doing their loving duty. The auspices cross the public and private sectors. With limited public resources targeted to those in need, and insufficient supply to meet the demand along the socioeconomic spectrum, the cost of early care and education is exorbitant, especially for parents of infants and toddlers. "Child Care Costs More than College in Illinois," Julie Blair announced on her *Early Years* blog at *Education Week* in the middle of one long summer break for parents of dependent young children.[27] A market on the verge of a nervous breakdown.

Anne Mitchell, cofounder of the Alliance for Early Childhood Finance, who has studied this patient for decades, sees quality rating and improvement systems as good medicine, no less than the framework for early childhood reform. As she outlined in a brief for the BUILD initiative, which works with ten state partners on the task at hand, these policy levers offer "clear, organized ways to assess, improve, and communicate the quality of early care and education programs."[28]

The systems have the potential, at least, to empower parents, offer policymakers grist for their decisions, ensure a reasonable level of accountability, provide professional development and incentives to practitioners, and promote children's health and development. Sounds like a plan, doesn't it? Mitchell concedes it's a visionary ideal. Still, she's been the ultimate champion of these initiatives. When based on a common set of standards, she argues, they help move us toward that evanescent quality based on best practice, regardless of funding source or auspice.

While theorists continue to ponder the complexities of construction, states have been joining the charge. Oklahoma, known for its early commitment to universal preschool, and oil mogul George Kaiser, were the first to jump on the QRIS bandwagon, in 1998. North Carolina, home of Smart Start and systems mecca for the nation, followed suit in 1999. The contagion soon spread, with the District of Columbia, Tennessee, Kentucky, and Vermont among the early millennial adapters.[29]

The next cohort got going in the second half of the first decade of the 2000s. Quality rating and improvement systems are now in place in 38 states, a substantial increase above the 25 that were operational in 2010. In recent years, the systems have moved to the front burner in laggard states, "incentivized," in the language of market-based reform, by one of the criteria in the Race to the Top–Early Learning Challenge grant competition. Kaiser, whose billions have seeded Educare, a year-round early childhood program, joined the U.S. Department of Education as the federal agency announced the details of its largesse.[30]

As always, the devil is in the details—debated vociferously among the systems scientists, who struggle with the yawning gaps between reality and results. "While we have the constructs linking child outcomes to quality, the mechanics are not clear," Kathryn Tout, a director of early childhood development at Child Trends, told me. "We're doing better at the higher end of quality, but it's harder to distinguish at the middle, where most children are." With the four or five levels that most systems have, this can be one painstaking process.

Tout cut her teeth as a student in developmental psychology videotaping infants for a study conducted by the National Institute of Child Health and Human Development. She then went on to work with Megan Gunnar, a psychobiologist at the University of Minnesota Institute of Child Development and pioneer in the arena of children and stress and the interplay between the environment and temperament. While she loved the experience, Tout was determined to get closer to the heart of policy shaping. Next stop was a summer internship at New York City's Administration for Children's Services, where she studied unlicensed child care providers in Brooklyn—the inspiration for her laser focus on quality improvement across all settings where children spend their days.

She talks about quality with the zest of a master chef. Tout obsesses about the ingredients of an effective system—standards, curriculum, instruction, practitioner skills, assessment, family engagement. She questions the assumption that the field has adequately defined quality, and she's concerned that the measurement tools may not be sophisticated enough to get there. Tout has spent some time in New Mexico, which has embarked on a third-generation system. Early on, she worried about embedding early learning standards into the delicate process of assessing children's progress. "Would the curriculum be aligned with the standards?" she wondered.

"Would they miss the link to practice?" But the state evolved, moving to the cutting edge, using its standards to design an assessment tool that incorporates observations and documentation of children's work. "This has the potential to support early development in a meaningful way," she said.

Tout remains cautiously optimistic, her own rating of the nation's rating systems between a "C" and a "B." Still, "quality rating and improvement systems are moving our policies in a direction that's focusing on quality," she conceded, leaving scientific skepticism behind for a brief moment.

VISIONARY IDEAL MEETS REALPOLITIK

The desire to make change drives today's system building. But construction is arduous, and the timeline excruciatingly slow. Architects navigate a polarized and dysfunctional political system. They're stymied by enduring ambivalence—among those who espouse "family values"—about government intervention in the early years of family life. Internecine squabbling is rife. The budget pie is miniscule, and priorities constantly shift. Most politicians couldn't care less about long-term outcomes; they won't be around to take credit. How anyone moves the needle is a wonder. Still, if you believe—as all converts do—that early childhood is the most powerful leverage point for changing the trajectory for children, then this is the mission that calls your name.

The inspiration may be born at any time. For Naomi Karp, who spent a decade at the U.S. Department of Education's Office of Educational Research, a lifelong worry that "other children do not have enough" surfaced in the budding consciousness of her earliest years. Harriet Dichter, known for her groundbreaking systems work in Pennsylvania, served on a mental health community board in adolescence. For many others, personal experience with early trauma and toxic stressors—a depressed mother, violence at home and outside, substance abuse, a parent in jail—fuels their work.

Joseph Jones, who heads up the Center for Urban Families, is in that last category. Raised in Baltimore by a mother with schizophrenia, he succumbed to the streets and heroin, doing his time in prison. "When I was about twelve my mom was hearing voices," he told a gathering of people who work on strengthening families in upstate New York. "The only person I felt comfortable calling was another drug addict, who told me, 'I think you need to talk to someone professional.'" Long back from the brink, he has brought hard-earned wisdom, which earned him a White House Champion of Change Award, to the young, Black fathers of his hometown. "It's exhilarating, and so gratifying to do the stuff that I like," he said.[31]

All architects are alchemists, their early experiences transmuted into the drive for reform. Lisa Stanley, at UCLA's Center for Healthier Children, Families, and Communities, grew up in San Francisco, in a public school system that "embodied everything that you wouldn't want for your kid"— violence, teacher burnout, indifference. As a child of the middle class, she was in the minority, an experience indelibly imprinted on her own career path. Young children attracted her like a magnet. As a college student in the late 1980s, Stanley focused on early childhood work in the public sector, the seeds for her later work with the Peace Corps in West Africa and as the lead evaluator for Ventura County's First 5 initiative.

In her work on the Transforming Early Childhood Community Systems initiative, the fruit of those seeds is blossoming. I first heard about TECCS at North Carolina's Smart Start conference, mecca for system aficionados. Information about children—from birth on up—is critical for the success of the enterprise. Yet, mining it is torturous, as is consensus about what exactly we should *know* about young children, families, and the programs that serve them. These people were actually interested in the whole child, and all those contextual factors, as researchers call them, that influence the outcomes we desperately seek. How illuminating. What a gorgeous idea— empirically based and eloquent.[32]

A partnership of the United Way Worldwide and UCLA's center—led by Neil Halfon, a pediatrician with a passion for public health policy—the initiative uses the Early Development Instrument, which allows communities to measure children's school readiness at the population level. The domains include physical health and well-being, social competence, emotional maturity, and language and cognitive skills as well as communication skills and general knowledge. The idea is that assessment of children's cognitive abilities isn't enough; family, school, and community need to be in the mix.

Today, more than 30 communities are implementing TECCS, including Magnolia Place, in Los Angeles. Its dashboard—a work of art and sweat— includes such indicators of readiness as the percentage of parents achieving family goals, reporting positive relationships with their children, and reading to youngsters daily.[33] Were he alive to see it, psychologist and Head Start cofounder Urie Bronfenbrenner would crow at this perfect incarnation of his bioecological systems theory, which nests children in the circles of society's institutions and values.

Bronfenbrenner's seminal proposition—in the scientist's clunky language—touts the importance of nurturing those early relationships:

> In order to develop—intellectually, emotionally, socially, and morally—a child requires participation in progressively more complex reciprocal activity on a

regular basis over an extended period of life, with one or more persons with whom the child develops a strong, mutual, irrational, emotional attachment and who is committed to the child's well-being and development, preferably for life.[34]

His lay translation—"Every child needs at least one adult who is irrationally crazy about him or her"—continues to resonate powerfully for those whose hearts beat, along with the children, in the innermost circle.[35]

Stanley is clear-eyed as she assesses the odds of ensuring this foundation. "It takes time for us to really start to see change," she said, acknowledging the need for more collaboration and integration between organizations, not to mention shared outcomes and alignment. "You don't see the long-term outcomes for the children." Like her fellow architects across the country, she's running fast to get up to speed, developing a survey to document outcomes, and breathing life into a research agenda, which will continue to buttress the evidence base for the work. "Now we've gotten our legs," Stanley said, "but system building is not for the faint of heart."

A BUDGET FOR CHILDREN OF THE STORM

When the Levees Broke, filmmaker Spike Lee's epic documentary, is a requiem for a city of lost dreams. The sign for Humanity Street, dislodged from the grid, bobs in the water. A yellow school bus has collapsed. Children seated in a delicate metal basket swing high above the surging waters. Piles of wood punctuate the neighborhoods of the vulnerable, remnants of the homes that were destroyed. "Help us," a handmade sign calls out. Of the Atlantic hurricanes in 2005, Katrina was the deadliest, our failure at protection the worst civil engineering disaster in U.S. history.[36] Prior to the storm, 40 percent of New Orleans's children under age five were living in poverty. After the deluge, that rate ascended to 65 percent.[37]

One June, just months before *Early Childhood Risk and Reach in Louisiana* was published, I found myself in Arizona, in a different natural and human ecosystem.[38] Geoffrey Nagle had come to weigh in on strong systems for early learning, the focus of an educational seminar I was leading with Didi Goldenhar, a consultant on social change initiatives. Then director of Tulane's Institute of Infant and Early Childhood Mental Health, he was buttoned up to the chin in shirt, tie, and suit. Oblivious to the heat, Nagle was in total command of policy minutiae. A new breed of systems geek, I thought. At the time, he was teaching psychiatry and behavioral health at

Tulane, while serving as the state director of BrightStart, Louisiana's Early Childhood Advisory Council.

An act of nature made change acceptable. "With Hurricane Katrina, everything was going through a massive rebuild and redesign," Nagle told me. "Before the storm, the state wasn't paying a lot of attention. Two months after the storm, they said, 'Remember that QRIS, you were talking about, how quickly can you do this?'" He swung into action, bringing to the table 200 stakeholders, including early childhood teachers, many fearful of the changes to come. How would they rate on new scale? By 2006, Louisiana's Quality Start was up and running. But Nagle wasn't finished. Advocacy then began for the state's school readiness tax credit, which he described as "a package with a little something for everyone—providers, business, parents, all different constituencies, all in the name of school readiness."

But the *pièce de résistance* was the early childhood system budget, which includes all slices of the state's pie for children. Like Magnolia Place's dashboard, this is a tool worth its weight in gold. "When you show that half of one percent of early childhood dollars are going to early childhood mental health, it jumps off the page," Nagle said. "Before, they would have said: 'What is early childhood mental health?' but now it's on the pie chart, and they go, 'Oh my God, we're doing nothing in mental health.'"

The conversation had shifted. Even better, the budget served as a quantitative touchstone for advocacy. The budget clearly showed $1.4 billion spent for young children in the state—a number on which the governor fixated in his push to redesign the early education system. When state legislators came up with their own calculations, reducing investment to $250 million, Nagle and his fellow advocates held lawmakers' feet to the fire. A victory to savor, though ephemeral. "Getting it used to inform policy remains a struggle," Nagle said. "It's difficult for legislators to put it into context. They want to know how this compares to other states." Nagle continues to struggle with the vicissitudes of making change, including the inevitable tensions between advocates and those "inside" the policymaking machine.

In 2007, the Head Start Reauthorization Act called for governors to establish early childhood advisory councils to improve the quality, availability, and coordination of programs and services for children birth to five.[39] As the Great Recession cut into already-meager investments in early childhood, Congress approved $100 million, through the American Recovery and Investment Act, to support the work of the councils. By September of 2010, the U.S. Administration for Children and Families had awarded a total of $92.8 million in grants—ranging from $500,000 to $11.2 million—to 45 states and five territories, among them Louisiana.[40] The move was heralded as a welcome, long-overdue acknowledgment of the need to bring order to the chaos of early childhood's dysfunctional system.

According to the agency's voluminous status report, issued six years after the congressional mandate, the states have made considerable progress—including the creation of data systems with unique child identifiers.[41] But Christina Satkowski, a policy researcher, had interviewed the council leaders when many of them were just a couple of years into the project. Her narrative was more in keeping with the spirit of realpolitik. Among the topic headings in her report was "A Sobering History of Collaboration."[42] While all of her sources had cited positive results, most expressed disappointment. She wrote of promising initiatives that were now below the radar or defunct. Others had been eliminated due to budget constraints and changes in political leadership. Many fell short of expectations for system transformation.

When Satkowski returned to her subject just after the agency had awarded its grants, she was troubled to find that five states had not been able to take advantage of the grant. They couldn't meet the requirement of a 70-percent match, an especially bitter loss for South Dakota, where less than a third of Native American students graduate from high school.[43]

Such work takes a significant emotional toll. Nagle, now the CEO of the Erikson Institute, a graduate school of early childhood education in Chicago, wistfully reminisced about the benefits of operating under stealth. "If you're in the system, you can't push it," he said. "The innovation is completely stifled. There is a grieving period, then you recalibrate your expectations. But in early childhood, five years is a generation. It's disheartening when you just nibble." The children are still waiting.

CHANGEMAKER: GERRIT WESTERVELT
Master Builder

Gerrit Westervelt is a policy wonk with energy as expansive as the Rockies he skis with his twin boys. His brain, too, ranges far and wide, extracting nuggets from the work of John Kingdon, who wrote the book on agenda setting, and Aaron Wildavsky, a Brooklyn-born political scientist, the author of the classic *Implementation*. "Go check them out," Westervelt told me when we last talked.

Most of the systems pioneers were rooted in early child development and education. Practitioners and researchers, among them former Head Start directors and founders of child care programs, they were inspired by their experiences in the field and by the research that exposed the great gaps between what they knew was best for children and conditions on the ground. What got Westervelt going was his work on education reform in the K–12 arena. "I was struck by the disconnect between the people I met in state government and the decisions they sometimes made," he said. "Why are all these smart people making bad decisions?" Policymakers focused on issues—say, teacher quality—in a vacuum, often clueless about how this might relate to the real lives and needs of educators and students. Often missing was a systemic approach.

"I realized that most of the K–12 reforms were not going to succeed unless we helped kids come to school able to perform to standard," he said. "It was a journey, and I thought early childhood was the place to invest." Westervelt's trajectory coincided with a changing political zeitgeist and the ascent of early childhood to the top of the national policy agenda—although he's quick to point out that where it is on the agenda depends on the day of the week and to whom you're talking.

From his home state of Colorado to the precincts of Albany, New York's notoriously challenging capital, he's spent his professional life thinking about, designing, and tweaking systems. At the Education Commission of the States, where he worked for the better part of the 1990s, the K–12 community was beginning to wake up to the prekindergarten set, with the help of a growing number of governors, including Jeanne Shaheen, Roy Romer, Jim Hunt, and Zell Miller. Westervelt then took a nosedive into the weeds, heading up Colorado's Qualistar, an early quality rating and improvement system. By the mid-2000s, he had returned to the national stage, as the leader of BUILD, an initiative that has sought to connect everyone, in all sectors of society, working on behalf of children and families. An ecological framework in the Bronfenbrenner mode.

BUILD's history embodies the frustrations and aspirations of a community that has long been politically marginalized. Launched by a high-powered group of foundations two years after the nation had missed another deadline for universal school readiness, the initiative represented a reimagining of the fractured programs, policies, and services that so often operated at cross-purposes, with anemic investment. They began modestly, working with leaders inside and outside of government. Nearly $1.5 million went to support policymakers, early childhood educators, and advocates from Illinois, New Jersey, Ohio, and Minnesota, planting the seeds for strategic early childhood system building.

The work has been slow but steady, their stable encompassing New York, Georgia, Arizona, Pennsylvania, Michigan, and Washington. Other states have been brought into the fold as learning partners, and in recent years, the initiative has expanded its reach further, in collaboration with the First Five Years Fund, to hold states' hands as they have applied for the federal Race to the Top–Early Learning Challenge grants, another one of our grand efforts in tinkering toward utopia.

Westervelt is a structural engineer, with an affinity for system parts, as well as the supports for keeping the work on track. He's followed the trends in the field. Now that prekindergarten has acquired legitimacy, he's moved down the spectrum to infants and toddlers, joining the Center for Child and Family Studies at WestEd, in California. He easily spews forth the terms of art in a system builder's lexicon—*connections, linkages, shared funding streams*—and he's convinced that early childhood's construction project is the frontier of education reform.

"Systems thinking has carried the day, it's become the dominant paradigm," he said. "Not all, but many, policymakers understand how putting money into pre-K programs isn't going to do it; they realize that this is more complicated." Westervelt is also an astute student, and critic, of policy design and implementation. He notes that we have spent more time and money on programs and components than we have on connecting and aligning them. He understands that you've got to have *something* to connect before you can create the links but worries about the lack of clarity in this mission.

"The field has evolved organically, like a garden, watering particular populations of kids and families," he observed. "If you pour water on these programs, you have wildflowers. The field has grown this way because of the reactive nature of politics. If you want policy to be implemented, then begin with end in mind." That end is nowhere in sight—at the moment. Westervelt reminded me that the K–12 system took a hundred years, and higher education, half a century. He sees another 20 or 30 years, at least, of construction work.

The biggest nut to crack is the nation's reluctance to establish early education as a public good, and the absence of those who teach young children in the national conversation. "ECE professionals are on the cutting edge of educational thought leadership, they're thinking way ahead of everyone else," he said. "The closer you get to the child, the more you know about what you need to do to move them forward. But we don't have opportunities to hear what they're saying."

Here, the policy wonk takes a page from *Horton Hears a Who*. Dr. Seuss's classic protagonist, an elephant with extraordinary auditory powers, hears a cry for help from the infinitesimal powerless creatures on a speck of dust and persuades them to be noisy and make their existence known. "Where are the elephant ears?" Westervelt asks. "How do we support local practitioners, enable the really smart people working with kids to have their voices heard?"

CHAPTER 6

The Machine in the Garden

On December 28th, I found myself at the Parkside Café, in Stinson Beach, California, up the coast from Apple's headquarters, in Cupertino. Across the room sat a man, woman, their daughter and a toddler son, howling inconsolably. His mother tinkered with her iPad, in search of a video to distract him. . . . The child's screams intensified. "Up," he said to his mother, her focus on the tablet. "We have books," said the maître'd to the father, who scooped up his son, removed him from the lunch table, and strolled over to the library.

—"Technology and Relationships,"
ECE Policy Matters

So much in this digital culture is beyond our control, but . . . our locus of power as parents, educators, and advocates for children remains essentially unchanged and it resides in the space of our relationship with them.

—Catherine Steiner-Adair, *The Big Disconnect*

One June, as the nation's youngsters squirmed in their sticky seats, yearning for summer, *Education Week* pondered the merits of virtual kindergarten. In the spotlight of the industry magazine was Christa Consadene. She had joined the corps of teacher forces led by Steven Guttentag, cofounder and chief education officer of Connections Education, a Baltimore-based curriculum provider. The company began offering instruction online for kindergartners in 2002.

Within a little more than a decade, enrollment was keeping pace with the other grades, growing between 20 percent and 25 percent a year. When last consulted, Consadene was checking into the possibility of offering live instruction. "There isn't such a thing," she said, "as being too young for online."[1]

The founder of the kindergarten movement is rolling over in his grave. As Eugene Provenzo noted in "Friedrich Froebel's Gifts: Connecting the Spiritual and Aesthetic to the Real World of Play and Learning," the 19th-century educator and his ideas are passé in the modern classroom.[2] But this virtual-kindergarten teacher, a new, if untested, species, is not alone in her thinking. Electronic media use in the United States is exploding, our preschoolers, and even babies, swiping their sweet, tiny fingers across a plethora of magnetizing screens.

BOMBARDED BY SCREENS

Chronicling this movement from analog to digital—a transformation, some say, on par with the huge leaps from oral to written language and onward to the printing press—is Common Sense Media. Don't you just love the name? Based in San Francisco, close to the action in Silicon Valley, the organization has branded itself as a trusted guide to parents "to help them navigate a world where change is the only constant." Helping the organization to fulfill its mission, among others, are Melinda and Bill Gates.

They can barely keep up the pace. In Common Sense Media's first report, released in 2011, Victoria Rideout breathlessly summed up the challenge:

> Today—20 years after the birth of the World Wide Web, 13 years after the launch of Google Search, eight years after the start of the first social networking site, six years after the first YouTube video, four years after the introduction of the first touch-screen smartphone, three years after the opening of the first "app" store, and a little over a year after the first iPad sale—the media world that children are growing up in is changing at lightning speed.[3]

By the time the second report emerged from the front two years later, Rideout was showing signs of battle fatigue, noting that she was "blown away by the rapidity of the change."[4] The findings represented an avalanche of digital adoption. Among families with children age eight and younger, ownership of tablet devices had increased fivefold, from 8 percent to 40 percent. During that same period, the percentage of children with access to some type of smart mobile device leapt from 52 percent to 75 percent. Usage of mobile media almost doubled, coming in at 72 percent. Most stunning of all the data was the revelation that nearly 40 percent of children under age two had used a mobile device—a fact emphasized in the report by the use of italics for the phrase *under two*.[5]

Digging down deeper, we find persistent trends, including a sizable digital divide, a decline in the amount of time children read or are read to daily, and the enduring lure of television. The gap, mirroring the rapid shifts in the landscape, had morphed into two distinct categories: the "traditional divide," reflecting access to high-speed Internet, and the "app gap," gestating amid the proliferation of mobile technologies.

While nearly half of our nation's poor children now have access to high-speed Internet, their more affluent peers continue to have the broadband advantage, with nearly 90 percent on intimate terms with the virtual world. Families with lower incomes are slowly edging up in their use of mobile media devices and apps. Smartphone access climbed from 41 percent to 63 percent in the two-year period between surveys; tablet ownership rose from a meager 2 percent to 20 percent, with reported use by 65 percent of lower-income children—a huge jump from 22 percent, two years earlier.[6]

FAMILIES IN TERRA INCOGNITA

From the crevices of this data dump arise the mounting questions of a community entrusted with raising the next generation. Is that video firing, or frying, the synapses of my child's brain? Will the green room in *Goodnight Moon* lose its magic on an electronic reader? Can little Olivia master, much less understand, equi-partitioning—the foundation for working with fractions—via a math app online?[7] And what about television, the preferred screen for millions of children from birth through the age of eight, especially among two- to four-year-olds, most prominently in Latino and African American families? Word has it that that the tube's background buzz is interfering with language development.[8]

"U.S. Parents Not Worried About Kids' Digital-Media Use," CNN announced, upon the release of *Parenting in the Age of Digital Technology*, by Ellen Wartella, Common Sense Media's Rideout, and colleagues at Northwestern's Center on Media and Human Development. According to this nationally representative survey of 2,300 parents of eight-year-olds and younger, nearly 80 percent of parents reported no family conflict over their children's media use, and just about 60 percent dismissed the idea that they might be worried about addiction to phones, tablet computers, or gaming devices. "Instead of a battle with children on one side and parents on the other," the authors wrote, "media and technology use has become a family affair."[9]

But the findings suggest the contours of a more complicated relationship with digital life, conveniently ignored by one of America's premier media outlets, ever striving for market share. While 55 percent of parents maintained that they were "not too" or "not at all" concerned about children's media use, almost a third of those surveyed thought otherwise, their worries rising from the deceptively placid waters of adaptation.

Anxiety and guilt, those defining staples of childrearing, are not going the way of the flip phone anytime soon. Lisa Guernsey, director of
the New America foundation's early education initiative, illuminates these
emotional land mines in the preface to her book, *Screen Time*, a pioneering journey into the technological zeitgeist. Written in the aftermath of
those harrowing days and nights of colic, she relates how her friend turned
her on to the Baby Einstein videos—or "crack" for moms. "With the inser-
tion of every DVD, I felt guilty," wrote Guernsey. "With every statement
about the videos stimulating my children's brains, I felt I was being taken
for a ride. And yet with every minute of quiet, I couldn't help but breathe
a sigh of relief."[10]

Today, such soul-baring testimony is as common—well, as colic—in the
blogosphere, that barometer of the parental psyche and virtual playground,
to which legions of the nation's nurturers repair, on their various screens, to
document the most intimate details of modern family life. Visual aids are in
no short supply for this ongoing conversation, including "A magazine is a
broken iPad!" on YouTube. The video depicts an infant repeatedly pressing
the pages of print—in search of the touch that will yield a reward for his
exploration.[11]

The video went viral just as Vinci, the first tablet computer targeted
to infants and toddlers, appeared on the market. At one point in the life
of the controversial device, the company's website promised "Windows of
Opportunity," to "ensure your children get the best start in life." A case of
Baby Einstein redux. "Amidst a cacophony of conflicting messages from
many diverse sources, parents must decide what constitutes an appropriate
'media diet,'" noted Sarah Vaala and her colleagues at the Annenberg Public
Policy Center.[12]

Such ambivalence and confusion fuel the creators, and purveyors, of
society's latest tools, caught between innovation, the market, and their
instincts—however inconvenient—about what is best for their own children. "At Google and all these places, we make technology as brain-dead
easy to use as possible," Alan Eagle confessed to a *New York Times* reporter
in 2011, as the digital assault persisted. "There's no reason why kids can't
figure it out when they get older."[13]

A communications executive at the company that has become synony-
mous with the quest for knowledge, he sent his own children to the Waldorf
School of the Peninsula, in northern California. Here, nature is an integral
part of nurture, educators look askance at mechanistic learning. Activities
such as knitting, gymnastics, foreign languages, and beeswax modeling fill
the days. Austrian philosopher and Waldorf progenitor Rudolf Steiner saw
this curriculum as an antidote to a "one-sided claim on the child's intellect

and the merely abstract acquisition of skills"—an opportunity for students to learn in a manner that calls upon their whole being.[14]

Other industry parents are navigating these shoals. At a conference of app developers in Monterey, California, journalist Hanna Rosin asked some of the participants about domestic rules for screen time. One woman, a former Montessori teacher, confessed to allowing no screen time during the week, with the exception of educational content; another designer restricted use to half an hour on Wednesdays and weekends; and the most permissive, to half an hour daily. "As technology becomes ubiquitous in our lives," Rosin wrote, "American parents are becoming more, not less, wary of what it might be doing to their children." She noted, too, how technological competence had now been added to the list of things that parents need to navigate in just the right way."[15]

THE SLOW PROCESS OF EVIDENCE GATHERING

I'm a "digital immigrant," a refugee from an earlier era, BiP, or "Before iPhone," a moniker whose origins are indeterminate, but one that would have tickled the Apple man himself.[16] I reared my own children on a zero-tolerance media policy, leaving them to their own devices, of the non-electronic kind. That time now seems like an age of innocence, before the revolution, when clicking, typing, texting, tweeting, messaging, friending, and podcasting irrevocably changed our syntax, and possibly our synapses. Not to mention Twitter, Tumblr, Instagram, Google+, and Pinterest, a tiny fraction of the burgeoning digital habitats that will be reinvented, if not obsolete, as the AiP (After iPhone) era whizzes by.

What does science tell us? Not a lot—or at least not enough to fully address the pressing, and growing, concerns of parents, educators, policymakers, and children's advocates. The evidence base continues to emerge, the research of a simpler technological age, in which television and video ruled, inadequate to the task of successful adaptation. But speed is not the forte of the academy. Some of the field's most prolific researchers, many of whom have been studying children's development for decades, have been scrambling to churn out the data.

"The timeline on which most people do research is many years, the timeline for the digital revolution is minutes," Kathy Hirsh-Pasek told me. She's an expert in language development, and coauthor, with Roberta Michnick Golinkoff, of a host of popular books, including *Einstein Never Used Flash Cards* and *How Babies Talk*. "People would say to me: 'So why haven't you studied the effects of ebook reading or the iPad on development?'"

she said. They have been on the job, indeed, but the evidence base is changing as rapidly as an infant in the first months of life.

She and Golinkoff had teamed up with Julia Parish-Morris and others, before the advent of the iPad, to investigate the effect of ebooks on the interactions between children and adults. They found that the bells and whistles—sound effects and a stylus for touching words and pictures—weren't helpful at all. Electronic devices, unlike books in print, thwarted children's reading comprehension. Rather than talking with them about the content, parents tended to tell kids what to do, to ensure that they moved chronologically through the story.[17] When I talked with Hirsh-Pasek, she and other researchers were shopping around an article for publication on toddlers' language learning from contingent and interrupted conversations—in other words, how cellphones disrupt that all-important dialogue at the heart of learning.

A growing number of scientists have been joining them, mapping children's learning at the intersection of technology and spawning a new lexicon as they go. In investigations of children's learning during the earliest years of development, the term *video deficit* pops up often, a leitmotif of the literature. The term is a nagging reminder of the gap between learning mediated by screens and human interactions. And the age at which this phenomenon disappears is the subject of intense debate.

Earlier researchers, who had studied children's television and video viewing, set it at two years, or even two and a half. But a team of investigators, including Kelly Dickerson and Rachel Barr, recently found that children as old as three had trouble putting together the pieces of a puzzle after watching a video demonstration.[18] As electronic media become more pervasive in the lives of infants and toddlers and the parents whose actions they're programmed to imitate, this question is hardly academic.

POLICYMAKING ON ANALOG TIME

In the policymaking precincts of our messy democracy, where the evidence comes to roost, incremental action is still the dominant modus operandi. As the nation's great love affair with screens was heating up, the American Academy of Pediatrics weighed in. On the eve of the new millennium, they issued their infamous decree, recommending that physicians "urge parents to avoid television viewing for children under the age of two years."[19] These words would haunt the physicians for a long time to come.

More than a decade later, they dredged them up in the abstract for an updated policy statement. Parsing their language like zealous defense attorneys, the academy blamed journalists for frequently misquoting them, translating the recommendation into an all-out ban. They continued to urge great caution in exposing children to the omnipresent screens during their most tender years. Conceding their historic cluelessness, they sent the document's lead author, pediatrician Ari Brown, to the media to exorcise the ghost once and for all. "The academy took a lot of flak for the first one," she said, "from parents, from industry, and even from pediatricians, asking, 'What planet do you live on?'" Such cognitive dissonance would no longer be tolerated.[20]

The academy, which puts the fear of God in parents across the land and still publishes its recommendations in the print journal *Pediatrics*—quaintly referring readers to its online version on the World Wide Web—was coming along. In yet another policy statement, issued in 2013 (note the slightly accelerated timeline), the doctors acknowledged the presence of electronic media as a dominant force in children's lives. They scratched it from the list of leading causes of major health problems and declared that media literacy and prosocial use would enhance knowledge, connectedness, and health. A far cry from an earlier position on media violence, which implicated TV, movies, music, and video games in a terrifying list of outcomes, including aggressive behavior, desensitization to violence, nightmares, and fear of being harmed.[21]

Meanwhile, the National Association for the Education of Young Children (NAEYC), the field's leading professional organization, had its hands full, shepherding its workforce of child care providers, preschool educators, and early elementary teachers through the weeds of No Child Left Behind. With its emphasis on accountability, standards, and assessment, the legislation was challenging some of early childhood's most cherished principles, including the social-emotional, relational foundations of learning.

Most vexing has been the assault on developmentally appropriate practice, the field's term of art for activities, curriculum, and experiences that "optimize the potential for children's learning and development," promoting relationships with adults and their peers.[22] NAEYC chose the Fred Rogers Center as a partner in drafting its belated position statement on the use of technology and interactive media in the nation's myriad settings serving children from birth through the age of eight. The benign television host, in his safe and child-proofed neighborhood, embodied the spirit of a slower, if not gentler, era.

The organization's platonic vision—a fragile bulwark against the onslaught of the new—wobbled on a platform of best intentions. They noted the dangers of passive use of technology and screen media, inappropriate replacements for active play and those critical human interactions with children and other adults. A couple of years later, in *The Village Effect*, psychologist Susan Pinker would observe the importance of face-to-face contact and how it could make us healthier, happier, and smarter.[23] But NAEYC knew that already. They cheered on their constituency, masters of highly attuned practice. Go, girls! they cried to the majority members of the early childhood workforce. You've got what it takes—knowledge, skill, and experience—to use technology well.

The Education Commission of the States, on which the nation's governors sit, was less fuzzy and warm. In a series of policy briefs, they reported on the progress of America's education system. Theirs was a bracing reality check, a "rethinking of education . . . in a world of increasing fiscal constraints." They saw a growing number of state leaders "under pressure to capitalize on these new technologies to improve productivity and help students excel."[24] In line with other silver-bullet seekers, the commission offered technology as a prescription for strengthening families and promoting success in school. They had singled out early childhood teachers, noting the daunting task that lies ahead. "Until recently," they observed, "most educators envisioned early learning as story time and hands-on activities with no technology in sight." But fortunately, the tech-savvy seemed to be getting the hang of it.[25]

LOSING A HUMAN KIND OF LEARNING

In the classrooms of the nation's early educators, this shift is well under way. But the old guard is skeptical. Weaned on psychologists Jean Piaget and Lev Vygotsky, they embrace as an article of faith the idea that young children learn best through their senses, exploring their surroundings with sensitive and engaging adults, and in the worlds they create with peers, in dramatic play.[26] Technology's virtual toys, from where they sit on their circle-time rugs, seem a poor substitute for the real thing. Digital education poses a significant risk, if not fully quantifiable, to teaching and learning.

Geralyn McLaughlin teaches three- and four-year-olds at Boston's Mission Hill School, the brainchild of progressive educator Deborah Meier, one of her prime mentors in a blossoming career as a teacher-activist. When she's not engaged with her lively and inquiring students, McLaughlin does duty as director of Defending the Early Years. The DEY project is rousing the early childhood community out of its slumber, urging well-reasoned arguments against the various, and growing, assaults on developmentally appropriate practice. When I first spoke with McLaughlin, she mentioned that iPads were already in use at Mission Hill for students with language delays. More would be making an appearance, in her classroom, in the fall—and she wasn't looking forward to their arrival.

"Young children don't need to use the technology now to learn the technology of tomorrow," she said, echoing Google executive Alan Eagle. She worries about the impact on children's capacity for imaginative play, the fount of self-regulation, more mature thinking, and innovation. She's seen imitative play—based on popular culture and regarded by purists as an inferior expression of creativity—become more common, even at Mission Hill. But a few years after the invasion of the iPads, McLaughlin was beginning to turn around. How could she ignore this lifeline for children struggling to speak?

She's following in a hallowed, if beleaguered, tradition. Child psychologist David Elkind issued an early battle cry in 1991 with *The Hurried Child*. The book served as a touchstone for those who found themselves increasingly at odds with the frenetic and programmed nature of contemporary childhood.[27] Among his acolytes was Joan Almon, a former kindergarten teacher, with a penchant for Rudolf Steiner's philosophy.

In 2000, as recounted in *Fool's Gold*, Almon and a group of like-minded colleagues had gathered in Spring Valley, New York, to found the U.S. branch of the Alliance for Childhood. A fervent, at times mystical, manifesto, the report articulated the organization's mission in a set of fundamental beliefs. The first reinforced childhood as a critical life stage, deserving of protection and time for unhurried experience. The second noted the importance of respect for each child as an individual, and the final tenet called for the alleviation of the tremendous stress of today's children, "suffering from allergies, asthma, hyperactive disorders, depression and autism."[28]

In a statement of the organization's raison d'etre, the Alliance for Childhood declared robust debate critical to the health of democracies, lamenting its absence amid the wide assumption that computers were essential in childhood. They argued that children and adults would be distracted from one another, losing face time or opportunities for language development. They worried that money would be diverted from the arts to expensive, unproven technology. Citing expertise from all corners, they painted an ominous picture of mechanistic and impersonal instruction, accompanied, in the words of child psychiatrist Stanley Greenspan, by "increasing levels of violence and extremism and less collaboration and empathy."[29]

In the first decade of 21st century, the alliance tenaciously documented violations of its tenets, waving red flags at all signs of vanishing childhood. In No Child Left Behind, they found the perfect target for their zeal:

education reform that sought to push its youngest students ahead to the detriment of their learning and well-being. The organization proclaimed a crisis in the kindergarten, quantifying the incursions against play and recess in classrooms in Los Angeles and New York City.[30]

They continued to tout the importance of children's connection to nature and to monitor their electronic diets, increasingly filled with fast-moving, commercially conjured images, leaving little to the imagination. Underlying the critique was a profound sense of loss. The alliance evoked *educare*, the Latin root of the word *educate*—to lead out, from darkness into light. The teacher as guide, as translator of the world's meaning, was dead. "Only a human being, not a machine, can model this uniquely human kind of learning," they said.[31]

Loss accompanies any profound societal shift. In ancient Greece, as Denise E. Murray wrote in the journal of *Language Learning and Technology*, Plato and Socrates agonized over the adoption of alphabetic writing. In Plato's *Phaedrus*, Socrates, his teacher, declares: "The fact is that this invention will produce forgetfulness in the souls of those who have learned it. They will not need to exercise their memories, being able to rely on what is written."[32] Whatever the century, a divide emerges—often two opposing camps—between those who fear the repercussions and those who extol the virtues of the new technology. Yet Murray dismisses the commonly held view that technology is revolutionary, arguing that it merely facilitates changes already beginning to take place in society.

When Almon returned to this subject more than a decade after the founding of the Alliance for Childhood, the ground was continuing to shift beneath her. In the foreword to *Facing the Screen Dilemma*, coauthored with Susan Linn and Diane Levin, leaders, respectively, of the Campaign for a Commercial-Free Childhood and Teachers Resisting Unhealthy Children's Entertainment, the tone is less defensive, even resigned. Reiterating the message of the earlier manifesto, they maintained that they were hardly Luddites, or technophobes. They confessed to tweeting, texting, blogging, and Skyping and enjoyment of all sorts of new technologies.[33]

Still, they hadn't given up on the question of how to find a "truly child-centered" solution to the screen dilemma. Buried deep within the section "Whether or Not You Use Screen Technology in Your Setting" was the beginning, at least, of an answer. A framework that resembled to a tee Lisa Guernsey's "3 Cs"—context, content, and child—or the prime factors that parents and teachers need to think about as they navigate this brave, new world. These recent converts to the pleasures of the realm had, unmistakably, taken a page from a digital pioneer.

EARLY EDUCATORS IN THE DIGITAL WILD WEST

When I visited Geralyn McLaughlin's classroom one September morning, the machines had entered the garden. In this bright, spacious sanctuary, with its smooth wooden blocks, yellow pencils for drawing, and the school's statement of purpose—"Without art, we are deprived"—securely fastened to the wall, two children had bright-colored, plastic iPads close at hand.

Maia, a four-year-old who does not yet speak, was at work on a drawing, while Angel Nasseh, her special education itinerant teacher, introduced me to the iChat app. "I want to eat" appeared with a light touch, offering a menu of both general (breakfast, lunch) and specific (fruit, milk) selections. She navigated to another option, "I feel," which listed a whole range of emotions, "sad" and "happy" among them. "Because of district policies, it took a year to get iPads and iChat," Angel told me. "My goal is to have Maia talk. If this is going to help her, I'm all for it. She vocalizes a lot, as if she wants to speak. What we don't know is if it slows her down."

According to the children's speech therapist, Aubrey Rubin, the device doesn't inhibit speaking. "But my role is not to get kids to talk," she told me. "My job is to get them to communicate." Rubin, whom I watched take a child from meltdown to calm in mere minutes—"Do you feel safe now?" she kept asking—views the iPad as a voice for the child. She talked about Henry, one of the three children with special needs in McLaughlin's inclusive classroom. "I don't want him to imitate an adult," she said; "he's got his device, they'll be *his* words."

She noted how Henry had outgrown Go Talk, a precursor to iChat, which had 25 buttons that he could press to retrieve words to make a sentence. One day, he was caught between his desire to be on the swings and at the usual morning gathering—an expression thwarted by the limitations of his machine. "That's when we got the iPad," Rubin said. "It had more than the 20 symbols, and we needed a tool to give him access." Professionals who work with young children with special needs are ahead of the curve. They see technology not as dehumanizing, but as a valuable adjunct to more traditional learning strategies, which often prove useless for students whose brains and bodies don't fit the mold. Some of their colleagues who play in the fields of typical development—many of them early childhood veterans— bring a different bias, along with a natural antipathy to change.

Chip Donohue, who oversees the TEC Center at the Erikson Institute, a graduate school of early childhood education in Chicago, is trying to bring them along. A former Montessori director in progressive Madison, Wisconsin, Donohue was, by turns, impatient, encouraging, and optimistic in his assessment of the situation. "We're using these tools in our personal lives," he said. "The jump isn't so big. But skepticism isn't okay anymore. We need to figure out ways to get more playful as adults so that we can start being more playful with children."

The charge to adapt had already been delivered by the Digital Age Teacher Preparation Council. Experts from the Joan Ganz Cooney Center at Sesame Workshop and the Stanford Center for Opportunity Policy in Education had issued a blueprint, *Take A Giant Step*. Noting the nation's dearth of high-quality early childhood programs, they highlighted the absence of innovative training models in their design. "Beginning with teachers of children aged three through eight, we can establish a cost-effective and productive pathway for learning in the 21st century," the authors wrote, echoing the language of the Education Commission of the States, with its emphasis on fiscal constraints and improving outputs.[34]

The distance between blueprint and implementation is considerable. In "Building the Plane While Flying It," posted to his blog, *Dangerously Irrelevant*, Scott McLeod, director of innovation for Iowa's Prairie Lakes Education Agency, asked, "How many of us have heard this phrase in presentations about the need for schools to move more quickly toward an uncertain and unknowable future?" While acknowledging the skeptics, McLeod plowed on. We have no choice, he wrote, urging support for educators and kids "who are ready to dive deep into hands-on, technology-infused learning experiences that emphasize cognitive complexity and student agency."[35]

Teachers of our youngest students are in the early stages of this aerodynamic experiment. A survey of technology use in early childhood classrooms, published in *Exchange*, an industry magazine, illuminates a landscape in transition. Of the 485 respondents, more than three-quarters of whom were teachers, the majority in public preschool, 65 percent had used technology. Nearly all reported the presence of a desktop or laptop computer in the classroom. Close to 40 percent had integrated tablet computers into their daily practice, although usage in each case was limited by the majority of teachers to less than 30 minutes daily. Interactive whiteboards are common—63 percent use them—as are multitouch devices, which are are popular with more than three-quarters of all practitioners.[36]

Smartphone use, while skyrocketing among parents, was still minimal among early childhood educators in the classroom, and screen time for children still emergent, with nearly 30 percent of their teachers reporting encounters three to four times a week. The study reveals a distinct change of consciousness. Of those teachers whose classrooms had remained low tech, the majority attributed the situation to budgetary restrictions and reported that they would have been happy to consider using interactive information processing technologies, if funding were available. Others cited concerns about developmental appropriateness and philosophical objections, with a small percentage dismissing the value added and a miniscule 5 percent noting parental opposition.[37]

Just choosing the games, apps and software—now proliferating online—is a formidable challenge. Among the guides is Erin Klein. A second-grade teacher at the Cranbrook schools in Bloomfield Hills, Michigan, and a blogger at Scholastic—a "Tweet loving, technology integrating mom of two with a passion for classroom design!"—she represents the new breed of purveyors of digital training. Her web-based CV describes her as "working in education, with a business background," someone who values "the importance of technology integration and global preparation into the learning environment." Klein's bachelor's degree, in elementary education, included a special endorsement in social studies, which would allow her to teach seventh- and eighth-graders, with a few courses in child development thrown in. Along the way, she picked up a master's degree in curriculum instruction.

Klein began the process of integration at home with her own two children. "I started with basic apps and just playing games," she recalled. She noticed her daughter, four at the time, sitting with her iPad and creating content. "I thought that was fantastic. It was like playing school, and she was having fun." Agnostic about the evidence base—there's research to support both sides, she asserts—Klein blithely dismisses the anxieties of her early childhood peers. "I think people resist what they're unaware of, or don't understand," she said. "They don't know that augmented reality can enhance a child's persuasive abilities, or abilities to retell a story."

As for the myriad options for entering this world, Klein remains nonplussed. She gives teachers an overview of the millions of apps, suggesting that they go for products that are free, easy to use, and extremely intuitive. The user interface also must offer "content creation," so that children are able to construct knowledge—an archaic term from the BiP, with which this digital native seemed unfamiliar.

Klein makes it sound so easy. Yet the findings of a scan of paid and free apps, electronic games, and websites, reviewed by the nation's watchdog, Common Sense Media, offer little encouragement. Digital products aimed at building literacy skills constitute a substantial segment of the market. But many made false claims about the educational benefits for young children. Scientific proof of their effectiveness was conspicuously absent from the product description. Most targeted only basic literacy skills—letters, phonics, and word recognition—omitting more advanced early reading competencies, such as grammar and comprehension. Ignoring the latest scientific findings—never mind that pleasure and discovery of reading—ebooks tended toward optional narration, embedded activities, and sound effects.[38]

PROFESSIONAL DEVELOPMENT GOES VIRAL

The learning curve for today's early childhood educators is steep. Those nasty apps are just the beginning. How do you even begin to promote higher order thinking and innovation? Erikson's Donohue has become a proselytizer for this cause, his TEC Center a hub for the technologically challenged. The desired outcome of the training—online and off—is confidence. He talks of "participation-contribution tools," and the power of peer-to-peer learning. Targeted to teachers trained in constructivist theory—which posits that young children learn best through full, hands-on exploration of their environments—the Early Childhood Investigations webinars combine the familiar language of inquiry-based pedagogy with soothing comparisons of digital technologies to pencils.

In one webinar on digital and media literacy, Faith Rogow, author of *The Teachers Guide to Media Literacy*, warned that while "knowing how to use digital devices is part of being literate . . . it isn't enough . . . where technology provides easy access to nearly unlimited information and resources, we need to expand the traditional "three Rs" to include reasoning and reflection."[39] Erikson also hosts a face-time series for those who still like their learning up close and personal. Here, in a TEC Conversation (@EriksonInst.), the keepers of the flame of developmentally appropriate practice can get their training in the bricks-and-mortar old-fashioned way—albeit from coaches whose credentials often evoke the cozy relationship between Silicon Valley and 21st-century education.

Among the panelists at one seminar, "Intentional Technology for Early Learners in Schools," was Jennifer Magiera, the digital learning coordinator for the Academy for Urban School Leadership. An Apple Distinguished Educator and Google Certified Teacher, she made no bones about her product commitment, describing herself as one who "explores how to leverage 1:1 devices such as Chromebooks and iPads to increase student metacognition, self-efficacy, and creativity."[40] But the short biography of her fellow panelist, Erin Stanfill, harked back to an earlier model of a preschool educator. A former Head Start teacher, she proclaimed her affinity for the philosophy of Reggio Emilia, a city in Italy that has become a mecca for constructivists, clinging to the wisdom of Piaget and Vygotsky.

TOWARD A THIRD WAY

"From the brightest of colors, sweetest of smells, feel and manipulation of every item, taste of each food and drink," Linda Mitchell wrote in the journal *Theory into Practice*, "children are guided into their worlds to uncover and create new knowledge and skills."[41] Joining a select few, Mitchell, a professor at Wichita State University in Kansas, had paid a visit to this city nestled in Emilia Romagna, a region with a history of political activism and a fervent belief in the primacy of the early years.[42]

Loris Malaguzzi, a native son of Reggio, had joined a movement, in the 1960s, begun after World War II, to create schools that would nurture high-level critical thinking—necessary for democracy's survival.[43] The first municipal preschool opened in 1963, earning Reggio Emilia, and Malaguzzi, a secure place in the vanguard of Italy's early childhood system building. But his idea that children are curious, capable beings, most creative in their relationships with adults, was hardly new. Twentieth-century philosopher and progressive education reformer John Dewey was writing about the "audacity of imagination" when Malaguzzi, himself, had barely left early childhood.[44]

Still, the Italian thinker and his Reggio colleagues captured the hearts of a global community of early childhood educators pining for pedagogy that would support them in translating the theory they hold dear into practice. They found irresistible the partnerships of inquiry among teachers, *atelieriste* (arts educators) and *pedagogiste* (education services coordinators), cultivating children's expression through a wide range of materials and media.[45]

Reggio's practitioners were early, if selective, technology users, documenting children's creative work through video—another native Italian product, nurtured in the Cinecitta film studios, outside of Rome. At the turn of the 20th century, as the digital age encroached, the city's infant-toddler centers and preschools flirted with American-style constructivism, collaborating with the Harvard Graduate School of Education on Project Zero, the brainchild of Nelson Goodman, a philosopher bent on exploring how children and adults learn through the arts.[46] Technology-based exploration was on the agenda, parents and teachers following children's interests in cybernetic objects—robots, remote-controlled cars and trucks, and small computers—and attempting to extend their students' learning.[47]

Yet something seems to have gotten lost in translation, from the *atelier*, where Plexiglas light tables illuminate children's work, to Cambridge, Massachusetts. As Reggio schools director Sergio Spaggiari warned the members of one of the celebrated study groups, technology is important, but "it lacks the feeling and visual encounters needed by young children."[48]

One cool, overcast morning, I sat in the lobby of the education and research center at New York City's Museum of Modern Art (MoMA). A group of students—girls in crisp uniforms, second- or third-graders—waited patiently and quietly for a tour. A mother with an infant strolled back and forth. Welcoming them was Cari Frisch. A young, hipsterish art and art history major, with a crash course on imaginative play at Sarah Lawrence under her belt, she readily concedes the gaps in her knowledge about child development. As she and her colleagues have developed a series of art labs, focused on color, line, shape, people, materials, and movement, Carla Englebrecht Fisher, who designed *Elmo's Musical Monsterpiece* for Nintendo Wii and DS, has served as their guide.

In its own *atelieri,* or studios, the museum aims to engage families with art and one another—and to promote the venerable institution, a star in New York City's cultural galaxy. Frisch emphasizes the family program's commitment to fostering parent-child interactions. But the labs, each of which has a shelf life of nearly a year, are also places for parents to relax, where children are left to explore, more or less, on their own. The museum has partnered with Microsoft, which developed the software for digital "paint" for the young artists.

MoMA's first venture into early childhood, an app hopefully named "Creative Play," was intended for parents to use at home with their children—a bridge to the artists, including Matisse, and the focus of a hands-on activity that directed children to cut out shapes. "What kind of app helps them see art, what detracts?" Frisch said. "I'd like to start a conversation. Is it appropriate to have technology? We are thinking about the kids. They need touch."

What they need to touch remains a subject of hot debate, of course. In the movement lab, a media installation beckoned with digital-age artist tools and palette, including charcoal—splattered in the style of Jackson Pollock—and paint, which children could remotely manipulate, viewing their creations on screen. Children can snap pictures of their work with their smartphones and email them home. A stop-motion animation project, intended for six- or seven-year-olds, and part of a space designed by Frisch and interpretive art museum fellow Desiree Gonzalez, has had staying power with older teens as well. Nascent filmmakers can upload their videos to YouTube for the world to see.

"We're constantly looking for the sweet spot, balancing tech and hands-on experiences," said Frisch, whose learning curve continues to flatten. A thomotrope, a toy that was popular in the 19th century, wowing children with optical illusions, did not light the fire of creativity. The movement lab also had discovery boxes, like those at the American Museum of Natural

History, further uptown, as well as blocks, a track for balls, and a video featuring a child in motion—to challenge the viewer to do one motion for 60 seconds. "We want the ideas of the lab to resonate with their daily lives," Frisch said.

When I visited, the children were in low-tech mode. One boy fiddled with the remote device for drawing, while another was finding his way with colored pencils. Someone was building with blocks, and a toddler was transfixed by the wires of an audio tape, which he proceeded to take apart, in the spirit of discovery. A six-year-old, headphones in ear, moved toward a wooden maze, riveted by the ball he had thrown on the path. Another toddler brought a board book over to her mother.

"A scaly lizard," she began to read, until her daughter, distracted, returned to get a set of balls from the shelf that held the blocks, maze, and other old-fashioned "manipulatives," as they are called in the early childhood field. No sooner had the child left than the mother's eyes were glued to her iPhone screen. When the toddler was ready to return to home base, the woman was deep in the digital universe, awakened only by her daughter's sobs—mid-meltdown—on the lab floor. She scooped the child into her lap, holding her close, her screen dark for the moment.

CHANGEMAKER: KRISTIN ENO

Authenticity and Awe in a Virtual World

Kristin Eno is a boundary crosser, straddling the analog and digital worlds. Her thoughts spew out in late-night emails. With children and husband asleep, and a quiet house, she is free to compose her life as artist, early childhood educator, and mother.

Like that of most artists, her path has been anything but linear. After college, Eno began teaching art to early elementary students—kindergarten through second grade—including a stint at the Reggio-inspired Brooklyn Charter School. She brought to her work a well-developed spirit of inquiry, embedded in the research base on child development. Where did her artistic work end, and the children's begin? Was it a collaboration? How could she maintain the integrity and autonomy of her young students? Those questions pushed her forward on her path as *atelierista*, or arts educator.

A painter intrigued by the creative potential of video, Eno learned how to shoot and edit, and embarked on a master's degree program in arts education at Columbia University's Teachers College. In 2004, she founded Digital Story Workshop, working with prekindergartners through third-graders in the classroom. Inspired by Vivian Paley, a MacArthur "genius" who recorded her observations of kindergarten children in a series of beloved books, Eno used her camera to document children's stories and imaginative play. What she found was a hostile climate. "I was the renegade," she told me. "I wanted to give these kids something to do free form, and all the principals wanted to know was: How does this fit into the curriculum?"

Eno moved on, creating and distributing her product through Little Creatures Films, which she established in 2008, while starting a family. After devoting major time and energy to *Spirit Ship*, a film with a young crew of 24, she felt a gnawing sense of dissatisfaction, cringing at the product nature of filmmaking. "The child is a thinking, feeling human being, not just an actor," she said. Her perspective shifted radically when she became a mother. Nurturing her firstborn, Eno began to imagine an alternate path through the digital universe. "As I witnessed my daughter beginning to communicate with the world through play," she said, "the last thing on my mind was placing technology in her hands, and I began to look with a much more critical eye at the media out there."

Eno's professional Waterloo awaited at the Fred Rogers Center in Latrobe, Pennsylvania. She had been invited to present her work in a showcase of organizations using technology and new media to nurture creativity, curiosity, and learning. But PBS declined to pick up her pilot. She watched as Angela Santomero, creator of *Blue's Clues*, showed some clips of a brand-new animated show. They had reduced "the Neighborhood of Make-Believe," Eno thought, to a drawn and colored world. She spoke up in a panel discussion, about the importance of nature and outdoor play. "I saw this weekend as the turning point in my career," she said. "One door closed on the opportunity to get my films out to children and families and another opened—to the important world of hands-on learning and tinkering."

Within a couple of years, now the mother of two, Eno sprang into action, joining Elisha Georgiou in the creation of Find & Seek. The two began conducting interactive lab classes around Brooklyn, engaging children in hands-on exploration and play. Their new project found a home in the public library in Red Hook, a gritty, underserved neighborhood on the waterfront. "We had pitched the program to parents of three- and four-year-olds," Eno said, "but many more families with younger children came, like a 'Mommy and Me' model. The parents wanted ideas that they could take back with them."

Eno is also a prime mover in the development of an infant-toddler center, an initiative spearheaded by Anna Allanbrook of the Brooklyn New School, a progressive outpost in an increasingly hostile climate. The initiative has attracted the borough's early childhood educators and those who train them, aware of the acute need to reach the city's students early with the kinds of experiences that enrich them. Meanwhile, Eno struggles as a parent to live by her principles.

At the beginning, she aligned her own screen rules with those of the American Academy of Pediatrics, which called for no screen time before the age of two. "I agreed that time was so much better spent playing, talking, singing, and simply living than watching others do these things," she said. She kept the screens out of reach—making an exception for her own film, *Spirit Ship*, and one of her favorite children's films, *Le Ballon Rouge*. Her daughters now watch a show or a movie once or twice a week, and she judiciously selects apps for their consumption.

But Eno's acutely aware of the power of the medium. She's read all the *Sesame Street* studies from the 1970s and other research on the effectiveness of television as a teaching tool. "I get it," she said. "I need only listen to my two-year-old singing 'use your words, use your words!' to the tune of a Daniel Tiger song." She concedes how tough it is to stay the course. "Making sure our kids get muddy daily is a tall order in Brooklyn," she said. "Media's like a pacifier, the one I can't provide when my girls and I are living through the 'witching hour,' and I need to make dinner. There is only so much Vygotskian-facilitated play that one mom can do every day."

Like *atelieristas* in Emilia Romagna, Eno and Georgiou, continue to bring the wisdom of the Russian psychologist to the youngest citizens of the borough. Through dialogue, inquiry, and video documentation, they fill in the missing pieces, importing the values of a vanishing civilization—captured in a 21st-century blog post, floating in the ether:

> Sheets of fall inspired golden silks and fiery organzas, lacy white packaging paper, glistening green bubble wrap and strands of fall leaf garlands were suspended from the ceiling's beams. We projected images of forest trees upon the walls, which also cast shadows, colors and lines across the fabrics in a most whimsical way. Upon the ground, earthy, velvety rugs in plum and avocado hues created warm spaces for laying down, stretching out, meeting in groups, telling stories and collecting objects.

Notes

Chapter 1

1. Patricia Kuhl and Andrew Meltzoff, "Brain Power: Why Early Learning Matters," NBC Education Nation Summit video, September 26, 2011, www.nbcnews.com/video/nbc-news/44672754#44672754.

2. Ibid.

3. Thomas Piketty, *Capital in the 21st Century* (Cambridge, MA: Belknap Press of Harvard University Press, 2014); Jennifer Schuessler, "Economist Receives Rock Star Treatment," *New York Times*, April 18, 2014, www.nytimes.com/2014/04/19/books/thomas-piketty-tours-us-for-his-new-book.html.

4. James K. Galbraith, "Kapital for the Twenty-First Century?" *Dissent,* Spring 2014, www.dissentmagazine.org/article/kapital-for-the-twenty-first-century.

5. B. F. Kiker, "The Historical Roots of the Concept of Human Capital," *Journal of Political Economy* 74 (1966): 481–499.

6. Ann Crittenden, *The Price of Motherhood* (New York: Henry Holt, 2001), 71.

7. Theodore W. Schultz, "Investment in Human Capital," *The American Economic Review* 51, no. 1 (March 1961): 1–17.

8. James Heckman, "Skills and Scaffolding," *Brookings Institution*, October 22, 2014, www.brookings.edu/research/papers/2014/10/22-skills-scaffolding-heckman.

9. See the Heckman Equation project, www.heckmanequation.org/content/resource/letter-national-commission-fiscal-responsibility-and-reform.

10. James Heckman, "White House Summit on Early Education, 'Going Forward Wisely,'" December 10, 2014, heckmanequation.org/content/resource/going-forward-wisely-professor-heckmans-remarks-white-house-summit-early-education.

11. David Hudson, "Invest in US: President Obama Convenes the White House Summit on Early Education," *The White House Blog*, December 10, 2014, www.whitehouse.gov/blog/2014/12/10/invest-us-president-obama-convenes-white-house-summit-early-education.

12. Robbie Crouch, "Cost of Military Jet Could House Every Homeless Person in U.S. with $600,000 Home," *Huffington Post*, July 11, 2014, www.huffingtonpost.com/2014/07/11/military-jet-spending_n_5575045.html.

13. ZERO TO THREE, "Spending on Children on Downward Slide," *Federal Policy Baby Blog*, July 23, 2012, zerotothreepolicy.tumblr.com/post/27852465186 /spending-on-children-on-downward-slide.

14. Julia Isaacs et al., *Kids' Share 2012: Report on Federal Expenditures on Children for 2011* (Washington, DC: Urban Institute, 2012), www.urban.org /UploadedPDF/412600-Kids-Share-2012.pdf.

15. Heather Hahn et al., *Kids' Share 2014*: Report on Federal Expenditures on Children Through 2013 (Washington, DC: Urban Institute, 2014), www.urban.org /UploadedPDF/413215-Kids-Share-2014.pdf.

16. Susan Ochshorn, "Russ Whitehurst's One-Man Crusade Against Early Childhood Education," *ECE Policy Matters*, February 5, 2014, www.ecepolicymatters .com/archives/2026.

17. OECD, "Social Expenditure Update: Insights from the OECD Social Expenditure Database (SOCX)," Directorate for Employment, Labour and Social Affairs, November 2014. www.oecd.org/els/soc/OECD2014-Social-Expenditure -Update-Nov2014-8pages.pdf.

18. OECD, "Social Expenditure Update," www.oecd.org/els/soc/OECD2014 -Social-Expenditure-Update-Nov2014-8pages.pdf; web.stanford.edu/group/scspi/ _media/pdf/pathways/winter_2008/Smeeding.pdf; www.usatoday.com/story/money /business/2014/05/21/rich-poor-widest-gap/9351639/.

19. Nancy Folbre, "Children as Public Goods," *American Economic Review* 84, no. 2 (1994): 86–90.

20. Janet C. Gornick and Marcia K. Meyers, *Families that Work: Policies for Reconciling Parenthood and Employment* (New York: Russell Sage Foundation, 2003), 40; Brian Faler, "5 Things to Know About Obama's Robin Hood Tax Plan," *Politico*, January 18, 2015, www.politico.com/story/2015/01/barack-obama-tax -plan-114367.html.

21. Anne-Marie Slaughter, "A New America that Cares," *A Woman's Nation Pushes Back from the Brink: The Shriver Report*, January 12, 2014, shriverreport .org/a-new-america-that-cares-ann-marie-slaughter/.

22. Nancy Folbre, *The Invisible Heart: Economics and Family Values* (New York: The New Press, 2001), 72; Jessica Grosse, "The Year Having Kids Became a Frivolous Luxury," *Slate*, December 22, 2014, www.slate.com/blogs/xx_factor /2014/12/22/the_cost_of_raising_children_why_we_now_see_parenting_as_a _frivolous_luxury.html.

23. Indradeep Ghosh and Riane Eisler, *Social Wealth Economic Indicators: A New System for Evaluating Economic Prosperity* (Pacific Grove, CA: Center for Partnership Studies, 2014), www.partnershipway.org/get-connected /social-wealth-indicators; caringeconomy.org/wp-content/uploads/2014/11/SWEI -Executive-Summary-and-Core-Indicators-2.pdf; see www.youtube.comwatch?v =HDdQHrLDLiE.

24. See *Syracuse.com*, "Defending Our Children: Marian Wright Edelman Talks About What's Gone Wrong in America's Relationship with Its Kids," Editorial Board, April 11, 2010, blog.syracuse.com/opinion/2010/04/defending_our _children_marian.html.

25. U.S. Department of Labor, *Infant Care*, Children's Bureau Publication No. 8, 1935, www.mchlibrary.info/history/chbu/3121-1935.PDF.

26. Ibid., 1.

27. John Locke, *An Essay Concerning Human Understanding* (Oxford, UK: Oxford University Press, 1975); J. Rousseau, *Emile, or On Education*, ed. Christopher Kelly and trans. Allan Bloom (Lebanon, NH: Dartmouth University Press, 2009).

28. See Elizabeth S. Spelke, "Core Systems and the Growth of Human Knowledge: Natural Geometry," in *The Proceedings of the Working Group on Human Neuroplasticity and Education: Vol. 117. Human Neuroplasticity and Education*, ed. A. M. Battro, S. Dehaene, and W. J. Singer (Vatican City: Pontifical Academy of Sciences, 2011), 73–99. For a recent profile of Spelke, see "Insights from the Youngest Minds," *New York Times*, April 30, 2012, www.nytimes.com/2012/05/01/science/insights-in-human-knowledge-from-the-minds-of-babes.html?pagewanted=all; Alison Gopnik, Andrew Meltzoff, and Patricia Kuhl, *The Scientist in the Crib: What Early Learning Tells Us About the Mind* (New York: William Morrow, 1999).

29. Gopnik, Meltzoff, and Kuhl, *Scientist in the Crib*.

30. Alison Gopnik, *The Philosophical Baby* (New York: Farrar, Straus and Giroux, 2009), 11. Although reading the book is a revelation, Gopnik does a fine synthesis in her TED talk, "What do babies think?" www.ted.com/talks/alison_gopnik_what_do_babies_think.html.

31. Anne Lamott, *Operating Instructions: A Journal of My Son's First Year* (New York: Random House 1993), 11.

32. Jack P. Shonkoff and Deborah A. Phillips, *From Neurons to Neighborhoods: The Science of Early Childhood Development* (Washington, DC: National Academies Press, 2000).

33. Robert Karen, *Becoming Attached: First Relationships and How They Shape Our Capacity to Love* (New York: Oxford University Press, 1998); A. F. Lieberman, *The Emotional Life of the Toddler* (New York: Free Press, 1993).

34. Erik H. Erikson, *Childhood and Society* (New York: W. W. Norton, 1950).

35. S. A. Kelley, C. A. Brownell, and S. Campbell, "Mastery Motivation and Self-Evaluative Affect in Toddlers: Longitudinal Relations with Maternal Behavior." *Child Development* 71, no. 4 (2000): 1061–1071.

36. Susan Ochshorn, "The Trouble with Grit," *ECE Policy Matters*, October 4, 2012, www.ecepolicymatters.com/archives/864; see Paul Tough, *How Children Succeed: Grit, Curiosity, and the Hidden Power of Character* (Boston: Houghton Mifflin Harcourt, 2012).

37. K. A. Ertel, J. W. Rich-Edwards, and K. C. Koenen, "Maternal Depression in the United States: Nationally Representative Rates and Risks," *Journal of Women's Health* 20, no. 11.

38. Francis Galton, *English Men of Science: Their Nature and Nurture* (London: MacMillan, 1874); "A devil, a born devil, on whose nature Nurture can never stick," wrote William Shakespeare of his character Caliban in *The Tempest*, Act IV, Scene 1 (Harmondsworth, UK: Penguin Books, 1987).

39. Anne Fausto-Sterling, "Letting Go of Normal," *Boston Review*, April 7, 2014, www.bostonreview.net/wonders/fausto-sterling-motor-development.

40. See Bill, Hillary, and Chelsea Clinton Foundation and Next Generation, toosmall.org/mission for a description of this initiative to support children from birth through five.

41. Karen Attiah, "Why Won't the U.S. Ratify the U.N.'s Child Rights Treaty?" *Washington Post*, November 21, 2014, www.washingtonpost.com/blogs/post-partisan/wp/2014/11/21/why-wont-the-u-s-ratify-the-u-n-s-child-rights-treaty.

42. United Nations, "Convention on the Rights of the Child," adopted and opened for signature, ratification, and accession by General Assembly resolution 44/25 of November 20, 1989, entry into force, September 1990, in accordance with article 49, www.ohchr.org/en/professionalinterest/pages/crc.aspx.

43. Amnesty International USA, "Convention on the Rights of the Child," www.amnestyusa.org/our-work/issues/children-s-rights/convention-on-the-rights-of-the-child-0.

44. Ibid.

45. World Health Organization, *Closing the Gap in a Generation: Health Equity Through Action on the Social Determinants of Health* (Geneva, Switzerland: World Health Organization, 2008), 1, www.who.int/social_determinants/final_report/csdh_finalreport_2008.pdf.

46. Clyde Hertzman, "Bridging a Population Health Perspective to Early Biodevelopment: An Emerging Approach," in *Nature and Nurture in Early Child Development*, ed. D. Keating (New York: Cambridge University Press, 2011), 217; For a definition of, and publications about, the social determinants of health, see Centers for Disease Control (www.cdc.gov/socialdeterminants/).

47. Shonkoff discussed his work at a forum sponsored by the Children's Health Fund, "Toxic Stressors, Child Development & Interventions to Improve Health," on March 28, 2011, in New York City.

48. Shonkoff and Phillips, *From Neurons to Neighborhoods*.

49. Guillermo Cantor (2014), "Thousands of U.S.-Citizen Children Separated from Parents, ICE Records Show," *Immigration Impact*, American Immigration Council, June 26, 2014, immigrationimpact.com/2014/06/26/thousands-of-u-s-citizen-children-separated-from-parents-ice-records-show/; see Hirokazu Yoshikawa, *Immigrants Raising Citizens: Undocumented Parents and Their Children* (New York: Russell Sage, 2012).

50. FindYouthInfo (updated, August 11, 2014), "Children of Incarcerated Parents." www.findyouthinfo.gov/youth-topics/children-of-incarcerated-parents.

51. Shonkoff, discussion at Children's Health Fund forum.

52. See Center on the Developing Child, Harvard University, "Toxic Stress Derails Healthy Development," developingchild.harvard.edu/resources/multimedia/videos/three_core_concepts/toxic_stress/; National Scientific Council on the Developing Child, *Excessive Stress Disrupts the Architecture of the Developing Brain, Working Paper 3,* updated ed. (2005; 2014), developingchild.harvard.edu/resources/reports_and_working_papers/working_papers/wp3/.

53. R. F. Anda et al., "Building a Framework for Global Surveillance of the Public Health Implications of Adverse Childhood Experiences," *American Journal of Preventive Medicine*, 39, no. 1: 93–98.

54. Nadine Burke Harris, "Iowa, Let's Kick Some ACEs!" Talk given at ACES 360 Conference, Des Moines, IA, October 14, 2013, www.youtube.com/watch?v=8AX6KJXyyxQ.

55. Urie Bronfenbrenner, *The Ecology of Human Development: Experiments by Nature and Design* (Cambridge, MA: President and Fellows of Harvard College, 1979), 7.

56. Ibid., 7

57. The Perryman Group, *Suffer the Little Children: An Assessment of the Economic Cost of Child Maltreatment* (Waco, TX: Author, 2014), 1, www.perrymangroup.com/wp-content/uploads/Perryman_Child_Maltreatment_Report.pdf.

58. M. Ray Perryman, "Cost of Child Abuse Is High, Economically and Physically," *Midland Reporter-Telegram*, November 22, 2014, www.mrt.com/business/article_eeef7e7e-72b2-11e4-881e-e7971e98756e.html.

59. Stephen Holden, "Images That Dare You to Turn Away," *New York Times*, November 11, 2014, www.nytimes.com/2014/11/12/movies/the-doc-nyc-film-festival-returns.html?_r=0.

60. Holbrook Mohr and Garance Burke, "AP: Abused Kids Die As Officials Fail to Protect," *Washington Times*, December 22, 2014, www.washingtontimes.com/news/2014/dec/22/ap-abused-kids-die-as-officials-fail-to-protect/?page=all.

61. Perryman, *Suffer the Little Children*, 9.

62. See the Perryman Group, *Hunger: Economic Effects and the Possibility of a Solution*, 2014, perrymangroup.com/wp-content/uploads/hunger_infographic.png, or *Hunger—Economic Perspectives or Sustainable Solutions* (Waco, TX: Author, 2014), 6–8, perrymangroup.com/wp-content/uploads/Perryman-Hunger-Report.pdf.

63. Ibid.

64. Feeding America, *Map the Meal Gap: Highlight of Findings for Overall and Child Food Insecurity* (Chicago, IL: Author, 2014), www.feedingamerica.org/hunger-in-america/our-research/map-the-meal-gap/2012/2012-mapthemealgap-exec-summary.pdf.

65. Ibid.

66. Ibid., 15; Susan Ochshorn, "Children in Poverty," *ECE Policy Matters*, February 10, 2011, www.ecepolicymatters.com/archives/446; R. Blank and M. Greenberg, "Improving the Measurement of Poverty" (Washington, DC: The Hamilton Project/Brookings Institution, 2008), www.brookings.edu/~/media/Research/Files/Papers/2008/12/poverty-measurement-blank/12_poverty_measurement_blank.PDF.

67. Alisah Coleman-Jensen, Christian Gregory, and Anita Singh, *Household Food Security in the United States in 2013*, Economic Research Service Report No. 173, U.S. Dept. of Agriculture, 2013, www.ers.usda.gov/media/1565415/err173.pdf.

68. Zoe Neuberger and Bob Greenstein, "The Impact of Sequestration on WIC: Will WIC Be Able to Serve All Eligible Low-Income Women and Young Children Who Apply?" (Washington, DC: Center on Budget and Policy Priorities, April 11, 2013), www.cbpp.org/files/2-26-13fa.pdf.

69. Ibid., 1–3

70. Ibid.

71. Shirley Burggraf, *The Feminine Economy and Economic Man: Reviving the Role of Family in the Postindustrial Age* (New York: Basic Books, 1996), 81.

72. Ibid., 1.

73. Ellen L. Bassuk et al., *America's Youngest Outcasts: A Report Card on Child Homelessness* (Waltham, MA: National Center on Family Homelessness at American Institutes for Research, 2014), www.homelesschildrenamerica.org /mediadocs/280.pdf.

74. Onion, "Report Finds More Americans Putting Off Children Until Companies Are Ready," June 24, 2014, www.theonion.com/articles/report-finds-more -americans-putting-off-children-u,36354/.

75. Susan Ochshorn and Curtis Skinner, "Strengthening 21st-Century Families: The Case for Paid Family Leave," *Spotlight on Poverty and Opportunity*, February 19, 2013, www.spotlightonpoverty.org/ExclusiveCommentary.aspx?id =c23d766a-de84-4620-b2da-7a6d3b681eab; Ann Crittenden, *The Price of Motherhood: Why the Most Important Job in the World is Still the Least Valued* (New York: Henry Holt, 2001), 2.

76. Human Rights Watch, *Failing Its Families: Lack of Paid Leave and Work-Family Supports in the U.S.*, 2011, www.hrw.org/sites/default/files/reports /us0211webwcover.pdf.

77. Helena Lee, "Why Finnish Babies Sleep in Cardboard Boxes," BBC *News Magazine*, June 4, 2013, www.bbc.com/news/magazine-22751415.

78. Ibid.

79. Troy Machir, "Babies Born at Columbus Hospital on Thursday to Get Special Bowl Gift," *Sporting News*, December 30, 2014, www.sportingnews.com /ncaa-football/story/2014-12-30/ohio-state-babies-beat-bama-blanket-new-years -day-sugar-bowl-college-football-playoff.

80. Brigid Schulte, "The 'Second Shift' at 25: Q & A with Arlie Hochschild," *Washington Post*, August 6, 2014, www.washingtonpost.com/blogs/she-the-people /wp/2014/08/06/the-second-shift-at-25-q-a-with-arlie-hochschild/.

81. Maria Shriver, *The Shriver Report: A Women's Nation Pushes Back from the Brink: Executive Summary,* January 12, 2014, shriverreport.org/a-womans -nation-pushes-back-from-the-brink-executive-summary-maria-shriver/

82. Jessica Spark, "New Dads Likely to Take Paternity Leave If Paid Time Is Offered," *Wall Street Journal*, July 8, 2014, blogs.wsj.com/atwork/2014/07/08 /new-dads-likely-to-take-paternity-leave-if-paid-time-is-offered/.

83. B. Harrington et al., *The New Dad: Take Your Leave*, Boston College Center for Work and Family. www.thenewdad.org/yahoo_site_admin/assets/docs /BCCWF_The_New_Dad_2014_FINAL.157170735.pdf.

84. Susan Ochshorn and Curtis Skinner (2012), *Building a Competitive Future Right from the Start: How Paid Leave Strengthens 21st Century Families* (New York: National Center for Children in Poverty, Mailman School of Public Health, Columbia University, 2014), 3–27, www.nccp.org/publications/pub_1071.html.

85. Koa Beck, "Be Jealous: A Week in a Finnish Mother's Maternity Leave," *Mommyish*, April 20, 2012, www.mommyish.com/2012/04/20/be-jealous-a-week-in-a-finnish-mothers-maternity-leave-300/.

86. Ibid.

87. National Partnership for Women and Families, *Expecting Better: A State-by-State Analysis of Laws That Help New Parents*, 2014, www.nationalpartnership.org/research-library/work-family/expecting-better-2014.pdf.

88. Ibid., 21.

89. Nina Totenberg, "Did UPS Discriminate Against a Pregnant Worker By Letting Her Go?" *Morning Edition*, National Public Radio, December 3, 2014, www.npr.org/2014/12/03/367835679/did-ups-discriminate-against-a-pregnant-worker-by-letting-her-go.

90. U.S. Department of Labor, "Working Families Across the Country: Highlights of the Department of Labor's Regional Forums," Fact Sheet, June 2014, www.dol.gov/wb/Regional_Forums_Summary.pdf.

91. Thomas E. Perez, "The Most Important Family Value," *White House Blog*, May 27, 2014, www.whitehouse.gov/blog/2014/05/27/most-important-family-value-0; S. Ochshorn, "A Moment of Conscience: Toward a Family-Friendly U.S.A.," *ECE Policy Matters*, June 23, 2014, www.ecepolicymatters.com/archives/2407.

92. Valerie Jarrett, "Why We Think Paid Family Leave Is a Worker's Right, Not a Privilege," *LinkedIn*, January 14, 2015, www.linkedin.com/pulse/why-we-think-paid-leave-workers-right-privilege-valerie-jarrett.

93. National Partnership for Women and Families, *Expecting Better*, (Washington, DC: Author, 2014)3, www.nationalpartnership.org/research-library/work-family/expecting-better-2014.pdf.

94. See Institute for Advanced Studies in Culture, "The Moral Lives of Children Project," www.iasc-culture.org/research_moral_lives_of_children.php.

95. Articles from *Hedgehog Review* 16, no. 3 (2014): Wilfrid M. McClay, "The Great War and the Future of Progress"; J. E. Davis, "Post-Prozac Pathography," both at www.iasc-culture.org/THR/hedgehog_review_2014-Fall.php.

96. L. D. Aslaugh, "Picturing the Poor: Photographs of Poverty in America," *Hedgehog Review* 16, no 3 (2014), www.iasc-culture.org/THR/hedgehog_review_2014-Fall.php

97. Robert Coles, *The Moral Intelligence of Children: How to Raise a Moral Child* (New York: Penguin Group, 1998); see "A Message from Ruby," Ruby Bridges Foundation, rubybridgesfoundation.org/welcome/a-message-from-ruby/.

98. Valerie Polakow, *Lives on the Edge: Single Mothers and Their Children in the Other America* (Chicago: University of Chicago Press, 1993), 46.

99. Ibid., 46.

100. Richard V. Reeves and Kimberly Howard, *The Parenting Gap*, introduction, Brookings Institution, 2013, www.brookings.edu/~/media/research/files/papers/2013/09/09%20parenting%20gap%20social%20mobility%20wellbeing%20reeves/09%20parenting%20gap%20social%20mobility%20wellbeing%20reeves.pdf; John Locke, "Some Thoughts Concerning Education," in *Library of Education, Volume I* (Boston: Gray & Bowen, 1830), 31.

101. Ibid., 4.

102. Ibid, introduction, n.p.

103. Isabel V. Sawhill and Joanna Venator, "Changing the Default to Improve Families' Opportunity," *Social Mobility Memos*, Brookings Institution, October 20, 2014, www.brookings.edu/blogs/social-mobility-memos/posts/2014/10/20-improve-families-opportunity-sawhill.

104. Erica Reischer, "When It Takes a Dentist's Chair to Disconnect," *Motherlode*, December 31, 2014, parenting.blogs.nytimes.com/2014/12/31/when-it-takes-a-dentists-chair-to-disconnect/.

105. Michael C. Barth, *Healthy Steps at 15: The Past and Future of an Innovative Preventive Care Model for Young Children* (Commonwealth Fund, 2010), 1, www.commonwealthfund.org/~/media/Files/Publications/Fund%20Report/2010/Dec/1458_Barth_Healthy_Steps_at_15.pdf.

106. Rahil D. Briggs et al., "Social-Emotional Screening for Infants and Toddlers in Primary Care," *Pediatrics*, January 9, 2012, doi:10.1542/peds.2010-2211, pediatrics.aappublications.org/content/129/2/e377.full.pdf.

Chapter 2

1. Susan Ochshorn, "Fishing Naked in Finland: What've PISA Scores Got to Do with It?" *Huffington Post*, November 30, 2011, www.huffingtonpost.com/susan-ochshorn/fishing-naked-in-finland-_b_1119626.html.

2. Christine Gross-Loh, "Finnish Education Chief: 'We Created a School System Based on Equality,'" *Atlantic*, March 17, 2014, www.theatlantic.com/education/archive/2014/03/finnish-education-chief-we-created-a-school-system-based-on-equality/284427/.

3. Barack Obama, "Inaugural Address," January 21, 2013, www.whitehouse.gov/the-press-office/2013/01/21/inaugural-address-president-barack-obama.

4. Susan Ochshorn, "Equity and the Opportunity Gap: The Heart of the Matter," *ECE Policy Matters*, November 18, 2013, www.ecepolicymatters.com/archives/1880.

5. Deroy Murdock, "Obama Proudly Declares Class War," *National Review*, October 3, 2011, www.nationalreview.com/articles/278930/obama-proudly-declares-class-war-deroy-murdock; See "Slumdogs vs. Millionaires." *The Daily Show with Jon Stewart*, January 9, 2014, thedailyshow.cc.com/videos/rlp7xz/slumdogs-vs-millionaires.

6. H. Luke Shaefer and Kathryn Edin, "Extreme Poverty in the United States, 1996 to 2011," Policy Brief 28, University of Michigan, Gerald R. Ford School of

Public Policy (National Poverty Center, 2012), www.npc.umich.edu/publications /policy_briefs/brief28/policybrief28.pdf.

7. UNICEF, "Child Well-Being in Rich Countries: A Comparative Overview," *Innocenti Report Card 11* (Florence, Italy: Office of Research, 2013), www.unicef-irc.org/publications/683; I. Gill, "Romania Has a Great Advantage on Developing Countries: It Is Part of the Most Important Economic Club in the World, the EU," *News,* World Bank, June 24, 2013, www.worldbank.org/en/news/opinion /2013/06/24/romania-has-a-great-advantage-on-developing-countries-it-is-part -of-the-most-important-economic-club-in-the-world-the-eu.

8. See the Declaration of Independence of the United States, 1776.

9. Cornel West and Tavis Smiley, *The Rich and the Rest of Us: A Poverty Manifesto* (New York: Smiley Books, 2012).

10. Emmanuel Saez, "Striking It Richer: The Evolution of Top Incomes in the United States," University of California, Berkeley, 2013, eml.berkeley.edu/~saez /saez-UStopincomes-2012.pdf.

11. Children's Defense Fund, *The State of America's Children,* 2014, www .childrensdefense.org/child-research-data-publications/state-of-americas-children/.

12. Schulyer Center for Analysis and Advocacy, "Growing Up in Poverty in America," Policy Forum, Albany, NY, November 7, 2013; Jonathan Kozol, *Savage Inequalities: Children in America's Schools* (New York: Random House, 1991).

13. See Jeff Yang, "Stephen Colbert, Racism, and the Weaponized Hashtag." *Wall Street Journal,* March 29, 2014, blogs.wsj.com/speakeasy/2014/03/29/stephen -colbert-racism-and-the-weaponized-hashtag/.

14. Stephen Bagnato et al., "Pay for Success Social Impact Finance: Theory and Practice," Human Capital and Economic Opportunity Global Working Group, October 7, 2013, hceconomics.uchicago.edu/sites/default/files/pdf/events /PayforSuccess2013Transcript.pdf.

15. Low Income Investment Fund "Low Income Investment Fund Releases First-of-its-Kind Social Impact Calculator Tool," September 4, 2014, www.liifund.org/ news/post/low-income-investment-fund-releases-first-of-its-kind-social-impact -calculator-tool/.

16. Center for Law and Social Policy, "What's Next? The Agenda for Reducing Poverty and Expanding Opportunity," 2014, www.clasp.org/whats-next; www .clasp.org/news-room/news-releases/clasp-launches-new-online-commentary.

17. Raj Chetty et al., *Is the United States Still a Land of Opportunity? Recent Trends in Intergenerational Mobility,* Working Paper 19844 (Cambridge, MA: National Bureau of Economic Research, 2014), 1–14, www.nber.org/papers/ w19844.

18. See the Equality of Opportunity Project, "Upward Mobility in the 50 Biggest Metro Areas: The Top Ten and Bottom Ten," www.equality-of-opportunity.org/.

19. See OECD, *Economic Policy Reforms 2010: Going for Growth* (OECD Publishing, 2010), www.oecd-ilibrary.org/economics/economic-policy-reforms-2010 _growth-2010-en.

20. Equality of Opportunity, "Upward Mobility."

21. Jens Manual Krogstad, "One-in-Four Native-Americans and Alaska Natives Are Living in Poverty," Pew Research Center, June 13, 2014, www.pewresearch.org /fact-tank/2014/06/13/1-in-4-native-americans-and-alaska-natives-are-living-in -poverty/.

22. Chetty et al., *Is the United States Still a Land of Opportunity?*

23. U.S. Department of Education, "Equity of Opportunity," webpage, www .ed.gov/equity.

24. Paul E. Barton and Richard J. Coley, *The Black-White Achievement Gap: When Progress Stopped*, (Princeton, NJ: Educational Testing Service, 2010), 7, www.ets.org/Media/Research/pdf/PICBWGAP.pdf.

25. Linda Darling-Hammond, *The Flat World and Education: How America's Commitment to Equity Will Determine Our Future*, (New York: Teachers College Press. 2010), 7–8.

26. Jimmy Carter, *Palestine: Peace not Apartheid*, (New York: Simon & Schuster, 2007).

27. Kelsey Sheehy, "Graduation Rates Dropping Among Native American Students." *U.S. News and World Report*, June 6, 2013, www.usnews.com/education /high-schools/articles/2013/06/06/graduation-rates-dropping-among-native -american-students; "2013 Data Kids Count Data Book: State Trends in Child Well-Being," Annie E. Casey Foundation (2013), www.aecf.org/m/resourcedoc /AECF-2013KIDSCOUNTDataBook-2013.pdf.

28. Darling-Hammond, *Flat World and Education*, 8.

29. Richard J. Colegy and Bruce Baker, *Poverty and Education: Finding the Way Forward*, (Princeton, NJ: Educational Testing Service, 2013), www.ets.org/s /research/pdf/poverty_and_education_report.pdf.

30. See "Education and Poverty: Confronting the Evidence," Helen Ladd's presidential speech to the Association for Public Policy Analysis and Management, *Journal of Policy Analysis and Management*, 31, no. 2 (2012): 203–227, files.eric .ed.gov/fulltext/ED536952.pdf

31. Lalita Clozel, "U.S. Schools Plagued by Inequality Along Racial Lines, Study Finds." *Los Angeles Times*, March 21, 2014, www.latimes.com/nation /la-na-schools-inequalities-20140322,0,4359998.story#axzz2wztewSsS.

32. U.S. Department of Education, "Expansive Survey of America's Public Schools Reveals Troubling Racial Disparities," 2014, www.ed.gov/news/press-releases /expansive-survey-americas-public-schools-reveals-troubling-racial-disparities.

33. Ibid.

34. Laura Yuen, "Years After Somali Men Left Minn., Youth Decry Extremism." Minnesota Public Radio, November 8, 2011, www.mprnews.org/story /2011/11/08/young-minnesota-somalis-decry-extremism.

35. See Isuroon, "The Somali Population in Minnesota: Characteristics and Disparities," www.isuroon.org/the-somali-population-in-minnesota/.

36. See ThirdEyeMom, "A New American: The Rise of Somalis in Minnesota," blog, September 9, 2013, thirdeyemom.com/2013/09/30/a-new-american-the-rise -of-somalis-in-minnesota/.

37. Ibid.

38. Annie E. Casey Foundation, *Race for Results: Building a Path to Opportunity for All Children*, 2014, www.aecf.org/m/resourcedoc/AECF-RaceforResults-2014.pdf.

39. Pew Research Center, *A Nation of Immigrants: A Portrait of the 40 Million, Including 11 Million Unauthorized*, Hispanic Trends Project, January 29, 2013, www.pewhispanic.org/2013/01/29/a-nation-of-immigrants/; see Hirokazu Yoshikawa, *Immigrants Raising Citizens: Undocumented Parents and Their Children* (New York: Russell Sage, 2012).

40. Annie E. Casey Foundation, *Race for Results*; F. Bass, "Nonwhite U.S. Births Become the Majority for First Time," *Bloomberg.com*, May 17, 2012, www.bloomberg.com/news/2012-05-17/non-white-u-s-births-become-the-majority-for-first-time.html.

41. Janet Currie and Robert Kahn, "Children with Disabilities: Introducing the Issue," in *The Future of Children: Children with Disabilities*, 22, no. 1 (2012), futureofchildren.org/futureofchildren/publications/docs/22_01_FullJournal.pdf; Roy Grant and Elizabeth A. Isakson, (2012), "Regional Variations in Early Intervention Utilization for Children with Developmental Delay," *Maternal and Child Health Journal* 15, no. 1 (2012).

42. Susan Ochshorn, "Political Correctness, or Equality, for Heather and Her Two Mommies?" *Huffington Post*, March 29, 2013, www.huffingtonpost.com/susan-ochshorn/political-correctness-or-_b_2966427.html.

43. See Marian Wright Edelman, "Ending the Cradle-to-Prison Pipeline and Mass Incarceration—the New American Jim Crow," *Child Watch*, 2012, www.childrensdefense.org/newsroom/child-watch-columns/child-watch-documents/ending-cradle-to-prison-pipeline.html; Foundation for Child Development, *Diverse Children: Race, Ethnicity, and Immigration in America's New Non-Majority Generation*, 2013, fcd-us.org/whats-new/diverse-children-race-ethnicity-and-immigration-americas-new-non-majority-generation; Lakota People's Law Project, "Lakota Child Rescue Project," website, lakotalaw.org/lakota-child-rescue-project.

44. Annie E. Casey Foundation, *The State of Washington's Children*, 2013, kidscountwa.org/wp-content/uploads/2013/06/State_of_Washington_Children_2013.pdf.

45. Ibid.

46. Sylvia L. M. Martinez and John L. Rury, "From 'Culturally Deprived' to 'At Risk': The Politics of Popular Expression and Educational Inequality in the United States, 1960–1985," *Teachers College Record* 114, no. 6 (2012); Cited in Diane Ravitch, *The Troubled Crusade: American Education, 1945–1980*, (New York: Basic Books, 1983) 152–153.

47. Barbara Bowman, "The State of the Black Child,", in *Being Black Is Not a Risk Factor: A Strengths-Based Look at the State of the Black Child* (Washington, DC: National Black Child Development Institute2013); Barbara T. Bowman, M. Suzanne Donovan, and M. Susan Burns, eds., (2000), *Eager to Learn: Educating Our Preschoolers* (Washington, DC: National Academy Press, 2000).

48. *Being Black Is Not a Risk Factor*, 2.

49. Susan Ochshorn, "Rewriting NCLB: The Promise of Neighborhoods." *Huffington Post*, March 17, 2011, www.huffingtonpost.com/susan-ochshorn/rewriting-nclb-the-promis_b_836710.html.

50. Sasha Abramsky, *The American Way of Poverty: How the Other Half Still Lives* (New York: Nation Books, 2013), 44.

51. Annette Lareau, *Unequal Childhoods: Class, Race, and Family Life* (Berkeley: University of California Press, 2003); Elementary and Secondary Education Act, 107th Congress Public Law print of PL 107-110, No Child Left Behind Act of 2001, www2.ed.gov/policy/elsec/leg/esea02/107-110.pdf.

52. Linda M. Espinosa, *Getting It Right for Young Children from Diverse Backgrounds: Applying Research to Improve Practice* (Boston, MA: Pearson, 2010), iii.

53. Felicia Delaney, *Being Black is Not a Risk Factor*, (Washington, DC: National Black Child Development Institute, 2013), 1, www.nbcdi.org/sites/default/files/resource-files/Being%20Black%20Is%20Not%20a%20Risk%20Factor_0.pdf.

54. Mark Hugo Lopez, "In 2014, Latinos Will Surpass Whites as Largest Racial/Ethnic Group in California," Pew Research Center web page, January 24, 2014, www.pewresearch.org/fact-tank/2014/01/24/in-2014-latinos-will-surpass-whites-as-largest-racialethnic-group-in-california/.

55. Robert Crosnoe, "Early Childcare and the School Readiness of Children from Mexican Immigrant Families," *International Migration Review* 41, no. 1 (2007): 152–181.

56. Linda M. Espinosa, *Challenging Common Myths About Young English Language Learners*, Foundation for Child Development, 2008, fcd-us.org/sites/default/files/MythsOfTeachingELLsEspinosa.pdf.

57. Julie Blair, "Sesame Street Explains Parents' Incarceration to Preschoolers," *Education Week*, April 4, 2014, blogs.edweek.org/edweek/early_years/2014/04/sesame_street_explains_parents_incarceration_to_preschoolers.html; Rebecca Klein, "The School-to-Prison Pipeline Can Start Even Before Kindergarten, Mother Points Out," *Huffington Post*, July 28, 2014, www.huffingtonpost.com/2014/07/28/racist-preschool-suspensions_n_5627160.html.

58. L. Layton and M. A. Chandler, "De Blasio Aims to Reverse Education Policies in New York," *Washington Post*, November 8, 2013, www.washingtonpost.com/local/education/de-blasio-aims-to-reverse-education-policies-in-new-york/2013/11/08/5de6d24c-47f2-11e3-b6f8-3782ff6cb769_story.html.

59. J. Hernandez, "A Mayoral Hopeful Now, de Blasio Was Once a Young Leftist," *New York Times*, September 22, 2013, www.nytimes.com/2013/09/23/nyregion/a-mayoral-hopeful-now-de-blasio-was-once-a-young-leftist.html; Susan Ochshorn, "Go West, Bill de Blasio: Land of Inequality-Busting," *Huffington Post*, December 4, 2013, www.huffingtonpost.com/susan-ochshorn/go-west-bill-de-blasio_b_4350966.html.

60. L. Mahapatra, "Billionaires: New York City Remains Favorite City for the Richest Individuals in the World," *International Business Times*, November 7,

2013, www.ibtimes.com/billionaires-new-york-city-remains-favored-city-richest-individuals-world-interactive-map-1461018.

61. Laird W. Bergad, "The Concentration of Wealth in New York City: Changes in the Structure of Household Income by Race/Ethnic Groups and Latino Nationalities 1990–2010," (New York: Center for Latin American, Caribbean and Latino Studies, Graduate Center, City University of New York, 2014), 10, clacls.gc.cuny.edu/files/2014/01/Household-Income-Concentration-in-NYC-1990-2010.pdf.

62. Robert Frank, "Cities with the Most Millionaires per Capita," CNBC, July 22, 2014, www.cnbc.com/id/101856833.

63. Tod Newcombe, "Can Mayors Really Be Robin Hood," *Governing the States and Localities Urban Notebook,* February 5, 2014, www.governing.com/columns/urban-notebook/col-mayor-robin-hood-income-equality-cities.html.

64. Patrick McGheehan, "De Blasio Taps a Goldman Executive as Deputy Mayor of Housing," *New York Times,* December 23, 2013, www.nytimes.com/2013/12/24/nyregion/de-blasio-taps-a-goldman-executive-as-deputy-mayor-of-housing.html.

65. Michael A. Rebell et al., *Making Prekindergarten Truly Universal in New York: A Statewide Roadmap*, Center for Children's Initiatives and the Campaign for Educational Equity, 2013, www.centerforchildrensinitiatives.org/images/Cheri/new%20york%20prek%20long%20report.pdf.

66. Susan Ochshorn, "Sophia Pappas: Sisyphus on a Pre-K Mission," *ECE Policy Matters*, May 19, 2014, www.ecepolicymatters.com/archives/2276.

67. See *Ready to Launch: New York City's Implementation Plan for Free, High-Quality, Full-Day Universal Pre-Kindergarten*, Office of the Mayor, Office of Management and Budget, January 2014, www1.nyc.gov/assets/home/downloads/pdf/reports/2014/Ready-to-Launch-NYCs-Implementation-Plan-for-Free-High-Quality-Full-Day-Universal-Pre-Kindergarten.pdf.

68. Citizens' Committee for Children of New York, "Snapshot of NYC Children and Families in 2013," 2014, www.cccnewyork.org/data-and-reports/publications/snapshot-of-nyc-children-and-families-in-2013/; Citizens Committee for Children, "Concentrated Poverty in New York City: An Analysis of the Changing Geographical Patterns of Poverty," April, 2012, www.cccnewyork.org/wp-content/publications/CCCReport.ConcentratedPoverty.April-2012.pdf; U.S. Census Bureau, Areas with Concentrated Poverty: 2006–2010, American Community Survey Briefs, December 2011, www.census.gov/prod/2011pubs/acsbr10-17.pdf.

69. Susan Ochshorn, "Planning for Pre-K Perfection," *Weekly Wonk* (Washington, DC: New America, September 18, 2014), weeklywonk.newamerica.net/articles/planning-pre-k-perfection/.

70. Errol Louis, "Segregation: Our Enduring Shame," *New York Daily News,* April 10, 2014, www.nydailynews.com/opinion/segregation-enduring-shame-article-1.1751241; For an analysis of equitable access to preschool in the early stages of implementation of de Blasio's initiative, see Bruce Fuller and Elise Castillo, *Expanding Preschool in New York City—Lifting Poor Children or Middling Families?* (Berkeley: Institute of Human Development, University of California,

Berkeley, March 2015), gse.berkeley.edu/sites/default/files/users/bruce-fuller/NYC _PreK_Expansion_Berkeley_Study_25_Feb_2015.pdf.

71. J. Kucsera and G. Orfield, "New York State's Extreme School Segregation: Inequality, Inaction and a Damaged Future," *Civil Rights Project*, March 26, 2014, civilrightsproject.ucla.edu/research/k-12-education/integration-and-diversity /ny-norflet-report-placeholder.

72. Louis, "Segregation: Our Enduring Shame."

73. W. S. Barnett, "Four Reasons the United States Should Offer Every Child a Preschool Education," in *The Pre-K Debates: Current Controversies and Issue*, ed. E. Zigler, W. S. Gilliam, and W. S. Barnett (Baltimore, MD: Paul H. Brookes, 2011), 34–39.

74. David L. Kirp, "The Benefits of Mixing Rich and Poor," *New York Times*, May 10, 2014, opinionator.blogs.nytimes.com/2014/05/10/the-benefits-of-mixing -rich-and-poor/; See also David L. Kirp, *Kids First: Five Big Ideas for Transforming Children's Lives and America's Future* (New York: PublicAffairs, 2011).

75. Amy Rothschild, "How Universal Will de Blasio's Universal Pre-K Be?" *Hechinger Report*, January 13, 2014, hechingerreport.org/content/how-universal -will-de-blasios-universal-pre-k-be_14425/.

76. Kate Tarrant, *Building the Pipeline for a Successful Early Childhood Workforce in New York: A New Policy Agenda* (New York: NYC Early Childhood Professional Development Institute, City University of New York, 2013) earlychild-hoodnyc.org/pdfs/Policy%20Brief%202013.pdf.; Susan Ochshorn and Maria Garcia, *Learning About the Workforce: A Profile of Early Childhood Educators in New York City's Community—and School-Based Centers* (NYC Early Childhood Professional Development Institute, 2007). www.earlychildhoodnyc.org/pdfs/eng /FinalReport.pdf.

Chapter 3

1. Laura J. Colker, "Twelve Characteristics of Effective Early Childhood Teachers," *Beyond the Journal* (March 2008): 1–6,: www.naeyc.org/files/yc/file/200803 /BTJ_Colker.pdf.

2. Haley Sweetland Edwards, "Rotten Apples: It's Nearly Impossible to Fire a Bad Teacher," *Time*, November 3, 2014, time.com/3533556/the-war-on-teacher -tenure/.

3. Rebecca Klein, "Parents, Teachers, Deliver over 100,000 Signatures to *Time* Magazine Demanding Apology," *Huffington Post*, October 30, 2014, www .huffingtonpost.com/2014/10/30/time-magazine-teacher-petition_n_6078092 .html.

4. Bill Raden and Gary Cohn, "The Man Behind *Vergara v. California*," *Capital & Main*, February 20, 2014, capitalandmain.com/david-welch-the-man-behind -vergara-versus-california/; Diane Ravitch, "What Was the Evidence in the Vergara Case? Who Wins? Who Loses?" *Diane Ravitch's Blog*, June 11, 2014, dianeravitch .net/2014/06/11/what-was-the-evidence-in-the-vergara-case-who-wins-who -loses/.

5. Raj Chetty, Jonah N. Friedman, and Jonah E. Rockoff, "Measuring the Impact of Teachers, I: Evaluating Bias in Teacher Value-Added Estimates," Working Paper 19423, National Bureau of Economic Research, Cambridge, MA, September 2013, www.hks.harvard.edu/fs/jfriedm/value_added1.pdf; Economic Policy Institute, "Problems with the Use of Student Test Scores to Evaluate Teachers," Briefing Paper 27, August 29, 2010, www.epi.org/publication/bp278/.

6. *The Verge* is one of a growing number of online media platforms that cover technology, science, art, and culture. Casey Newton, "Why Twitter's New Head of Product Could Be the One to Fix It," *The Verge*, October 30, 2014, www.theverge.com/2014/10/30/7134235/why-twitters-new-head-of-product-could-be-the-one-to-fix-it.

7. See U.S. Department of Education, "Laws and Guidance/Elementary and Secondary Education," www2.ed.gov/policy/elsec/leg/esea02/beginning.html.

8. Linda Darling-Hammond and Gary Sykes, "Wanted: A National Teacher Supply Policy for Education: The Right Way to Meet the 'Highly Qualified Teacher' Challenge," *Education Policy Analysis Archives* 11, no. 33 (September 17, 2003): 2, epaa.asu.edu/ojs/article/viewFile/261/387.

9. Charles Coble, "No Child Left Behind FAQ: How Will States Define 'Highly Qualified' Teachers?" Education Commission of the States, 2002, www.ecs.org/html/Document.asp?chouseid=4155.

10. Ibid.; See Title IX, Para. A, Sec. 9101, of Public Law 107-110—January 8, 2002, 115 Stat. 1425, www2.ed.gov/policy/elsec/leg/esea02/107-110.pdf.

11. Lisa Delpit, *Other People's Children* (New York: New Press, 2006), 124.

12. National Council for Accreditation of Teacher Education, *Transforming Teacher Education Through Clinical Practice: A National Strategy to Prepare Effective Teachers*, Executive Summary, 2010, ii, www.ncate.org/LinkClick.aspx?fileticket=zzeiB1OoqPk%3D&tabid=715.

13. Ibid., 2.

14. Jal Mehta, "Why American Education Fails: And How Lessons from Abroad Could Improve It," *Foreign Affairs*, May/June 2013, www.foreignaffairs.com/articles/139113/jal-mehta/why-american-education-fails.

15. National Council on Teacher Quality, *Teacher Prep Review* (2013 Report), 6, www.nctq.org/dmsView/Teacher_Prep_Review_2013_Report.

16. Valerie Strauss, "Why the NCTQ Teacher Prep Ratings Are Nonsense," *Washington Post*, June 18, 2013, www.washingtonpost.com/blogs/answer-sheet/wp/2013/06/18/why-the-nctq-teacher-prep-ratings-are-nonsense/. Strauss regularly invites others to publish commentary at her blog, *The Answer Sheet*. This post was written by Linda Darling-Hammond, chair of the California Commission on Teacher Credentialing.

17. Jeff Archer, Kerri A. Kerr, and Robert C. Pianta, "Why Measure Effective Teaching," in *Designing Teacher Evaluation Systems: New Guidance from the Measures of Effective Teaching Project*, ed. Thomas J. Kane, Kerri A. Kerr, Robert C. Pianta (San Francisco: Jossey-Bass, 2014), 1–5.

18. Ibid., 5.

19. Arna H. Jónsdóttir and Marianne Coleman, "Professional Role and Identity of Icelandic Preschool: Effects of Stakeholders' Views," *Early Years* 34, no. 3 (2014), www.academia.edu/7410033/Professional_role_and_identity_of_Icelandic _preschool_teachers_Effects_of_stakeholders_views_2014_; Jennifer J. Chen and Sonja de Groot Kim, "The Quality of Interactive Conversations with Preschoolers from Low-Income Families During Small-Group and Large-Group Activities," *Early Years* 34, no. 3 (2014); Debra Harwood, Audrey Klopper, Ajike Osanyin, and Mary-Louise Vanderlee, "'It's More than Care': Early Childhood Educators' Concepts of Professionalism," *Early Years* 33, no. 1 (2013).

20. Susan Ochshorn, "Shifting the Paradigm of ECE Professionalism," *ECE Policy Matters*, January 20, 2012, www.ecepolicymatters.com/archives/685.

21. Susan Ochshorn, "Preschool Teacher Sells Chili to Make Ends Meet: Where Are Our Values?" *Huffington Post*, February 26, 2012, www.huffingtonpost.com /susan-ochshorn/early-childhood-care_b_1255574.html. For an extended discussion of the early childhood field's identity crisis, see Stacie G. Goffin and Valora Washington, *Ready or Not: Leadership Choices in Early Care and Education* (New York: Teachers College Press, 2007).

22. Rachel Langford, "Making a Difference in the Lives of Young Children: A Critical Analysis of a Pedagogical Discourse for Motivating Young Women to Become Early Childhood Educators," *Canadian Journal of Education* 31, no. 1 (2008): 78–101.

23. Ibid., 87.

24. I discuss this battle in "Shifting the Paradigm of ECE Professionalism," *ECE Policy Matters*, January 20, 2012, www.ecepolicymatters.com/archives/685.

25. Nancy Folbre, *The Invisible Heart: Economics and Family Values* (New York: New Press, 2002), 9.

26. Ibid., xiii, xx.

27. Ibid., 73.

28. See caringeconomy.org/about/for a discussion of the Caring Economy Campaign's mission ; Riane Eisler and Kimberly Otis, "Unpaid and Undervalued Care Work Keeps Women on the Brink," *Shriver Report: A Woman's Nation Pushes Back from the Brink*, January 22, 2014, shriverreport.org/unpaid-and-undervalued-care -work-keeps-women-on-the-brink/; Riane Tennenhaus Eisler, *The Real Wealth of Nations: Creating a Caring Economics* (San Francisco, CA: Berrett-Koehler, 2008).

29. For this brief discussion of the feminization of the teaching workforce, I am indebted to Dana Goldstein's *The Teacher Wars: A History of America's Most Embattled Profession* (New York: Doubleday, 2014), which helped me unpack the identity of the "Mother-Teacher." See Catharine Beecher, "An Essay on the Education of Female Teachers," *Classics in the Education of Girls and Women* (1834): 285–295.

30. See Melissa Sherfinski, "Contextualizing the Tools of a Classical and Christian Homeschooling Mother-Teacher," *Curriculum Inquiry* 4, no. 2 (March 2014): 169–203, onlinelibrary.wiley.com/doi:10.1111/curi.12046/abstract, and Milton Gaither, "Classical and Christian: A Case Study of One Mother-Teacher,"

International Center for Home Education Research Reviews, April 4, 2014, icher.org /blog/?p=1202.

31. Goldstein, *Teacher Wars*, 15.

32. Horace Mann, *A Few Thoughts on the Powers and Duties of Woman: Two Lectures* (Syracuse, NY: Hall, Mills, 1853), 38

33. Redding S. Sugg, *Motherteacher: The Feminization of American Education* (Charlottesville: University of Virginia Press, 1978), 81, cited in Goldstein, *Teacher Wars*, 26.

34. "In the School of Anti-Slavery, 1895–1906," in *The Selected Papers of Elizabeth Cady Stanton and Susan B. Anthony, vol. 1*, ed. Ann D. Gordon (New Brunswick, NJ: Rutgers University Press, 1997), 57–58.

35. Marcy Whitebook and Rory Darrah, "Raises and Respect for Early Childhood Teachers: A Four-Decade Perspective," *Exchange*, July/August 2013, 16–22; for an extended discussion, see Marcy Whitebook, *Working for Worthy Wages: The Child Care Compensation Movement, 1970–2001*, revised ed. (University of California, Berkeley, Institute of Industrial Relations, Center for the Study of Child Care Employment, 2002).

36. Marcy Whitebook, Carollee Howes, and Deborah Phillips, *Who Cares? Child Care Teachers and the Quality of Care in America, Final Report: National Child Care Staffing Study* (Berkeley, CA: Child Care Employee Project), 49, www .irle.berkeley.edu/cscce/wp-content/uploads/2010/07/Who-Cares-full-report.pdf.

37. Ibid., 67; for a discussion of the effects of high job turnover in child care programs on the healthy development of children, especially for those from families of low socioeconomic status, see National Scientific Council on the Developing Child, *Excessive Stress Disrupts the Architecture of the Developing Brain: Working Paper 3*, updated ed., developingchild.harvard.edu/resources/reports_and_working _papers/working_papers/wp3/.

38. Marcy Whitebook, Deborah Phillips, and Carollee Howes, *Worthy Work: STILL Unlivable Wages: The Early Childhood Workforce 25 Years After the National Child Care Staffing Study, Executive Summary*, (Berkeley: Center for the Study of Child Care Employment, University of California, Berkeley, 2014), www .irle.berkeley.edu/cscce/wp-content/uploads/2014/11/ReportFINAL.pdf.

39. Ibid., 2; see also Susan Ochshorn, "Preschool Teacher Sells Chili to Make Ends Meet: Where Are Our Values?" *Huffington Post*, February 6, 2012, www .huffingtonpost.com/susan-ochshorn/early-childhood-care_b_1255574.html.

40. Whitebook et al., *Worthy Work: STILL Unlivable Wages—The early childhood workforce 25 years after the National Child Care Staffing Study* (Executive Summary, Berkeley: Center for the Study of Child Care Employment, Institute for Research on Labor and Employment, University of California, Berkeley, 2014), 5, www.irle.berkeley.edu/cscce/wp-content/uploads/2014/11/Executive -Summary-Final.pdf.

41. For a history of the child care compensation movement, including the Worthy Wage Campaign, see Whitebook, *Working for Worthy Wages*, 29, www.irle .berkeley.edu/cscce/wp-content/uploads/2010/07/worthywages.pdf.

42. TNTP, *Fast Start: Training Better Teachers Faster with Practice, Focus and Feedback*, 2014, tntp.org/publications/view/fast-start-training-better-teachers -faster-with-focus-practice-and-feedback and tntp.org/about-tntp.

43. Laura Bornfreund, *Getting in Sync: Revamping Licensing and Preparation for Teachers in Pre-K, Kindergarten, and the Early Grades* (Washington, DC: New America Foundation, 2011), www.newamerica.net/publications/policy/getting_in _sync; see also Whitebook et al., *By Default or By Design? Variations in Higher Education Programs for Early Care and Education Teachers and Their Implications for Research Methodology, Policy, and Practice*, (Berkeley: Center for the Study of Child Care Employment, University of California, Berkeley, 2012), www.irle.berkeley.edu /cscce/wp-content/uploads/2012/01/ByDefaultOrByDesign_FullReport_2012.pdf.

44. Susan Ochshorn, *Forging a New Framework for Professional Development: A Report on "The Science of Professional Development in Early Childhood Education: A National Summit,"* (Washington, DC: ZERO TO THREE, 2011), 1.

45. Ibid., 10.

46. Susan Ochshorn, "To B.A. or not to B.A.: That Is Not the Question," *ECE Policy Matters*, March 18, 2011, www.ecepolicymatters.com/archives/471.

47. Stephen Herzenberg, Mark Price, and David Bradley, *Losing Ground in Early Childhood Education: Declining Workforce Qualifications in an Expanding Industry, 1979–2004*, (Washington, DC: Economic Policy Institute, 2005), s2.epi .org/files/page/-/old/studies/ece/losing_ground-full_text.pdf.

48. Ibid., 1, 13.

49. U.S. Office of Planning, Research, and Evaluation, "Number and Characteristics of Early Care and Education (ECE) Teachers and Caregivers: Initial Findings from the National Survey of Early Care and Education," NSECE Research Brief No. 38, October 2013, www.researchconnections.org/childcare/resources /26496/pdf.

50. Marcy Whitebook, *Building a Skilled Teacher Workforce: Shared and Divergent Challenges in Early Care and Education and in Grades K–12* (Bill and Melinda Gates Foundation, 2014), www.irle.berkeley.edu/cscce/wp-content/uploads /2014/09/Building-a-Skilled-Teacher-Workforce_September-2014_9-25.pdf.

51. See Marisa Bueno, Linda Darling-Hammond, and Danielle Gonzales, *A Matter of Degrees: Preparing Teachers for the Pre-K Classroom* (Washington, DC: Pew Center on the States, 2010); W. Steven Barnett, "Better Teachers, Better Preschools: Student Achievement Linked to Teacher Qualifications," *Preschool Policy Matters* (New Brunswick: National Institute for Early Education Research, Rutgers State University of New Jersey, 2005), nieer.org/resources/policybriefs /2.pdf; Barbara T. Bowman, M. S. Donovan, and M. S. Burns, *Eager to Learn: Educating Our Preschoolers* (Washington, DC: National Academy Press, 2000).

52. Susan Ochshorn, "Charter Ed for the Early Childhood Workforce: A Recipe for Disaster," *Huffington Post*, September 15, 2011, www.huffingtonpost .com/susan-ochshorn/charter-ed-for-the-early-childhood-workforce_b_963189 .html; Kevin Carey and Sara Mead, "Beyond Bachelor's: The Case for Charter Colleges of Early Childhood Education," Brookings Institution and

Rockefeller Foundation, August 2011, www.brookings.edu/~/media/research/files/papers/2011/8/25%20education%20mead%20carey/0825_education_mead_carey.

53. See Institute for Health and Human Potential, "Free EQ Quiz," www.ihhp.com/free-eq-quiz/.

54. Andy Hargreaves, "Mixed Emotions: Teachers' Perceptions of Their Interactions with Students," *Teaching and Teacher Education* 16 (2000): 811–826.

55. Ibid., 812; Arlie Hochschild, *The Managed Heart: The Commercialization of Human Feeling* (Berkeley: University of California Press, 1983).

56. Hargreaves, "Mixed Emotions," 824.

57. See Tovah Klein, *How Toddlers Thrive: What Parents Can Do Today for Children Ages 2–5 to Plant the Seeds of Lifelong Success* (New York: Simon and Schuster, 2014); see interview with Tunette Powell, "My Three-Year-Old Was Suspended from Preschool Five Times," *HuffPost Live*, 2014, live.huffingtonpost.com/r/archive/segment/53d808c0fe34445fa2000179.

58. Francis Wardle, "The Challenge of Boys in Our Early Childhood Classrooms," *Early Childhood News*, n.d., www.earlychildhoodnews.com/earlychildhood/article_view.aspx?ArticleID=414; see Grace Manning-Orenstein, *Building Blocks for Reflective Communication: A Guide for Early Care and Education Professionals* (Berkeley, CA: She Writes Press, 2014), for a discussion on emotions and practice.

59. William S. Gilliam, "Implementing Policies to Reduce the Likelihood of Preschool Expulsion," *FCD Policy Brief: Advancing PK–3* (January 7, 2008): 7.

60. Lisa S. Goldstein and Debra Freedman, "Challenges Enacting Caring Teacher Education," *Journal of Teacher Education* 54, no. 4 (November/December 2003): 441–454.

61. Nel Noddings, *The Challenge to Care in Schools: An Alternative Approach to Education*, 2nd ed. (New York: Teachers College Press, 2005), 17.

62. Lisa S. Goldstein and Debra Freedman, "Challenges Enacting Caring Teacher Education," 441.

63. Ibid., 447.

64. Franita Ware, "Warm Demander Pedagogy: Culturally Responsive Teaching that Supports a Culture of Achievement for African American Students," *Urban Education*, 41, no. 4 (July 2006): 438; see also Elizabeth Bondy and Dorene D. Ross, "The Teacher as Warm Demander," *Educational Leadership* 66, no. 1 (2008): 54–58, 438.

65. Franita Ware, "Warm Demander Pedagogy," 438.

66. Tyler Thigpen, "Taking a Relationship-Centered Approach to Education, *Education Week* (September 11, 2013), impact.sp2.upenn.edu/ostrc/doclibrary/documents/TakingaRelationship-CenteredApproachtoEducation.pdf.

67. Carrie R. Leana, "The Missing Link in School Reform," *Stanford Social Innovation Review* (Fall 2011): 2, www.ssireview.org/articles/entry/the_missing_link_in_school_reform.

68. Ibid., 5.

69. Edna K. Shapiro and Nancy Nager, "The Developmental-Interaction Approach to Education: Retrospect and Prospect" (Occasional Paper Series, Bank Street College of Education, New York, April 1999), 5.

70. Conference Group, Bank Street College of Education, October 29, 2014.

71. Stanley I. Greenspan with Nancy Thorndike Greenspan, *The Learning Tree: Overcoming Learning Disabilities from the Ground Up* (Philadelphia, PA: DaCapo Press/Lifelong Books, 2010).

72. See website of the consulting firm Applied Behavioral Strategies (www .appliedbehavioralstrategies.com/what-is-aba.html).

73. See Andrew Krugly, Amanda Stein, and Maribel G. Centeno, "Demystifying Data: Designing and Implementing Data-Driven Systems and Practices for Continuous Quality Improvement," *Zero To Three* 34, no. 3 (2014): 11–19.

Chapter 4

1. For this brief discussion of the origins of the preschool movement, I am indebted to Barbara Beatty, *Preschool Education in America: The Culture of Young Children from the Colonial Era to the Present* (New Haven, CT: Yale University Press, 1995); Johann Amos Comenius, "Comenius' School of Infancy: An Essay on the Education of Youth During the First Six Years," *DC Health* 27 (1828): 3.

2. Shiv Malik, "Early Schooling Damaging Children's Wellbeing, Say Experts." *The Guardian*, September 12, 2013, www.theguardian.com/education /2013/sep/12/early-years-schooling-damaging-wellbeing.

3. Susan Ochshorn, "Racing to the Top and Leaving the Love of Learning Behind," *Huffington Post*, December 10, 2013, www.huffingtonpost.com /susan-ochshorn/racing-to-the-tophttpsblo_b_4412040.html.

4. Susan Ochshorn, "To the Man with the Audacity of Hope: Let's Make Good on Cradle to Career," *Huffington Post*, January 28, 2011, www.huffingtonpost .com/susan-ochshorn/to-the-man-with-the-audac_b_815170.html.

5. Scott Gillum, "Could Falling Test Scores Be A Good Thing?," *Forbes*, January 6, 2014, www.forbes.com/sites/gyro/2014/01/06/could-falling-test-scores-be-a -good-thing-for-the-u-s/

6. Yong Zhao, *World Class Learners: Educating Creative and Entrepreneurial Students* (San Francisco, CA: Corwin Press, 2012).

7. Ken Robinson, "Do Schools Kill Creativity?" YouTube video of a lecture recorded at a TED Conference, January 6, 2007, www.youtube.com/watch?v =iG9CE55wbtY.

8. David Kirp, "Teaching Is Not a Business." *New York Times*, August 16, 2014, www.nytimes.com/2014/08/17/opinion/sunday/teaching-is-not-a-business.html? _r=0; see also Jill Lepore, "The Disruption Machine," *The New Yorker*, June 23, 2014, www.newyorker.com/magazine/2014/06/23/the-disruption-machine.

9. Susan Sirigatti, "Gesturing Predicts School Success," *A Smarter Beginning* (2014), asmarterbeginning.com/gesturing-predicts-childrens-future-success -school/#sthash.m7fX6kam.dpuf.

10. See Sleep'n Sync, website, www.sleepnsync.com/.

11. Julie Blair, "Preschool Game Predicts Academic Success, Researchers Say," *Education Week*, October 8, 2013; see also Megan M. McClelland et al., "Predictors of Early Growth in Academic Achievement: The Head-Toes-Knees-Shoulders Task." *Name: Frontiers in Psychology* 5 (2014): 599.

12. Ibid.

13. Linda Darling-Hammond et al., "Evaluating Teacher Evaluation." *Education Week*, February 29, 2012, www.edweek.org/ew/articles/2012/03/01/kappan _hammond.html; "Progress, Adequate Yearly," *Education Week*, revised, July 18, 2011, www.edweek.org/ew/issues/adequate-yearly-progress/; New York State Education Department, *Annual Professional Performance Review Plan (APPR)*, usny .nysed.gov/rttt/teachers-leaders/plans/docs/mattituck-cutchogue-appr-plan.pdf; New York State Education Department, *Guidance on New York State's Annual Performance Review for Teachers and Principals to Implement Educational Law and the Commissioner's Regulations,* updated July 16, 2014, www.engageny.org/sites /default/files/resource/attachments/appr-field-guidance.pdf.

14. Diane Ravitch, "Breaking News: NEA Delegates Call for Arne Duncan's Resignation." *Diane Ravitch's Blog*, July 4, 2014, dianeravitch.net/2014/07/04 /breaking-news-nea-delegates-pass-resolution-calling-for-arne-duncans -resignation/.

15. Diane Ravitch, "As of Today, More Than 14 Million Page Views on This Blog!" *Diane Ravitch's Blog*, August 18, 2014, dianeravitch.net/2014/08/18/as-of-1 -p-m-today-more-than-14-million-page-views-on-this-blog/ Arne Duncan, "A Back-to-School Conversation with Teachers and School Leaders," *Homeroom: The Official Blog of the U.S. Department of Education*, 2014, www.ed.gov/blog/2014 /08/a-back-to-school-conversation-with-teachers-and-school-leaders/.

16. David Tyack and Larry Cuban, *Tinkering Toward Utopia: A Century of Public School Reform* (Cambridge, MA: Harvard University Press, 1995).

17. Ibid., 1.

18. National Commission on Excellence in Education, *A Nation at Risk: The Imperative for Educational Reform*, (Washington, DC: Author, 1983), datacenter .spps.org/uploads/sotw_a_nation_at_risk_1983.pdf.

19. See National Aeronautics and Space Administration website, Sputnik 1: NSSDC/COSPAR ID: 1957-001B, nssdc.gsfc.nasa.gov/nmc/spacecraftDisplay .do?id=1957-001B.

20. See "Sputnik Crisis," en.wikipedia.org/wiki/Sputnik_crisis.

21. National Education Goals Panel, *Data for the National Education Goals Report, Vol. 2. State Data*, 1995, govinfo.library.unt.edu/negp/reports/goalsv2.pdf.

22. Congress, U. S. "Goals 2000: Educate America Act," *Public Law* (1994): 103–227, www.govtrack.us/congress/bills/103/hr1804; S. L. Kagan, "Readiness 2000: Rethinking Rhetoric and Responsibility," *Phi Delta Kappan*, 72, no. 4 (1990): 272.

23. Susan Ochshorn, *Partnering for Success: Community Approaches to Early Learning*, (New York: Child Care Action Campaign, 2000), 6, files.eric.ed.gov /fulltext/ED439819.pdf.

24. Kagan, "Readiness 2000," 274.

25. National Center for Education Statistics, "Readiness for Kindergarten: Parent and Teacher Beliefs." *Statistics in Brief*, 1995.

26. Beatty, *Preschool Education in America*, 8.

27. Susan Ochshorn, "Books of Wonder: Parental Anxiety in the Post-NCLB Age," *ECE Policy Matters*, October 15, 2010, www.ecepolicymatters.com /archives/272.

28. C. Cybele Raver, "Emotions Matter: Making the Case for the Role of Young Children's Emotional Development for Early School Readiness," *Social Policy Report* 16, no. 3 (2002), steinhardt.nyu.edu/scmsAdmin/uploads/001/784 /Raver%20SPR%20Emotions%20Matter.pdf; Clancy Blair and C. Cybele Raver, "Closing the Achievement Gap Through Modification of Neurocognitive and Neuroendocrine Function: Results from a Cluster Randomized Controlled Trial of an Innovative Approach to the Education of Children in Kindergarten," *PLOS ONE* 9, no. 11 (2014), e112393, journals.plos.org/plosone/article?id=10.1371 /journal.pone.0112393.

29. National Center for Education Statistics, "Back to School Statistics," the NCES website fact sheets, 2014, nces.ed.gov/fastfacts/display.asp?id=372.

30. Tamara Halle et al., *Disparities in Early Learning and Development: Lessons from the Early Childhood Longitudinal Study—Birth Cohort (ECLS-B)*, (Executive Summary, Child Trends and Council of Chief State School Officers, 2009), www .childtrends.org/wp-content/uploads/2013/05/2009-52DisparitiesELExecSumm .pdf.

31. S. Daily, M. Burkhauser, and T. Halle, "A Review of School Readiness Practices in the States: Early Learning Guidelines and Assessments," *Child Trends: Early Childhood Highlights* 1, no. 3 (June 17, 2010), www.childtrends.org/wp -content/uploads/2013/05/2010-14-SchoolReadinessStates.pdf.

32. Bridget K. Hamre and Robert C. Pianta, "Early Teacher-Child Relationships and the Trajectory of Children's School Outcomes Through Eighth Grade." *Child Development* 72, no. 2 (March/April 2001).

33. Timothy R. Konold and Robert C. Pianta, "Empirically Derived, Person-Oriented Patterns of School Readiness in Typically Developing Children: Description and Prediction to First Grade Achievement." *Applied Developmental Science* 9, no. 4 (2005), 174–187, www.tandfonline.com/doi/abs/10.1207 /s1532480xads0904_1#.VKzT9WTF-1Q.

34. Christopher P. Brown, "Pivoting a Prekindergarten Program Off the Child or the Standard? A Case Study of Integrating the Practices of Early Childhood Education into Elementary School," *Elementary School Journal* 110, no. 2 (2009).

35. Oregon Department of Education, Office of Student Learning and Partnership, 2003, www.ode.state.or.us/gradelevel/pre_k/ecborntolearnecfoundations .pdf.

36. Ohio Department of Education, Early Learning and Development Standards, website, 2014, education.ohio.gov/Topics/Early-Learning/Early-Learning-Content -Standards/The-Standards.

37. William Gilliam, "Prekindergarteners Left Behind: Expulsion Rates in Pre-kindergarten Programs." *FDC Policy Brief Series*, no. 3 (New York: Foundation for Child Development, 2005), fcd-us.org/resources/prekindergartners-left-behind-expulsion-rates-state-prekindergarten-programs; U.S. Department of Education Office for Civil Rights, *Data Snapshot: School Discipline*, Issue Brief No. 1, March 2014 www2.ed.gov/about/offices/list/ocr/docs/crdc-discipline-snapshot.pdf; M. D. Smith, "The School-to-Prison Pipeline Starts in Preschool." *The Nation*, March 28, 2014, www.thenation.com/blog/179064/school-prison-pipeline-starts-preschool#.

38. Jennifer M. Stedron and Alexander Berger, *NCSL Technical Report: State Approaches to School Readiness Assessment*(Denver, CO: National Conference of State Legislatures, updated August, 2010), www.ncsl.org/research/education/ncsl-technical-report-state-approaches-to-school.aspx.

39. Ibid, 5.

40. Maryland State Education Association, "Too Many Tests!" *Action Line* 15, no. 2 (December 2014); Maryland State Education Association, "MSEA Calls for Immediate Suspension of Kindergarten Readiness Assessment," December 16, 2014, www.marylandeducators.org/press/msea-calls-immediate-suspension-kindergarten-readiness-assessment.

41. Asa Hilliard, Standards, "Decoy or Quality Control," *Rethinking Schools* 12, no. 4 (1998).

42. George Madaus and Michael Russell, "Paradoxes of High-Stakes Testing." *Journal of Education* 190, no. 1/2 (2010/2011), 21.

43. Diane Ravitch, *The Death and Life of the Great American School System: How Testing and Choice Are Undermining Education* (New York: Basic Books, 2010), 151.

44. Walker Percy, "Diagnosing the Modern Malaise," in P. Samway (Ed.), Walker Percy: *Signposts in a Strange Land: Essays* (New York: Farrar, Straus and Giroux, 1991), cited in George Madaus and Terence-Lee St. John, "Standardized Testing: Unheeded Issues that Impact Children's Learning," in *Defending Childhood: Keeping the Promise of Early Education*, ed. B. Falk (New York: Teachers College Press, 2012), 152.

45. A. A. Milne, *Autobiography* (New York: Dutton), 112, cited in Madaus and St. John, "Standardized Testing," 162; see S. Ochshorn (2012), "Testing 1,2,3: Accountability Run Amok," ECE Policy Matters, April 24, 2012, www.ecepolicymatters.com/archives/757.

46. National Early Childhood Accountability Task Force, *Taking Stock: Assessing and Improving Early Childhood Learning and Program Quality*, 2013, 11, policyforchildren.org/wp-content/uploads/2013/07/Taking-Stock.pdf.

47. Economist Intelligence Unit, *Starting Well: Benchmarking Early Education Across the World*, 2012, www.lienfoundation.org/pdf/publications/sw_report.pdf.

48. Tyack and Cuban, *Tinkering Toward Utopia*.

49. National Early Childhood Accountability Task Force, *Taking Stock*, 76.

50. Ibid., 79; see Samuel J. Meisels et al., "The Work Sampling System: Reliability and Validity of a Performance Assessment for Young Children," *Early Childhood Research Quarterly* 10, no. 3 (1995): 277–296.

51. For a history of Head Start, see Elizabeth Rose, *The Promise of Preschool: From Head Start to Universal Pre-Kindergarten* (New York: Oxford University Press, 2010).

52. Administration for Children and Families, *The Head Start Path to Positive Child Outcomes*, 2003, eclkc.ohs.acf.hhs.gov/hslc/hs/resources/eclkc _bookstore/pdfs/f0567be74aee74e7f53e332565c15383.pdf; National Women's Law Center, *Head Start: Supporting Success for Children and Families* (2011), www.nwlc.org/sites/default/files/pdfs/head_start_fact_sheet_2011.pdf.

53. Samuel J. Meisels, *Accountability in Early Childhood: No Easy Answers*, Occasional Paper No. 6, Herr Research Center for Children and Social Policy, Erikson Institute, 2006, 12, www.erikson.edu/wp-content/uploads/opmeisels2006.pdf.

54. Administration for Children and Families, *The Head Start Path to Positive Child Outcomes*, updated (summer), Department of Health and Human Services, 2003, eclkc.ohs.acf.hhs.gov/hslc/hs/resources/eclkc_bookstore/pdfs /f0567be74aee74e7f53e332565c15383.pdf.

55. Sara Rimer, "Now, Standardized Tests in Head Start," *New York Times*, October 29, 2003, www.nytimes.com/2003/10/29/education/29STAR.html; see also D. L. Kirp, "Teaching Is Not a Business," *New York Times*, August 16, 2014, www.nytimes.com/2014/08/17/opinion/sunday/teaching-is-not-a-business.html.

56. Meisels, *Accountability in Early Childhood*.

57. Evelyn Moore and Raul Yzaguirre, "Head Start's National Reporting System Fails Our Children. Here's Why," *Education Week*, June 9, 2004, www.edweek .org/ew/articles/2004/06/09/39moore.h23.html.

58. For discussion of Head Start and accountability, see S. Quinton, "The Accountability Revolution Comes to Head Start," *National Journal*, April 23, 2014, www.nationaljournal.com/next-america/early-childhood/the-accountability -revolution-comes-to-head-start-20140423; M. Severns, "Reforming Head Start: What 'Re-Competition' Means for the Federal Government's Pre-K Program," New America Foundation, 2012, earlyed.newamerica.net/sites/newamerica.net/files /policydocs/Reforming_Head_Start_2012_NAF.pdf; S. Garland, "In Mississippi, Will Competition Cure Head Start—or Kill It?" *Time.com*, November 30, 2012, nation.time.com/2012/11/30/in-mississippi-will-competition-cure-head-start-or -kill-it/; S. Knafo, "Head Start Agencies Sue over Obama's Recompetition Rules." *Huffington Post*, March 28, 2012, www.huffingtonpost.com/2012/03/28 /head-start-recompetition-rules-lawsuit_n_1385051.html.

59. U.S. Government Accountability Office, *Head Start: Further Development Could Allow Results of Test to be Used for Decision Making*, 14, www.gao.gov /products/GAO-05-343; Meisels, *Accountability in Early Childhood*.

60. Quinton, "Accountability Revolution."

61. Melvin Konner, *The Evolution of Childhood* (Cambridge, MA: First Belknap Press of Harvard University Press, 2010), 500.

62. Ibid., 501.

63. Edward Miller and Joan Almon, *Crisis in the Kindergarten: Why Children Need to Play in School* (College Park, MD: Alliance for Childhood, 2009), files.eric .ed.gov/fulltext/ED504839.pdf.

64. Carollee Howes and A. G. Wishard, "Revising Shared Meaning: Looking Through the Lens of Culture and Linking Shared Pretend Play Through Proto-Narrative Development to Emergent Literacy," in *Children's Play: The Roots of Reading,* ed. E. F. Zigler, D. G. Singer, and S. Bishop-Josef (Washington, DC: ZERO TO THREE Press, 2004).

65. Ageliki Nicolopoulou, "The Alarming Disappearance of Play from Early Childhood Education." *Human Development* 53, no. 1 (2010): 1–4.

66. P. Bronson and A. Merryman, "The Creativity Crisis," *Newsweek,* July 10, 2010, www.newsweek.com/creativity-crisis-74665.

67. Kathy Hirsh-Pasek et al., *A Mandate for Playful Learning: Presenting the Evidence* (New York: Oxford University Press, 2009), 15.

68. C. Cook, N. D. Goodman, and L. E. Schulz, "Where Science Starts: Spontaneous Experiments in Preschoolers' Exploratory Play," *Cognition* 120 (2011): 341–349, eccl.mit.edu/papers/CookGoodmanSchulz2011.pdf.

69. Jerome Bruner, *Child's Talk: Learning to Use Language* (New York: Norton, 1983), quoted in Hirsh-Pasek, *A Mandate for Playful Learning,* 30.

70. D. K. Dickinson and P. O. Tabors (eds.), *Beginning Literacy with Language: Young Children Learning at Home and School* (Baltimore, MD: Paul H. Brookes, 2001), cited in Hirsh-Pasek, *A Mandate for Playful Learning,* 30.

71. Hirsh-Pasek, *A Mandate for Playful Learning,* 8.

72. K.-H. Seo and H. P. Ginsberg, "What Is Developmentally Appropriate in Early Childhood Mathematics Education? Lessons from New Research," in *Engaging Young Children in Mathematics: Standards for Early Childhood Mathematics Education,* ed. D. H. Clements, J. Sarama, and A. M. DiBiase (Mahwah, NJ: Lawrence Erlbaum, 2004), 91–104.

73. R. Gelman, "Young Natural-Number Arithmeticians," *Current Directions in Psychological Science* 15 (2006): 193–197, cited in Hirsh-Pasek, *A Mandate for Playful Learning,* 35.

74. Deborah Leong, "The Power of Play-Based Education for Young Children: The Link Between Self-Regulation and Executive Function," paper presented at Giving Young Children the Right Start: Effective Practices for Experiential Learning, U.S. Department of Education, sponsored by Gesell Institute, Alliance for Childhood, Office of Early Learning, May 8, 2012.

75. L. E. Berk and A. B. Meyers, "The Role of Make-Believe Play in the Development of Executive Function: Status of Research and Future Directions," *American Journal of Play* 6, no. 1 (2013); E. Bonawitz et al., "The Double-Edged Sword of Pedagogy: Instruction Limits Spontaneous Exploration and Discovery," *Cognition* (2010), doi:10.1015/j.cognition.2010.10.001, files.eric.ed.gov/fulltext /EJ1016170.pdf.

76. A. Diamond et al., Preschool Program Improves Cognitive Control, *Science* 318 (2007): 1387–1388, cited in Hirsh-Pasek, *Mandate for Playful Learning,* 29.

77. P. Morris et al., *Impact Findings from the Head Start CARES Demonstration: National Evaluation of Three Approaches to Preschoolers' Social and Emotional Competence*, Executive Summary, OPRE Report 201-44 (Washington, DC: Office of Planning, Research, and Evaluation, Administration for Children and Families, U.S. Department of Health and Human Services, 2014), www.acf.hhs.gov/programs/opre/resource/impact-findings-from-the-head-start-cares -demonstration-national-evaluation-of-three-approaches-to-improving -preschoolers-social; D. Willingham, "Tools of the Mind: Promising Pre-K Curriculum Looks Less Promising," *Science and Education* (blog), August 27, 2012, www .danielwillingham.com/daniel-willingham-science-and-education-blog/promising -pre-k-curriculum-looking-less-promising.

78. Selma H. Fraiberg, *The Magic Years: Understanding and Handling the Problems of Early Childhood*, (New York: Charles Scribner's Sons, 1959).

79. Beverly Falk (ed.), *Defending Childhood: Keeping the Promise of Early Education*, (New York: Teachers College Press, 2012).

80. Daphna Bassok and Anna Rorem, "Is Kindergarten the New First Grade? The Changing Nature of Kindergarten in the Age of Accountability" (*EdPolicy Works Working Paper Series*, No. 20), 2014, curry.virginia.edu/uploads/resourceLibrary /20_Bassok_Is_Kindergarten_The_New_First_Grade.pdf; L. A. Shepard and M. L. Smith, "Escalating Academic Demand in Kindergarten: Counterproductive Policies," *Elementary School Journal* 89, no. 2 (1988), nepc.colorado.edu/files /EscalatingAcademicDemand.pdf.

81. Bassok and Rorem, "Is Kindergarten the New First Grade?," 21.

82. Lesley Koplow, *Creating Schools that Heal: Real-Life Solutions* (New York: Teachers College Press, 2002).

83. Motoko Rich, "Unlikely Allies Uniting to Fight School Changes," *New York Times*, May 26, 2014, www.nytimes.com/2014/05/27/us/unlikely-allies-uniting -to-fight-school-changes.html; Susan Ochshorn, "Rejecting the Common Core of Childhood," *ECE Policy Matters*, May 4, 2014, www.ecepolicymatters.com /archives/2165; Elizabeth Phillips, "We Need to Talk About the Test," *New York Times*, April 9, 2014, www.nytimes.com/2014/04/10/opinion/the-problem-with-the -common-core.html.

Chapter 5

1. Jonathan Cohn, "The Hell of American Day Care," *The New Republic*, April 15, 2013, www.newrepublic.com/article/112892/hell-american-day-care.

2. U.S. Department of Health and Human Services, "HHS Announces Actions to Improve Safety and Quality of Child Care," May 16, 2013, press release, www .hhs.gov/news/press/2013pres/05/20130516a.html.

3. Federal Register, May 20, 2013, s3.amazonaws.com/public-inspection .federalregister.gov/2013-11673.pdf.

4. U.S. Department of Health and Human Services, "Characteristics of Families Served by Child Care and Development Fund (CCDF)," based on preliminary FY 2013 data, Nov 17, 2014, www.acf.hhs.gov/sites/default/files/occ/data_fact_sheet _preliminary_fy_2013.pdf.

5. Edward Zigler, Katherine Marsland, and Heather Lord, *The Tragedy of Child Care in America* (New Haven, CT: Yale University Press, 2009).

6. For information about regulatory policy in the states, see Child Care Aware, *America State Fact Sheets and Licensing Information*, website, naccrrapps.naccrra .org/map/, and Child Care Aware, *We Can Do Better: State Child Care Center Licensing, 2011 Update*, www.naccrra.org/about-child-care/state-child-care -licensing/we-can-do-better-state-child-care-center-licensing.

7. Sharon Lynn Kagan and Nancy E. Cohen, *Not by Chance: Creating an Early Care and Education System for America's Children*. Quality 2000 Initiative (New Haven, CT: Bush Center in Child Development and Social Policy, Yale University, 1997), 103–112.

8. Ibid., 6–7.

9. Ibid., 9.

10. Child Care Aware, "Child Care in America: 2014 State Fact Sheets," www .naccrra.org/public-policy/resources/child-care-state-fact-sheets-0.

11. Lynda Laughlin, "Who's Minding the Kids? Child Care Arrangements: Spring 2011," U.S. Census Bureau, U.S. Department of Commerce, April 2013, www.census.gov/prod/2013pubs/p70-135.pdf.

12. For the persistence of this problem over time, see Judy David, Susan Ochshorn, and Anne Mitchell, "An Assessment of the Integrated Early Childhood Program in Three Settlement Houses," (United Neighborhood Houses of New York, 1996).

13. Early Childhood Data Collaborative, *2013 State of States' Early Childhood Data Systems*, February 2014, www.ecedata.org/files/2013%20State%20of %20States%27%20Early%20Childhood%20Data%20Systems.pdf.

14. Karen Hill Scott, "Perspectives and Visions of Early Childhood Systems," in *Early Childhood Systems: Transforming Early Learning*, ed. Sharon Lynn Kagan and Kristie Kauerz (New York: Teachers College Press, 2012), 23.

15. Anne W. Mitchell, "Foreword," in *The Quest for Quality: Promising Innovations for Early Childhood Programs*, ed. P. W. Wesley and V. Buysse (Baltimore, MD: Paul Brookes Publishing, 2010), xiii.

16. Sharon Lynn Kagan and Kristie Kauerz, "Early Childhood Systems: Looking Deep, Wide, and Far," in Kagan and Kauerz, *Early Childhood Systems*, p. 5.

17. Robert Ajemian, "Where Is the Real George Bush?" *Time*, January 26, 1987.

18. See Stacie Goffin and Valora Washington for a discussion of this phenomenon in *Ready or Not: Leadership Choices in Early Care and Education* (New York: Teachers College Press, 2007).

19. Susan Ochshorn, "Paid Family Leave: A Work Unfinished," *ECE Policy Matters*, February 19, 2013, www.ecepolicymatters.com/archives/1061.

20. See *CNNPolitics*, "The 44th President First Hundred Days: Obama Wants to Overhaul Education from 'Cradle to Career,'" March 10, 2009, www.cnn .com/2009/POLITICS/03/10/obama.education/.

21. Susan Ochshorn, "Preschool: A Nonpartisan No-Brainer," *Huffington Post*, February 22, 2013, www.huffingtonpost.com/susan-ochshorn/preschool-a -nonpartisan-nobrainer_b_2736218.html.

22. California Department of Education, "RTT-ELC Implementation: California's Race to the Top—Early Learning Challenge (RTT-ELC) Grant Award," April 18, 2013, www.cde.ca.gov/sp/cd/rt/rttelcapproach.asp.

23. Patricia W. Wesley and Virginia Buysse, "Changing Times and the Quest for Quality," in *The Quest for Quality: Promising Innovations for Early Childhood Programs*, ed. Patricia W. Wesley and Virginia Buysse (Baltimore, MD: Paul Brookes, 2010), 2.

24. See QRIS National Learning Network Newsletter, March 28, 2014, qrisnetwork.org/sites/all/files/lt/private/2nd%20Web%20Posting%20March%20 2014.pdf; Steven Johnson, *Where Good Ideas Come From: The Natural History of Innovation* (New York: Riverhead Books, 2010); Eleanor Duckworth, *The Having of Wonderful Ideas: And Other Essays on Teaching and Learning*, 3rd ed. (New York: Teachers College Press, 2006).

25. *CBS Morning News*, "Earning the Good Housekeeping Seal of Approval," March 24, 2013, www.cbsnews.com/news/earning-good-housekeepings-seal-of -approval/.

26. Stacie G. Goffin and W. Steven Barnett, "Assessing QRIS as a Change Agent," *Early Childhood Research Quarterly* 30 (2015): 179–182.

27. Julie Blair, "Child Care Costs More than College in Illinois," *Early Years blog, Education Week*, July 9, 2013. blogs.edweek.org/edweek/early_years/2013 /07/if_youve_just_had_a.html

28. Anne W. Mitchell, *Quality Rating and Improvement Systems as the Framework for Early Care and Education System Reform*, BUILD Initiative, 2009, 3, www.earlychildhoodfinance.org/downloads/2009/QRISasSystemReform _2009.pdf.

29. Christopher Helman, "George Kaiser's $10 Billion Bet," *Forbes*, September 21, 2011, www.forbes.com/forbes/2011/1010/forbes400-11-passions-kaiser-bet -poorest-kids-helman.html; Gail Zellman and Michal Perlman, *Child Care Quality Rating and Improvement Systems in Five Pioneer States: Implementation Issues and Lessons Learned* (Santa Monica, CA: RAND Corporation, 2008).

30. Cameron Brenchley, "A Major Investment in Helping Students Get Off on the Right Foot," *Homeroom Blog*, U.S. Department of Education, May 2011, www .ed.gov/blog/2011/05/; Susan Ochshorn, "Early Learning: Center Stage," *ECE Policy Matters*, May 28, 2011, www.ecepolicymatters.com/archives/572.

31. Joseph T. Jones, Stronger Families Leadership Forum, Poughkeepsie, New York, January 31, 2013.

32. For a thumbnail description of the work of the intiative, Transforming Early Childhood Community Systems (TECCS), housed at the Center for Healthier Children, Families, and Communities, see www.healthychild.ucla.edu/ourwork /teccs/.

33. See Magnolia Place Dashboard, edsila.org/wp-content/uploads/2011/10 /EDSI-in-Magnolia-Place1.pdf.

34. Urie Bronfenbrenner, "Who Cares for the Children?" in *Resources for Early Childhood: A Handbook*, ed. H. Nuba, M. Searson, and D. L. Sheiman

(New York: Garland, 1994), 113–129 (edited paper from an individual address to UNESCO, Paris, September 7, 1989); Urie Bronfenbrenner, *The Ecology of Human Development: Experiments by Nature and Design*, (Cambridge, MA: Harvard University Press, 1979).

35. Quoted in L. K. Brendtro, "The Vision of Urie Bronfenbrenner: Adults Who Are Crazy about Kids," *International Child and Youth Care Network*, no. 141, November 2010, www.cyc-net.org/cyc-online/cyconline-nov2010-brendtro.html.

36. Spike Lee, *When the Levees Broke: A Requiem in Four Acts*, (New York: 40 Acres and a Mule/HBO, 2006); J. Chang, "Duty of Civil Engineers Following Natural Disasters," Technical Paper, ASCE Ohio Valley Student Conference, Carnegie Mellon University, March 1, 2014.

37. Sasha Abramsky, *The American Way of Poverty: How the Other Half Still Lives* (New York: Nation Books, 2013), 156.

38. LSU/Tulane Early Childhood Policy and Data Center, *Early Childhood Risk and Reach in Louisiana*, Fall 2012, www.gov.state.la.us/assets/2012_Risk_and _Reach_Report_online-correctedWEBSITE.pdf.

39. National Association for the Education of Young Children, "Head Start Collaboration: State Early Childhood Education and Care," www.naeyc.org/policy /statetrends/ecac/HeadStartAct.

40. U.S. Administration for Children and Families, *Early Childhood State Advisory Councils: Status Report April 2013*, 3, www.acf.hhs.gov/sites/default/files /ecd/508_sac_report_3.pdf.

41. Ibid, 13.

42. Christina Satkowski, *The Next Step in System-Building: Early Childhood Advisory Councils and Federal Efforts to Support Policy Alignment in Early Childhood* (Washington, DC: New America Foundation, 2009), education .newamerica.net/sites/newamerica.net/files/policydocs/Early_Childhood _Advisory_Councils_Nov_09_0.pdf.

43. Christina Satkowski, "Four Years Later: Progress and Pitfalls for State Advisory Councils on Early Childhood," *Early Education Watch*, May 28, 2013, earlyed.newamerica.net/blogposts/2013/four_years_later_progress_and_pitfalls _for_state_advisory_councils_on_early_childhood; K. Sheehy, "Graduation Rates Dropping Among Native American Students," *U.S. News and World Report* (online), June 6, 2013, www.usnews.com/education/high-schools/articles/2013/06/06 /graduation-rates-dropping-among-native-american-students.

Chapter 6

1. Robin L. Flanigan, "Is Virtual Kindergarten a Good or Bad Idea?" *Education Week*, June 11, 2013, www.edweek.org/dd/articles/2013/06/12/03kindergarten.h06 .html.

2. Eugene F. Provenzo, "Friedrich Froebel's Gifts: Connecting the Spiritual and Aesthetic to the Real World of Play and Learning," *Journal of Play*, Summer 2009, www.journalofplay.org/sites/www.journalofplay.org/files/pdf-articles/2-1-article -friedrich-froebels-gifts.pdf

3. Victoria Rideout, *Zero to Eight: Children's Media Use in America 2011*, Common Sense Media website, 2011, www.commonsensemedia.org/research/zero -to-eight-childrens-media-use-in-america.

4. Tamar Lewin, "New Milestone Emerges: Baby's First iPhone App," *New York Times*, October 28, 2013, www.nytimes.com/2013/10/28/us/new-milestone -emerges-babys-first-iphone-app.html?_r=0.

5. Victoria Rideout, (2013), *Zero to Eight: Children's Media Use in America 2013*, Common Sense Media, www.commonsensemedia.org/research/zero-to-eight -childrens-media-use-in-america-2013

6. Ibid., 29; Susan Neuman and Donna Celano, *Giving Our Children a Fighting Chance: Poverty, Literacy and the Development of Information Capital* (New York: Teachers College Press, 2012).

7. Lisa Guernsey, "Field-Testing the Math Apps," *New York Times*, September 3, 2013, www.nytimes.com/2013/09/03/science/field-testing-the-math-apps .html?pagewanted=all.

8. Rachel Barr et al., "Infant and Early Childhood Exposure to Adult-Directed and Child-Directed Television Programming: Relations with Cognitive Skills at Age Four," *Merrill-Palmer Quarterly 56*, no. 1 (2010): 21–48.

9. Brandon Griggs, "U.S. Parents Not Worried About Kids' Digital-Media Use," *CNN.com*, June 4, 2013. www.cnn.com/2013/06/04/tech/gaming-gadgets/parenting -digital-devices-study/; E. Wartella, E., V. Rideout, A. Lauricella, and S. Connell et al., *Parenting in the Age of Digital Technology: A National Survey* (Evanston, IL: Northwestern University Center of Media and Human Development, 2013), vjrconsulting.com/storage/PARENTING_IN_THE_AGE_OF_DIGITAL _TECHNOLOGY.

10. Lisa Guernsey, *Screen Time: How Electronic Media—from Baby Videos to Educational Software—Affects Your Young Child* (New York: Basic Books, 2012), xvi.

11. "Baby Thinks Magazine is Broken iPad!," YouTube video, 2011, www. youtube.com/watch?v=aXV-yaFmQNk.

12. S. E. Vaala, A. Bleakley, and A. B. Jordan, "The Media Environments and Television-Viewing Diets of Infants and Toddlers," *ZERO TO THREE*, March 2013: 18–24.

13. Matt Richtel, "A Silicon Valley School that Doesn't Compute, *New York Times*, October 22, 2011, www.nytimes.com/2011/10/23/technology/at-waldorf- school-in-silicon-valley-technology-can-wait.html?pagewanted=all.

14. Association of Waldorf Schools of North America, "The Waldorf Curriculum," website, www.whywaldorfworks.org/02_W_Education/curriculum.asp; R. Steiner, "An Introduction to Waldorf Education: An Essay by Rudolf Steiner from GA 24", 1985, originally published in the collected edition of Rudolf Steiner's works in *Aufsatze Uber die Dreigleiderung der sozialen organismus und zur Zeitlage 1915– 1921* (vol. 24 in the Bibliographic Survey, 1961). E-text edition provided with the cooperation of the Anthroposophic Press, wn.rsarchive.org/Books/GA024/IntWal _index.html.

15. Hanna Rosin, "The Touch-Screen Generation" *The Atlantic*, March 20, 2013, www.theatlantic.com/magazine/archive/2013/04/the-touch-screen-generation /309250/; Kyla Calvert, "For Toddlers, It's the Quality of the Screen Time that Matters, Study Reveals," *PBS Newshour*, October 30, 2014, www.pbs.org/newshour /rundown/screen-time-toddlers-parents-dont-feel-guilty/.

16. Roberta Michnick Golinkoff and Kathy Hirsh-Pasek, "Life in the AiP Era: Finding the Education in Educational Apps for Children," *Huffington Post*, July 9, 2012, www.huffingtonpost.com/roberta-michnick-golinkoff/educational -apps_b_1632281.html.

17. Sarah Roseberry et al., "Live Action: Can Young Children Learn Verbs from Video?" *Child Development* 80, no. 5 (2009): 1360–1375.

18. K. Dickerson et al., "Age-Related Changes in Learning Across Early Childhood: A New Imitation Task." *Developmental Psychobiology*, 2012, doi:10.1002 /dev.21068, www.ncbi.nlm.nih.gov/pmc/articles/PMC2821208/.

19. American Academy of Pediatrics, "Media Education," Committee on Public Education, 1999, pediatrics.aappublications.org/content/104/2/341.full.

20. Ari Brown, "Media Use by Children Younger than 2 years." *Pediatrics* 128, no. 5 (2011): 1040–1045, pediatrics.aappublications.org/content/early/2011/10/12 /peds.2011-1753; Benedict Carey, "Parents Urged Again to Limit TV for Youngest." *New York Times*, October 18, 2011, www.nytimes.com/2011/10/19/health /19babies.html.

21. American Academy of Pediatrics, "Media Violence." *Pediatrics* 108, no. 5 (2001): 1222–1226.

22. National Association for the Education of Young Children, "Technology and Interactive Media as Tools in Early Childhood Programs Serving Children from Birth Through Age 8." Position Statement with the Fred Rogers Center, January 2012, www.naeyc.org/files/naeyc/file/positions/PS_technology_WEB2.pdf.

23. Susan Pinker, *The Village Effect: How Face-to-Face Contact Can Make Us Healthier, Happier, and Smarter* (New York: Random House, 2014).

24. Education Commission of the States, "Technology in Early Education." *Progress of Education Reform* 13, no. 4 (2012), 1 www.ecs.org/clearinghouse /01/03/00/10300.pdf.

25. Ibid., 1.

26. Jean Piaget, *To Understand Is to Invent* (New York: Grossman, 1973); Lev Vygotsky, *Mind in Society* (Cambridge, MA: Harvard University Press, 1978).

27. David Elkind, *The Hurried Child: Growing Up Too Fast Too Soon* (Cambridge, MA: Da Capo Press, 2006).

28. Edward Miller and Colleen Cordes (eds.), *Fool's Gold: A Critical Look at Computers in Early Childhood*, Alliance for Childhood, 1999, 1, files.eric.ed.gov /fulltext/ED445803.pdf.

29. Ibid., 28.

30. Edward Miller and Joan Almon, *Crisis in the Kindergarten: Why Children Need to Play in School*, Alliance for Childhood (NJ3a), 2009, www.allianceforchildhood .org/sites/allianceforchildhood.org/files/file/kindergarten_report.pdf.

31. Miller and Cordes, *Fools Gold*, 10.

32. Denise E. Murray, "Changing Technologies, Changing Literacy Communities?" *Language Learning and Technology* 4, no. 2 (2000), 43–58, llt.msu.edu /vol4num2/murray/default.html.

33. Susan Linn, Joan W. Almon, and Diane E. Levin, *Facing the Screen Dilemma: Technology, Children, and Early Education*, Alliance for Childhood and Campaign for a Commercial-Free Childhood, 2012, www.allianceforchildhood.org/sites /allianceforchildhood.org/files/file/FacingtheScreenDilemma.pdf.

34. Brigid Barron et al., *Take a Giant Step: A Blueprint for Teaching Young Children in a Digital Age*, The Joan Ganz Cooney Center at Sesame Workshop and Stanford University, 2011, 2, www.joanganzcooneycenter.org/Reports-31.html.

35. Scott McLeod, "Building the Plane While Flying It," *Dangerously Irrelevant*, May 13, 2013, dangerouslyirrelevant.org/2013/05/building-the-plane-while -flying-it.html.

36. Fran Simon, Karen Nemeth, and Lilla Dale McManis, "Technology in ECE Classrooms: Results of a New Survey and Implications for the Field," *Exchange*, September/October 2013, www.slideshare.net/FSSimon/ccie-survey-article -final-213simonnemethmc-manis.

37. Ibid.

38. Lisa Guernsey et al., *Pioneering Literacy in the Digital Wild West: Empowering Parents and Educators*, Campaign for Grade-Level Reading, 2012, gradelevelreading.net/wp-content/uploads/2012/12/GLR_TechnologyGuide _final.pdf.

39. Faith Rogow, "Digital and Media Literacy—Practical Pedagogy Behind Successful Technology Integration in ECE—A TEC Track Webinar," Early Childhood Webinars, Erikson Institute, www.earlychildhoodwebinars.com/presentations /digital-media-literacy-the-practical-pedagogy-behind-successful-technology -integration-in-ece/.

40. Jennifer Magiera, Tricia Fuglestad, and Erin Stanfill, "Intentional Technology for Early Learners in Schools; A TEC Conversation," April 6, 2013, www.erikson.edu/news/events/2013/intentional-technology-for-early-learners -in-schools-a-tec-conversation/.

41. Linda M. Mitchell, "Using Technology in Reggio Emilia-Inspired Programs," *Theory into Practice* 46, no. 1 (2007), 32–39; S. Philips, Special needs or special rights? in *Experiencing Reggio Emilia: Implications for Preschool Provision*, ed. L. Abbott and C. Nutbrown, (Philadelphia: Open University Press, 2001).

42. Rebecca Staples New, *Reggio Emilia: Catalyst for Change and Conversation*, ERIC Clearinghouse on Elementary and Early Childhood Education, University of Illinois, 2000.

43. For a brief history of the evolution of the Reggio approach and the work of Loris Malaguzzi, see www.reggiokids.com/the_reggio_approach.html.

44. John Dewey, *The Quest for Certainty: A Study of the Relationship Between Knowledge and Action* (New York: Kessenger Publishing, 2005). First published 1929.

45. North American Reggio Emilia Alliance, "Frequently Asked Questions," reggioalliance.org/resources/faqs/.

46. Claudi Giudici, Carla Rinaldi, and Mara Krechevsky, "Making Learning Visible: Children as Individual and Group Learners," Project Zero, Harvard Graduate School of Education, 2001, webpage, cited in Linda M. Mitchell, "Using Technology in Reggio Emilia-Inspired Programs, 36.

47. Mitchell, "Using Technology in Reggio Emilia-Inspired Programs," 36.

48. Ibid., 3.

Index

About the Author

Susan Ochshorn is the founder of the consulting firm ECE PolicyWorks (www.ecepolicyworks.com). She has served in a number of advisory positions, including on the council of the Early Learning Initiative at the Education Commission of the States. A former journalist, Ochshorn has written for *Parenting*, the *Los Angeles Times*, and other publications. She blogs at the *Huffington Post* and *ECE Policy Matters,* the go-to place for early childhood teachers, those who train them, and the decisionmakers who determine their professional course.